OLLOWING GOD
HARACTER SERIES
BLE STUDY

An informative **12 WEEK BIBLE STUDY** of life principles for today, to guide the church and the Christian's walk.

Life Principles from the Prophets of the Old Testament

LEARNING LIFE PRINCIPLES
FROM THE PROPHETS
OF THE OLD TESTAMENT

A Bible Study by

Wayne Barber
Eddie Rasnake
Richard Shepherd

Chattanooga, TN 37421

Following God

Learning Life Principles from the Prophets of the Old Testament

Published by AMG Publishers.

First Printing, 2024

ISBN: 978-1-61715-622-9

Cover design by Marc Whitaker, MTW Design, Dickson, TN
Editing and layout by Rick Steele,

Printed in United States of America
POD

As the prophets lived and spoke the truth to their generations and beyond, may our children do so in their generation. With thanksgiving to God for the children with whom He has blessed us, we dedicate this book to them:

Steven Barber and Erik and Stephanie (Barber) Christensen and grandchildren, Hollen and Jonathan Christensen

Lauren, Blake, Michael, and Chandler Rasnake

Joshua, Talitha, Lydia, and Sarah Beth Shepherd

"I have no greater joy than to hear that my children are walking in the truth" 3 John 1:4 (NIV).

Acknowledgments

This work goes forth to those who have encouraged us in the publication of the first three books in this series: Life Principles from the Old Testament, Life Principles from the Kings of the Old Testament, and Life Principles from the Women of the Bible. We are especially grateful to the body of believers at Woodland Park Baptist Church in Chattanooga, Tennessee, who have walked through many of these studies with us and have been a continual source of encouragement as the writing of new studies progresses. Thanks to the folks at AMG, especially Warren Baker, Trevor Overcash, Dale Anderson, Phillip Rodgers, and Rick Steele. Thanks to Robin Currier for her help with proofreading. Most of all, we remain grateful to the Lord Jesus, who continues to teach us and lead us in what it means to follow Him with a whole heart.

The Authors

Wayne Barber

Wayne Barber was a renowned national and international conference ministry speaker, his primary goal of ministry was to spread the message of "the sufficiency of Christ." People around the world connected with Wayne's unique ability to make God's Word come alive through his honest and open "real-life" experiences. For more than twenty years he served as Senior Pastor-Teacher of Woodland Park Baptist Church. And for many of those years in Chattanooga, Wayne co-taught with noted author Kay Arthur of Precept Ministries and has studied under Dr. Spiros Zodhiates, who was one of the world's leading Greek scholars. On August 29, 2016, Wayne passed away suddenly after a short illness. He is survived by his wife and two grown children and several grandchildren.

Wayne was one of the founding authors of the Following God© series.

Rick Shepherd

Richard L. Shepherd has served in churches in Florida, Texas, and Tennessee, and ministered over fifteen years as Team Strategist for the Prayer and Spiritual Awakening Team of the Florida Baptist Convention. He holds M.Div and Ph.D degrees from Southwestern Baptist Theological Seminary. He has been married to his wife Linda Gail since 1977. They have four children and nine grandchildren. They are always glad to encourage believers, and witness to listening hearts wherever they go. They now make their home in Rolesville, North Carolina.

Rick is one of the founding authors of the Following God© series.

Eddie Rasnake

Eddie Rasnake graduated with honors from East Tennessee State University. He and his wife, Michele, served 7 years with Cru at UVa, James Madison, and as campus director at the University of Tennessee. Eddie left Cru to join Wayne Barber at Woodland Park Baptist Church where he still serves as Senior Associate Pastor. He has authored dozens of books and Bible studies and has published materials in Afrikaans, Albanian, German, Greek, Italian, Romanian, Russian and Telugu. Eddie and his wife Michele live in Chattanooga, Tennessee.

Eddie is one of the founding authors of the Following God© series.

Preface

The prophet Isaiah said almost 3000 years ago, *"truth has stumbled in the street, and uprightness cannot enter. Yes, truth is lacking"* (59:14b-15a). "Truth is lacking"—That is the banner headline over much of our world today, even over churches in some cases. When we look for truth we must always go to the Lord and His Word **first**. He has not been silent, and He has not left Himself without witness. He has sent many men and women throughout the centuries to proclaim His message—His truth. Let us introduce you to some of these messengers, the prophets of the Old Testament, as well as to The Prophet, Jesus Christ.

These prophets ministered at very different times in the life of the nation of Israel—times of famine and drought, times of economic prosperity, times of decline and corruption, and times of spiritual renewal. They came from very different backgrounds—we find priests, a judge, a farmer and a shepherd. Some were friends of the king; some were enemies of the king; and some had unknown backgrounds. The prophets who marched through the centuries lived very different lifestyles. Elijah was fed by the ravens for a time. Isaiah was a regular guest in the king's palace. Each prophet had different ministry assignments. Jonah's assignment was to go to Nineveh and, after a brief Mediterranean diversion, he completed that short assignment. Isaiah prophesied for over forty years during the reigns of four kings!

The prophets had many differences in their lives, but they all had one thing in common: they brought the truth of God to the people. They heard the Word of God clearly and spoke it faithfully. The people did not always like what the prophets said, and they certainly did not always obey what they said, but the people could never say that God had not made Himself clear. He always spoke the truth through His prophets. There were many who claimed to be prophets but they spoke lies, half-truths, and deceptions out of their own hearts. God spoke against them and continued to uphold His prophets and the message He had given them.

In the days and lives of the prophets we see mirrored many of our own present-day situations. We certainly see the need for truth to prevail at a time when truth is "stumbling" in the streets. Many people do not want to hear the truth if it's the least bit inconvenient, uncomfortable, or "politically incorrect," but that doesn't change our need to hear the truth or the need for the truth to prevail. Truth needs to be the foundation of our service for Christ.

Sadly though, many lives, many families, many nations, even many churches today have built on wrong foundations, and, for some, they have gone past mere structural damage. They have crashed and someone is having to try and clean up the mess. If only truth had been the first thing on the list of building materials. This study is all about coming back to the truth, tearing out crumbling foundations, and replacing them with rock-solid truth. We have it recorded not as the word of men but as the very Word of God—*"for no prophecy was ever made by an act of human will, but men moved by the Holy Spirit spoke from God"* (2 Peter 1:21). Concerning that "prophetic word" Peter exhorts us, *"to which you do well to pay attention as to a lamp shining in a dark place, until the day dawns and the morning star arises in your hearts"* (2 Peter 1:19). Jesus is at the center of all prophecy as Revelation 19:10 reminds us, *"For the testimony of Jesus is the spirit of prophecy."* With this study of *Following God: Life Principles from the Prophets of the Old Testament,* may you see the light and truth of Jesus and follow Him more faithfully, more fully, and more truthfully.

Following Him,

Wayne A. Barber

WAYNE A. BARBER

Richard L. Shepherd

RICHARD L. SHEPHERD

Eddie Rasnake

EDDIE RASNAKE

Table of Contents

Timeline of the Prophets

United Kingdom — Southern Kingdom (Judah) — Northern Kingdom (Israel)

The names in **bold** are kings in Israel or Judah. The names in all caps are PROPHETS.

1050 | 1000 | 950 | 900 | 850

SAMUEL
Judge and Prophet
GAD
NATHAN

Saul
1051–1011
David
1011–971
Solomon
971–931

Ishbosheth ruled over Israel
1011–1004
960—Temple finished

David ruled over Judah from Hebron
1011–1004

David ruled over all Israel and Judah from Jerusalem
1004–971

SHEMAIAH IDDO Hanani the Seer
ODED
AZARIAH
OBADIAH JOEL
Jahaziel the Levite

Rehoboam
931–913
Asa
911–870
Abijam
913–911
Jehoshaphat
873–848
Jehoram
(Joram)
853–841
Ahaziah
841
Athaliah
841–835
Joash
835–796

Jeroboam I
931–910
Nadab
910–909
Elah
886–885
Zimri
885
Baasha
909–886
Tibni
885–880
Ahab
874–853
Omri
885–874
Ahaziah
853–852
Jehu
841–814
Jehoram
(Joram)
852–841

AHIJAH the Shilonite
"A man of God from Judah"
A prophet from Samaria in Bethel
JEHU, son of Hanani
MICAIAH
ELIJAH
ELISHA

Hiram I of Tyre
981–947
Benhadad I of Syria
900–860
Benhadad II of Syria
860–841

---

800 | 750 | 700 | 650 | 600

"A Prophet"
(sent to Amaziah)
ISAIAH
MICAH
NAHUM ZEPHANIAH HABAKKUK
HULDAH (a prophetess)
JEREMIAH

Amaziah
796–767
Azariah(Uzziah)
790–739
Jotham
750–735
Ahaz
735–715
Hezekiah
715–686
Manasseh
697–642
Amon
642–640
Josiah
640–609
Jehoahaz
609
Jehoiakim
609–598
Jehoiachin
(Jeconiah)
598–597
Zedekiah
597–586

Jehoahaz
814–798
Joash
(Jehoash)
798–782
Jeroboam II
793–753
Zechariah
753–752
Menahem
752–742
Hoshea
732–722
Shallum
752
Pekahiah
742–740
Pekah
752–732

JONAH
AMOS
HOSEA
ODED

There are no more kings or prophets in the Northern Kingdom.
Foreign peoples are resettled into the land.

605—1st Captivity
DANIEL
Hananiah
Mishael
Azariah
597—2d Captivity
EZEKIEL
Nebuchadnezzar
605–562

Tiglath-pileser I
745–727
722—Assyria takes Israel into captivity
Shalmaneser V
727–722
Sennacherib
705–681
612—Fall of Nineveh

---

550 | 500 | 450 | 400

HAGGAI
ZECHARIAH
MALACHI

Zerubbabel
536—First Return
536—Rebuilding the Temple
516—Temple completed

Ezra
458—Second Return
Rebuilding the people

Nehemiah
445—Third Return
Rebuilding the walls
and the city of Jerusalem

The Jews are without a prophet, living under foreign rulers, and **AWAITING THE MESSIAH, THE GREATEST PROPHET OF ISRAEL.**

586—Final Captivity
Jerusalem and Temple destroyed

538–Decree of Cyrus to return

Queen Esther

Amel-Marduk
(Evil-Merodach)
562–560
Cyrus
539–530
Darius I
522–486
Xerxes
486–464
Artaxerxes
464–423
Socrates
470–399
Plato
428–348
Aristotle
384–322

Samuel

HEARING GOD—FOLLOWING HIS WORD

Samuel was a gift of God to Hannah and Elkanah as well as to the nation of Israel at a pivotal time in the chronicles of God's people. Placed as a bridge between two epochs in Israel's history, Samuel brought the long period of the judges to a close and ushered in the new era of government by kings. Samuel lived over 90 years and served as a prophet, judge, and priest for most of those years. He proved to be a strong leader and a stabilizing force at a time of great turmoil and transition. Samuel's ministry as the last of the judges and the first of the prophets brought Israel into days of unprecedented prominence which continued through the leadership of kings Saul, David, and Solomon.

Samuel is often spoken of as a great example of prayer and intercession on behalf of the people of God. His example serves as an encouragement to each of us. An even greater encouragement to us is the underlying foundation of prayer that marked his life—a surrendered heart that readily obeyed when he heard God speak. God taught Him that true prayer is always based first on surrender to the will of God, not on the need of man. Samuel shows us what it means to pray the way God wants. He shows us what it means to seek God and His will.

As we study the life of Samuel, we will not only learn about prayer, but also

Samuel ministered in Israel from around 1102 BC before the era of the kings to approximately 1012 BC during the reign of Saul. It is likely that portions of I Samuel were written by him.

WHEN DID HE PROPHESY?

1050	1000	950	900	850
SAMUEL GAD		SHEMAIAH IDDO	Hanani the Seer	OBADIAH JOEL
Judge and Prophet	NATHAN	ODED	Jahaziel the Levite	
			AZARIAH	
		Rehoboam 931–913 Asa 911–870	Jehoshaphat 873–848 Jehoram (Joram) 853–841	Ahaziah 841 Joash 835–796
Saul 1051–1011 David 1011–971	Solomon 971–931	Abijam 913–911		Athaliah 841–835
		Jeroboam I 931–910 Nadab 910–909	Elah 886-885 Zimri 885 Ahaziah 853–852	Jehu 841–814
Ishbosheth ruled over Israel 1011–1004	960—Temple finished	Baasha 909–886	Tibni 885-880 Ahab 874–853 Jehoram (Joram) 852–841	
David ruled over Judah from Hebron 1011–1004		AHIJAH the Shilonite	Omri 885–874	
David ruled over all Israel and Judah from Jerusalem 1004–971		"A man of God from Judah" A prophet from Samaria in Bethel	JEHU, son of Hanani MICAIAH	
			ELIJAH	ELISHA
	Hiram I of Tyre 981–947		Benhadad I of Syria 900–860 Benhadad II of Syria 860–841	

As we study the life of Samuel, we will not only learn about prayer, but also about walking in line with God's Word. Samuel's life and ministry paint a picture of dependence upon the Lord in the midst of a people who were spiritually weak. His testimony gives us a clear call to seek the Lord in all things, to listen to the voice of God, and to obey His Word. Samuel followed God and shows us how we, too, can follow Him—hearing His voice and obeying His Word.

Samuel DAY ONE

GIVEN TO THE LORD IN A DAY OF SPIRITUAL DECLINE

The people of Israel were ruled by judges for over 300 years after Joshua died. The theme of the book of Judges is found in the last verse of the book: *"In those days there was no king in Israel; everyone did what was right in his own eyes"* (21:25). That statement sums up the desperate state of the nation into which Samuel was born.

Read 1 Samuel 1:1–9. What characterized this home? Give a brief summary of what you find.

____

____

____

____

____

____

Did You Know?

THE TABERNACLE AT SHILOH

The area of the Tabernacle at Shiloh was a complex of structures that included housing for Eli and his family as well as places for others who served there. The Tabernacle was brought into Israel from the wilderness at the time of Joshua (ca. 1398 BC; Joshua 18:1).

Elkanah and his two wives, Hannah and Peninnah, lived in the hill country of Ephraim in Ramathaim-zophim, also called Ramah, about 5 miles north of Jerusalem. First Chronicles 6:22–28, 33–38 identifies Elkanah as a descendant of Levi. Elkanah's family was a household who sought to follow the Lord, being faithful in going each year to worship in Shiloh (20 miles north of Jerusalem) where the Tabernacle was located. Though his oldest wife, Hannah, was barren, Elkanah loved her dearly. But he had several children by his wife, Peninnah, and this was a cause of tension between Peninnah and Hannah, especially when the family traveled to Shiloh each year. As a result Hannah became very melancholy—even resentful, weeping and refusing to eat. Elkanah's efforts to comfort her did little to ease her sorrow.

How did Hannah handle her sorrow? Read 1 Samuel 1:9–18. What do you see about the heart of Hannah, the mother of Samuel?

____

____

____

____

____

The first thing she did was **pray**. She brought her distress and her tears to the Lord at the Tabernacle and vowed that if the Lord would give her a son, she would give him to the Lord for His service. This son would be set apart even to the point that a razor would never come upon his head. Hannah likely promised to set her child apart for service according to the guidelines of the Nazarite vow as mentioned in Numbers 6. When Eli saw her in such distress, he accused her of being drunk. She exclaimed that it was not true but that she had poured out her soul "before the LORD"—she was seeking Him with all her heart. Eli responded with his blessing that God would grant her petition, thus enabling her to go her way with a changed heart and a joyful countenance.

The Lord soon gave Elkanah and Hannah a son, and they named him Samuel which means "name of God." When Samuel was weaned, probably around age 3, Hannah and Elkanah took him to serve in Shiloh with Eli the priest. The offering they brought was that which was prescribed for the fulfillment of a vow (see Numbers 15:8–10). Hannah continued to thank the Lord for His gift of a son.

Read 1 Samuel 2:1–10, and note any other insights into the heart of Samuel's mother. What do you think Samuel learned from her during those three years at home?

____

____

____

____

____

She was God-centered and exalted the Lord and only the Lord. Her heart overflowed with praise to the God who is the one who gives victory over every enemy. She exalted Him as holy, as a Rock who judges the actions of men. He is the God who raises up the humble, strengthens the weak, and humbles the proud. With Him are the powers over life and death, riches and poverty, exaltation and humiliation. He stands as Creator and Arranger of all of life, the one who places people where He wants and where He knows best. He watches over His "godly ones" to protect and give victory. It is *"not by might"* that a man prevails, but by the Lord who fights those who contend with Him. He is the judge who will strengthen and exalt His King. These truths flowed from the heart of Hannah. They were the things a mother would sing to her child, speak to her child, and seek to explain to her child in many different ways, in many different stories, and in testimonies of the past. Samuel would have known many things by the time he moved to the Tabernacle in Shiloh.

Read 1 Samuel 2:12–26. What was the spiritual atmosphere around the Tabernacle?

____

____

____

____

____

Did You Know?

SAMSON AND SAMUEL

Both men were born during the period of the judges to mothers who had been previously barren. Both served as judges over Israel and dealt with the Philistines as the enemies of Israel. They were also both under a Nazarite vow from birth (Judges 13:5, 7; 1 Samuel 1:11). In the vow Hannah made, she offered to give Samuel back to the Lord so that he could serve the Lord all of his life. Her statement about a razor never touching his head was very similar to the requirements for a Nazarite. In addition, a Nazarite never ate nor drank anything from the vine (grape juice, wine, grapes, raisins) and never touched anything dead (Numbers 6:1–8).

Put Yourself In Their Shoes

FULFILLING A VOW

In Numbers 15:1–3, 8–10 are given certain regulations for fulfilling a vow. One would bring a young bull along with a grain offering and a drink offering. The bull was sacrificed and burnt on the altar. With it the grain and oil were offered up in the sacrificial fire, and then, on all of that the offering of wine was poured out. In each offering is the picture of wholehearted surrender and brokenness: a bull sacrificed, its life poured out on the altar, grain crushed into flour, oil from the crushed olives, and wine from the beaten grapes. As the offering was burned and the wine poured out, there was a sweet aroma of the smoke ascending to the heavens, a very Jewish picture of the fully surrendered heart offering a gift of love to the Lord in heaven.

Word Study
SONS OF BELIAL

In I Samuel 2:12, Hophni and Phinehas are called *"corrupt"* or *"worthless men,"* literally, *"sons of Belial."* The meaning of Belial has two possibilities. The first takes this Hebrew word as rooted in *bly*, "to swallow" referring to *Sheol* or Death as the "Greatest Swallower" of life, thus bringing destruction. A second perspective combines the two words *beli* and *ya'al* to form the word, *beliya'al*, meaning "without value" or "worthless," and thus wicked. Therefore *Ben Belial* would be translated "son of worthlessness." In the New Testament, Belial became associated with Satan (2 Corinthians 6:15). The sons of Eli were wicked men who did not know the LORD.

The sons of Eli who lived and ministered at the Tabernacle were labeled as *"worthless men"*—literally, "sons of Belial," a term used of Satan in 2 Corinthians 6:15 and referring to wickedness in nature and action. Eli's sons did not know the Lord nor the way of fellowship, nor obedience. Neither did they know the Word of God nor the *"custom of the priests."* Rather, they were gluttonous, wanting more than their share of the offerings and taking the fat that was to be burned in sacrifice to the Lord, ever seeking to please themselves. They despised the offering of the Lord and the Lord Himself, and, in addition, were immoral with the women who served at the door of the Tent of Meeting (Exodus 38:8). The atmosphere here was more akin to the atmosphere at Canaanite altars (indulging in the sensual and the immoral) than to the ways of the Lord, ways marked by holiness and the fear of the Lord.

📖 Contrast the actions and attitudes of Samuel in 1 Samuel 2:11, 18–21, 26. (You may wish to compare Luke 2:52.)

____

____

____

____

From the start Samuel *"ministered to the LORD,"* wearing a linen ephod, the garment of a priest. As Samuel ministered before the Lord, he grew physically and spiritually, in favor with the Lord and with men. His relationship with Eli and those who lived in Shiloh, as well as those who came to offer sacrifices at the Tabernacle, was ever growing. People could see the good character of this young boy as he grew into a young man. The statement in verse 26 is remarkably like that spoken of the Lord Jesus as a boy becoming a young man. He too grew in stature and in favor with God and man. Luke adds that Jesus *"kept increasing in wisdom"* (2:52), which, it is evident, was also true of Samuel.

Hannah gave Samuel to the Lord, and she devoted him to God with a grateful heart. She dedicated him to the service of the Lord of Hosts, the Lord of Israel. At the appropriate time, she fulfilled her vow and Samuel began his service. He did so in the midst of a needy place—a place in need of the Word of God, in need of the Spirit of God, and in need of the Work of God in the hearts of the people. We have seen all the Lord did in preparing His servant. How did God work through this young servant of His? We will begin to see that in Day Two.

GIVEN TO THE WORD OF THE LORD AS PROPHET, PRIEST, AND JUDGE

During the young boyhood of Samuel an unnamed *"man of God"* brought God's word to Eli. God knew the sinful ways of Eli and his sons, Hophni and Phinehas, and He promised to deal with them. In the midst of that environment, Samuel *"was growing in stature and in favor both with the LORD and with men."* Then, God's call came.

📖 Read 1 Samuel 2:27–36. What did the "man of God" speak concerning the sins of Eli and his sons?

____

____

____

____

What did he say about the consequences for that sin (2:30–34)?

____

____

____

What did *"the man of God"* say about the plans of God for His ongoing work (2:35)?

____

____

____

____

Eli and his sons failed to honor God as God. They despised Him, His word, and His work. As a result Hophni and Phinehas would die on the same day, and the house of Eli would eventually perish. The Lord promised to raise up *"a faithful priest who will do according to what is in My heart and in My soul."* Samuel certainly did that in his ministry, but this was ultimately fulfilled in the line of Zadok of the family of Eleazar. His line will one day walk before the Messiah ("My anointed") during His triumphant millennial reign (Ezekiel 44:15).

What did the Lord do after the "man of God" gave his message to Eli (3:1–14)?

____

____

____

Samuel was now a boy about twelve or thirteen years of age. Soon after the *"man of God"* delivered the message of the Lord to Eli, the Lord came to Samuel in a vision telling him of the coming judgment on Eli's house. Samuel had seen the wickedness and ways of Eli's sons, but the Lord wanted Samuel to know His ways. Now he saw the consequences of sin more clearly. God entrusted this truth to him as the first of many truths for the good of Israel and the glory of God.

📖 Read 1 Samuel 3:10, 15–20. How did Samuel respond to this revelation from the Lord?

____

____

____

____

Put Yourself In Their Shoes

THE GARMENTS OF SAMUEL

Samuel wore a linen ephod, the clothing of a priest. It was a sleeveless, vest-like garment designed for use in the service of the Tabernacle (Exodus 28:5–14). Later in Israel's history, the Lord made it clear that the priests were to wear linen garments in the Temple and never wear wool so that they would not sweat in their service (Ezekiel 44:15–19). He wanted no uncleanness of the flesh in any ministry He gave them to do. This applied to Samuel as well.

What was his first assignment? What did he have to do with this truth?

Did You Know?

THE COVENANT GOD OF ISRAEL

The name of the LORD, *Yahweh* or *Jehovah*, is the personal covenant name for God. This is the God who could be known or experienced in daily life. Hophni and Phineas never experienced God. They only experienced interaction with their own wicked hearts. Samuel as well as Elkanah and Hannah were different—they truly knew God personally and sought to bring others to that knowledge.

As a man with a true servant's heart, Samuel listened carefully and attentively to all the Lord spoke to him. He then faithfully told Eli all that God had said and thus began his ministry as a prophet to Israel. Over the next months and years he walked with the Lord, and when the Lord gave him a message, he spoke it faithfully, fully, and truthfully. That is what a prophet does, and because he speaks a message from the Lord, it **always** comes to pass. The sure sign of a false prophet is "hit-and-miss" prophecies. Elijah was a true prophet who walked in the presence of God—*"the LORD was with him"*—and God confirmed His Word through Samuel (3:19). None of his words failed—literally, none *"fell to the ground."* The people of Israel from Dan (northernmost region) to Beersheba (southernmost region) knew that Samuel was a prophet of God as God "confirmed" or established him and his ministry.

APPLY Are you being faithful in listening to and applying what God is speaking to you in His Word? Ask the Lord to reveal any areas where you are not honoring Him or His Word.

Read 1 Samuel 3:21; 4:1a with Psalm 99:6–7 and Jeremiah 15:1. With whom does the Lord group Samuel?

Doctrine

WHAT ABOUT FALSE PROPHETS?

What did God have to say about false prophets? First of all, if what they said did not agree with what God had already spoken, it was not from Him. Deuteronomy mentions a prophet who speaks of a sign or wonder that comes true, but leads the people after other gods. That is a false prophet. But what about those prophets whose words did not come true? Deuteronomy 18:21–22 states that God did not send them. There were serious consequences for speaking presumptuously in God's name, for saying something God did not command him to speak, or for speaking in the name of another god. *"That prophet shall die"* (Deuteronomy 18:20).

What characterized Samuel?

The Lord grouped Samuel with Moses and Aaron, men who were marked by a heart knowledge of God. They had fervently sought the LORD, heard His Word, and sought to lead the people of God by that Word. Psalm 99:6–7 says Samuel was characterized as one of those *"who called on His name"* and received His answer. He heard them when they prayed. The Lord spoke to these men in the pillar of cloud, and they obeyed what He said. What was this "pillar of cloud"?

First Samuel 3:21 states, *"And the LORD appeared again at Shiloh."* The Tabernacle rested at Shiloh, and the mention of the Lord appearing there seems to indicate that the Lord revealed Himself as He did with Moses and

Aaron at the Tabernacle in the wilderness. The Hebrew word for *"appeared"* in 3:21 has the same root as *"appearance"* in Numbers 9:15 which speaks of the Cloud of Glory that rested over the Tabernacle—a cloud by day and a pillar of fire by night. There the Lord spoke and gave specific directions for the Israelites—when to move, where to move, and how long to stay. He was walking with them and training them in the Wilderness. They needed to know and walk in His Word and His ways, not the thoughts and ways of Egypt. In Samuel's day, once again the people desperately needed the Word of the Lord, just as we need God's Word in this present day.

📖 Contrast 1 Samuel 3:1 with 3:21—4:1a. What difference do you see?

____

____

____

____

First Samuel 3:1 states that *"word from the LORD was rare in those days, visions were infrequent."* The same passage in the New King James Version is translated, *"there was no widespread revelation."* God raised up Samuel, a man who would hear God and respond with faithful obedience. When the Lord revealed truth, Samuel proclaimed that truth. From Dan to Beersheba the word went forth so that *"the word of Samuel came to all Israel."* Samuel was so clear in his proclamation that to mention *"the word of Samuel"* was the same as hearing *"the word of the LORD,"* because he only spoke what God gave him to speak. [Compare Jesus' words in John 8:28.] The Israelites would need to hear the Lord, for they had enemies to deal with. We will see that more clearly in Day Three.

GIVEN TO THE WILL OF THE LORD

Though the Word of the Lord spread throughout the land, Israel faced a constant threat from the Philistines, a coastal people who had entered the land around 1200 BC. Their "iron technology" gave them a superior advantage over the Israelites, who were a rural, agricultural people. The Philistines desired to conquer the land of Canaan and came against the Israelites. How would the Israelites go into battle? What would they do about this Philistine menace?

📖 Read 1 Samuel 4:1–11. What did Israel do and what were the results?

____

____

____

____

____

____

First Israel was defeated with the loss of 4,000 men in battle. Then, they decided to take the Ark of the Covenant, the sign of the presence and power

WHO WERE THE PHILISTINES?

The Philistines were originally a sea people from the Aegean and Mediterranean Sea region (Crete) who settled in Canaan around 1200 BC. They were localized in five cities—Ashdod, Ashkelon, Gaza, Ekron, and Gath (the chief city)—with each one ruled by a "lord" (1 Samuel 6:17–18). A cultured people, utilizing considerable skills both on land and on sea (1 Samuel 6:4, 8, 17–18 and 13:19–22), the Philistines worshiped the idols Dagon (a fish god), Ashtaroth (a fertility goddess), and Baalzebub ("lord of the flies"), one of the Baal gods (Judges 16:21–30; 1 Samuel 5:1-7; 31:10; 2 Kings 1:1–16). The modern word "Palestine" is from the Assyrian root words for Philistine.

of God, into battle. When they removed it from Shiloh and marched into battle, the Philistines captured it, and 30,000 Israelites died—including Eli's sons Hophni and Phinehas. Trusting God was not their first thought, but an afterthought.

Renowned pastor and Christian teacher, Adrian Rogers, has shown keen insight in describing how God responded to the actions of Israel and the Philistines concerning the Ark. The Israelites found that God would not be **used** like a superstitious charm (4:5–11). The Philistines soon found that the God of Israel could not be **captured.** Their cities were terrorized by the presence of the Ark of the Covenant. After seven months they sent the Ark back to Israel (5:1–2; 6:1–18). The people of Beth-shemesh found that God would not be **trivialized.** When they looked into the Ark against the clear commands of Scripture many men died (6:19–21). The Ark was to be handled only by the priests and in a prescribed manner. While the Ark rested at the house of Abinadab in Kiriath-jearim, the people still had no rest, and for twenty years *"all the house of Israel lamented after the LORD"* while the Ark was there (7:2). One lesson that could be drawn from that: The Lord cannot be **ignored** by His people if they want to walk in His joy.

Did You Know?

THE ARK OF THE COVENANT

The ark of the covenant was a wooden chest covered with gold. Its cover lid, known as the mercy seat, had two golden cherubim one at each end with their wings arching toward the center. Inside the ark were the two tablets of the Law, the golden jar of manna from the wilderness, and Aaron's almond rod that budded, all symbols of the covenant relationship between God and His people Israel. The ark was the sole piece of furniture in the Holy of Holies in the Tabernacle. The ark had four rings, one on each corner, and was to be carried on poles on the shoulders of the priests (Exodus 25:10–22; Hebrews 9:4).

At that time Samuel called on the people to turn to the Lord with all their hearts and remove the foreign gods from their midst. They thought it was enough to worship the Lord some of the time while at the same time worshiping some of the gods of the Canaanites. Samuel called them to serve God **alone**, and *"He will deliver you from the hand of the Philistines"* (7:3).

📖 Read 1 Samuel 7:4–6. Record what happened.

____

____

____

____

____

____

What was the focus of Samuel?

____

____

____

____

____

The people did remove the Baals and the images of Ashtaroth and chose to serve the Lord alone. At that point Samuel called them to gather to Mizpah where they drew water and poured it out before the Lord—a symbol of repentance and surrender to the Lord as evidenced when they humbled themselves through fasting and confessed, *"We have sinned against the LORD."* Verse 6 says Samuel judged Israel at Mizpah and implies that as they were gathered together for this meeting with the Lord, Samuel dealt with any offenses, disputes, sins, or questions that the people brought to him. He wanted them to know the Word of the Lord and obey Him fully.

When the Philistines heard Israel had gathered at Mizpah, they mustered their troops to battle with them. Read 1 Samuel 7:7–12. What was the people's response?

____

____

____

____

____

What did Samuel do? How did he lead the people?

____

____

____

____

____

How did the Lord respond?

____

____

____

____

____

The people called on Samuel to *"cry to the LORD our God for us, that He may save us"* (7:8). Samuel offered a lamb as a burnt offering, a symbol of total surrender to the Lord and His ways. He cried out to the Lord and the Lord answered and sent a tremendous thunder that confused the Philistines and led to their defeat by the Israelites. Thereafter, Samuel set up a stone of remembrance and named it "the stone of help" (*Ebenezer*) and declared, *"Thus far the LORD has helped us."* It was quite a change from the way they had tried to use God and the Ark several years before.

Think about what happened to Israel as a result of being led by a man of God who followed the Word of God. Think about how differently the people responded to the Philistine threat this time—no seeking to use Him or the Ark, no superstition. This time they followed the truth of the Word and came to the Lord with a surrendered heart. They were seeking to walk in line with His character and His will, and He responded with His power and provision. After this the menace of the Philistines lessened. During Samuel's days as Judge, the hand of the Lord continued to be against the Philistines, and Israel recovered the territory taken by the Philistines. The Lord also gave peace between Israel and the Amorites (7:13–14).

Samuel's ministry as Judge continued for several years. He traveled annually as a circuit judge to Bethel, Gilgal, and Mizpah, judging Israel at each location. The people faithfully heard the Word of the Lord and were able to deal with their disputes and problems. When he was not on this circuit, Samuel ministered in his hometown of Ramah (7:15–17).

Word Study

THE FALSE GODS BAAL AND ASHTAROTH

The Canaanites worshiped Baal as lord of nature (rain, thunder, crops, and fertility), and often practiced immoral rites associated with that worship. Some even sacrificed children in the fires of the altar to Baal. The word Baal means "lord" or "husband" and was sometimes combined with other names such as Baal-zebub (later Beelzebul, Matthew 10:25) or with place names such as Baal-Peor. Ashtoreth (plural, Ashtaroth), a Canaanite goddess of fertility, was the wife of Baal and daughter of El and Asherah, who were also Canaanite deities. The Canaanites, the Philistines, and the Sidonians all worshiped these false gods in some form, often placing a figure or an Asherah pole in front of an altar (1 Samuel 7:3–4; 12:10; 31:10; 2 Kings 3:2; 10:27), a practice prohibited by the Lord (Leviticus 26:1; Deuteronomy 16:21–22).

"THE LORD THUNDERED"

The Philistine god Dagon (half fish and half man) was the father of Baal, who was the god of nature, especially of the storm, or thunder and rain. Baal was sometimes pictured with a lightning bolt in his hand. In 1 Samuel 7:10, the Lord, the God of Israel, revealed who was truly God over thunder and God over all. He was the God and protector of His covenant people Israel.

GIVEN TO THE WAYS OF THE LORD IN HIS CHOICE OF KING

When Samuel grew older he appointed his two sons, Joel and Abijah, as judges. However, they did not judge as he did but chose to accept bribes, thus perverting justice (8:3). The people came to Samuel and confronted him with this issue. Not only that, but they also asked him to appoint a king over them, to judge them and to fight their battles for them. They wanted to be like the nations around them. What was Samuel to do?

Read 1 Samuel 8:4–20. What was Samuel's first response, and what did he do about it?

____

____

____

____

____

Put Yourself In Their Shoes

WAS IT WRONG FOR ISRAEL TO WANT A KING?

Israel's request for a king was not wrong in and of itself. In fact, the Law made provision for the appointment of a king. In Genesis 49:10, Jacob prophesied that kings from Judah would one day rule over Israel. In Numbers 24:17, Balaam prophesied that a king from Israel would even rule over other nations. In Deuteronomy 17:14–15, the issue comes into balance. There the assumption is made that Israel would want a king, and instructions are given on how to select a king and what he should be like. The most important thing we see there is that God is to select the king.

What was the Word from the Lord concerning this matter?

____

____

____

____

Samuel was displeased because he saw evil in their request. When he took it to the Lord, the Lord told him to listen to the people because they were rejecting God as King, not Samuel as judge. God instructed Samuel to inform them of what it would be like to have a king—what it would cost them, what it would mean, what it would take to support a king and his kingdom. Samuel again faithfully conveyed all the Word of the Lord to the people, but they refused to listen to his warnings or to the warnings of the Lord through him. They still wanted a king—someone to judge them, fight their battles for them, and make them like the other nations around them.

According to 1 Samuel 8:21–22, how did Samuel respond?

____

____

____

____

Samuel listened to all the words of the people and then went to the Lord and repeated to Him everything the people had said. The Lord simply instructed him to give them what they wanted. Since Samuel trusted God and His ways, he obeyed and began looking for the Lord's choice as king.

Through a search for his father's donkeys, a man by the name of Saul and his servant came to Ramah, where the Lord had revealed to Samuel that Saul would be coming. The Lord had told Samuel to anoint Saul as king (9:15–16), and had promised that through Saul He would deal with the Philistines for the sake of His people and in answer to their cries (9:16). Once Samuel had obeyed the instructions of the Lord and anointed Saul as Israel's king, he once again addressed the people concerning their desire for a king. He rebuked them for the wickedness of their request and called upon the Lord to send thunder and rain on the wheat harvest as a sign of their wickedness. The Lord answered with thunder and rain *"and all the people greatly feared the LORD and Samuel"* (12:18).

"As for me, far be it from me that I should sin against the LORD by ceasing to pray for you; but I will instruct you in the good and right way." I Samuel 12:23

Then Samuel called on them to follow the Lord and His ways with all their hearts and not to turn aside to *"futile things."* He also promised that the Lord would continually watch over His people *"on account of His great name"* (12:22). In 1 Samuel 12:23, Samuel made his personal promise—a promise that characterized his life: *"As for me, far be it from me that I should sin against the LORD by ceasing to pray for you; but I will instruct you in the good and right way"* (12:23). As the prophet, judge, and priest he was, Samuel could not let an opportunity pass to direct the heart of the people to the LORD. After his promise to pray for them, he exhorted them, *"only fear the LORD and serve Him in truth with all your heart; for consider what great things He has done for you. But if you still do wickedly, both you and your king shall be swept away"* (12:24–25). [See 1 Samuel 9–11 about the choice of Saul as king. Also see the in-depth study of the life of Saul in *Following God: Life Principles from the Kings of Israel*—Lesson 1, "Saul: The Folly of Not Following God," pp. 1–16.]

After anointing Saul as king, Samuel gave him clear instructions about what to do. Part of those instructions included going to Gilgal and waiting on Samuel for seven days after which Samuel would offer burnt offerings and peace offerings and give further instruction to Saul (10:2–8).

Read 1 Samuel 13:8–14. What did Saul do?

____

____

____

____

What were the consequences?

____

____

____

____

Put Yourself In Their Shoes

WHAT WENT WRONG WITH SAUL?

In confronting the disobedience of Saul, Samuel spoke of rebellion, divination, insubordination, iniquity, and idolatry. Rebellion is saying no to authority and making oneself the authority. Divination is seeking what is not God and what is contrary to the nature and character of God, while insubordination is honoring self as god. Iniquity is choosing what is deceptive and empty, which is readily associated with idolatry—the following of a false, lifeless, hollow image. Samuel's assessment was that Saul's heart was rooted in these five sins.

Saul grew impatient waiting for Samuel, especially since it was the seventh day and many of his men were leaving or hiding from the approaching Philistines. Saul, neither knowing nor honoring the ways of the Lord, took matters into his own hands and offered the sacrifices. As soon as he finished, Samuel came and rebuked Saul for his foolishness and told him that his kingdom would not last. Furthermore, the Lord was seeking a man *"after His own heart"* who would obey all He said.

Some time later the Lord instructed Samuel to order Saul to destroy the Amalekites for their wickedness. Read 1 Samuel 15:1–35. What do you see about the ways of Saul?

"The LORD has sought out for Himself a man after His own heart." I Samuel 13:14

What about the responses of Samuel?

Record your insights about the outcome of this event.

Saul killed all the Amalekites except king Agag, and he and his troops spared "the best" of the livestock for sacrifice, something the Lord had **not** commanded. Samuel confronted Saul for his disobedience and pronounced the Lord's judgment, which was that the kingship would be taken from Saul and given to another. In verse 26, Samuel gets to the heart of the matter, *"you have rejected the word of the Lord"*; and therefore, the Lord had rejected Saul as king over Israel. Samuel *"hewed Agag to pieces"* in judgment on his sins, and then traveled back to Ramah where he *"grieved over Saul."*

Put Yourself In Their Shoes

WHAT WAS RIGHT ABOUT DAVID?

When Samuel went to anoint the next king over Israel, the Lord further instructed him in a truth he knew in part. *"Do not look at his appearance . . . for God sees not as man sees, for man looks at the outward appearance, but the Lord looks at the heart"* (1 Samuel 16:7). The Lord wants loving obedience from the heart, and Samuel had seen that in his father, Elkanah, and his mother, Hannah, while it was missing in Hophni and Phinehas. Samuel instructed the people to live in obedience (12:24), and there at Bethlehem the Lord showed him once again a portrait of loving obedience in the young lad David, *"**A man after My heart,** who will do all My will"* (Acts 13:22).

The Lord was not finished with Samuel. After some time He called Samuel to go to Bethlehem and anoint the Lord's choice as king. This man was to be a man after His heart who would do His will. This was another opportunity for Samuel to learn more about the ways of God and the importance of listening to Him and following Him in those ways.

Read 1 Samuel 16:1–13, and record the central truth Samuel learned on that eventful day of David's anointing as king.

Samuel learned that man's outward appearance is secondary at best. *"The LORD looks on the heart,"* (16:7) and makes His decisions along the lines of the heart. If Samuel would look to the Lord about the man He wanted as king, He would find the right man, and that is exactly what Samuel did. After years of ministry, he still had a teachable, humble heart (the two always go together), and he discovered a new depth of joy and satisfaction in the ways and will of God.

[For an in-depth look at the life of David see *Following God: Life Principles from the Kings of Israel*—"David: A Man After God's Own Heart," pp. 17–34. For further details about Samuel's life, see the chart titled, "A Look at the Life of Samuel" at the end of this lesson.]

According to 1 Samuel 25:1, *"Samuel died; and all Israel gathered together and mourned for him, and buried him at his house in Ramah."* Samuel lived a long life of service. From boyhood he was a servant to the Lord in the Tabernacle, and then from his youth he began to serve as a prophet as well as judge and priest for the entire nation. His life was marked by **prayer** and a surrender to living and proclaiming **the Word of God.** He was a testimony of the sufficiency of the Lord in a day of spiritual decline. God used him to bring Israel to the threshold of some of her greatest days as Saul began his exit and David received the kingship and prepared to reign.

For Me to Follow God

Samuel was given to the Lord before he was born, and as he grew it became evident he was given to the Word of the Lord, to His will, and to His ways. He walked with God first through the word of his father and mother, then through the priestly instruction of Eli at the Tabernacle. There at the Tabernacle the Lord Himself began to give Samuel revelation of His will. In Samuel's life we see that he was, first, available; from the age of around three, he ministered before the Lord with Eli at the Tabernacle and stayed there for many years. He was also teachable; when he first heard the voice of the Lord he listened with a heart that said, *"Speak, for Thy servant is listening"* (see 1 Samuel 3:9–10), and he carried that attitude throughout his life. Samuel was faithful; he followed the Lord and His Word season after season, year after year, and he led the people in following God—ever faithful in prayer, ever careful to intercede for the people of God.

What about your life? Are you marked by being "available" to the Lord? Have you surrendered to Him? If not, now is the perfect time to bring your heart and life to him in surrender. Raise the "white flag" of surrender over the battlefield of your heart. He is a gracious General to follow, and being a bondservant in His army assures you of true victory in life.

Are you available and teachable?

Are you teachable? A disciple is defined as a "learner." Do you have a learner's heart, or do you think you already know all you need to know? Jesus said, *"Come to Me, all who are weary and heavy-laden, and I will give you rest. Take* **My yoke** *upon you, and* **learn from Me,** *for I am gentle and humble in heart; and* **you shall find rest for your souls.** *For My yoke is easy, and My load is light"* (Matthew 11:28–30). Pause right now, and ask the Lord to show you where you are "unteachable," and ask Him to begin the teaching process.

The disciples asked Jesus to teach them to pray. Perhaps that's where you should start. Samuel's mother, Hannah, started there, and it is evident that Samuel learned some things about prayer.

Samuel also knew the Word of God. That is where you and I will learn much from the Lord. If you have come this far in this study, you are on the right track to learning some of the things the Lord wants to teach you about following Him. Keep it up. Don't let distractions (the world system, the flesh, the devil) block your road to following God.

Are you faithful? Are you surrendered to the Lord's will? Someone has defined "faithful" using an acrostic from the word "faith." In other words the letters **"F-A-I-T-H"** can represent the meaning, "**F**orsaking **A**ll, **I** **T**rust **H**im." It means day-by-day, moment-by-moment, I forsake my way and trust His way; I forsake my agenda and take His agenda; I surrender my opinion and trust His Word. As you and I do that, we walk in faithfulness to Him.

Are you facing some "Philistines" in your life, things that rob you of your joy, your peace, and your time? Deal with them according to the Word of God. What applications do you see for your life?

____

____

____

____

____

Are there ways in which you have acted like the Israelites when they tried to use the Ark of the Covenant like a "good-luck charm"? Have you tried to use God to get your will on earth approved in the courts of heaven, to get your will, your way? Have you tried to **capture** God and imprison Him in your scheme of things?

____

____

____

____

"Only fear the LORD and serve Him in truth with all your heart; for consider what great things He has done for you." I Samuel 12:24

Have you **trivialized** God or the things of God in your life?

____

____

____

Have you **ignored** God and His Word?

____

____

____

____

Take some time to let the Lord search your heart. Ask Him to show you where any of these questions show up on your doorstep.

____

____

____

____

Lord, speak to me, for Your servant is needy, and I'm listening. Open my eyes that I might see the wonderful truths in Your Word, in the Creation around me, in the wise counsel of those godly friends (or friend) you have placed in my life. I find myself battle-weary over those "Philistines" in my life. Strengthen me with Your strength, make me wise with Your wisdom from above. Make me especially sensitive against using You or trying to box You into my plans. Forgive me for trivializing who You are or ignoring You, acting as if I could get along without You. Lord, You are my life. May I keep growing in hearing You, in obeying You, and in experiencing You in my daily life. In Jesus' Name. Amen.

In light of all you have learned this week write a prayer letter to the Lord or make a journal entry that serves as a mile marker in the journey on which the Lord has brought you.

____

____

____

____

____

____

____

____

____

____

A Look at the Life of Samuel

DATE	EVENTS	SCRIPTURE
	Hannah's desire for a son	1 Samuel 1:1–8
	Hannah's prayer for a son	1 Samuel 1:9–18
ca. 1105 BC	God's answer in the birth of Samuel—"asked of God"	1 Samuel 1:19–20
1105–02 BC	Samuel lived at home with Hannah until he was weaned (age 3).	1 Samuel 1:21–23
1102/01 BC	Samuel came to the House of the Lord at Shiloh (age 3 or 4).	1 Samuel 1:24–28
	Hannah's song of rejoicing	1 Samuel 2:1–10
As a Boy	Samuel began ministering to the Lord before Eli the Priest. [Contrast Eli's sons—2:12–17, 22–25.]	1 Samuel 2:11, 18–21
ca. 1093 BC	Samuel grew in stature and in favor with the Lord and man (around age 12). [Compare Luke 2:52.]	1 Samuel 2:26
	God pronounced judgment on Eli, his sons, and his house.	1 Samuel 2:27–36
	Samuel heard from God (around age 13 or 14).	1 Samuel 3:1–14
	Samuel prophesied to Eli.	1 Samuel 3:15–18
	Samuel began prophesying.	1 Samuel 3:19–21; 4:1
	War with the Philistines	1 Samuel 4:2–10
	Eli (age 98), Hophni, and Phinehas died. The Philistines captured the ark of the covenant.	1 Samuel 4:11–22
ca. 1073 BC	The Philistines were terrorized by the ark of the covenant.	1 Samuel 5
	The Philistines returned the ark to Israel after 7 months.	1 Samuel 6
1073–1053	The ark remained at Kiriath-jearim 20 years. Israel lamented.	1 Samuel 7:1–2
	Samuel confronted the people's idolatry.	1 Samuel 7:3–4
ca. 1053 BC	At Mizpah, Samuel served as judge of Israel and prayed for deliverance from the Philistines. God sent great thunder, and the Philistines were defeated.	1 Samuel 7:5–12
	Samuel set up a stone of remembrance and named it the "stone of help" (*Ebenezer*) because the Lord was their help.	1 Samuel 7:12
	"The hand of the Lord was against the Philistines all the days of Samuel," and there was peace with the Amorites.	1 Samuel 7:13–14
	Samuel governed Israel as a circuit judge in the cities of Bethel, Gilgal, Mizpah and Ramah.	1 Samuel 7:15–17
	Samuel was "old" (62?). Samuel appointed his sons, Joel and Abijah, as judges in Beersheba.	1 Samuel 8:1–3
ca. 1052 BC	The elders of Israel spoke of the injustice of Samuel's sons, and they requested a king. Samuel prayed.	1 Samuel 8:4–9
	Samuel warned the people about having a king, but the people insisted, and God granted them a king.	1 Samuel 8:10–22
	Saul came to Samuel at Ramah.	1 Samuel 9:1–14
	Samuel heard from God about Saul before he arrived.	1 Samuel 9:15–17
	Samuel met Saul.	1 Samuel 9:18–27
ca. 1051 BC	Samuel anointed Saul as king at Ramah.	1 Samuel 10:1–16
	Saul was chosen as king by lot at Mizpah.	1 Samuel 10:17–27
	War with the Ammonites was led by Saul and Samuel (11:7).	1 Samuel 11:1–11
	Some sought revenge against the Israelites who were disloyal to Saul.	1 Samuel 11:12–13
	Samuel led the people to Gilgal to affirm Saul as king.	1 Samuel 11:14–15
	Samuel rebuked the people for rejecting God as King and admonished and warned them to fear and follow the LORD.	1 Samuel 12:1–25
	War with the Philistines	1 Samuel 13:1–7
	Samuel and Saul at Gilgal—Saul disobeyed Samuel's word from the Lord, and judgment was pronounced. The kingdom was about to be taken from Saul.	1 Samuel 13:8–14
	Samuel at Gibeah. Saul prepared to battle the Philistines.	1 Samuel 13:15–23
	Jonathan and the Israelites defeated the Philistines.	1 Samuel 14:1–23
	Saul displayed foolish leadership which resulted in limited victory over the Philistines.	1 Samuel 14:24–34

DATE	EVENTS	SCRIPTURE
	Saul threatened to execute his son over eating honey, but Jonathan was rescued from death by the people.	1 Samuel 14:35–46
	Saul and his leaders faced warfare.	1 Samuel 14:47–52
	Samuel sent Saul to destroy the Amalekites.	1 Samuel 15:1–9
	At Gilgal, Samuel confronted Saul over his disobedience in sparing Agag and some of "the best" of the livestock.	1 Samuel 15:10–31
	Samuel slew Agag king of the Amalekites.	1 Samuel 15:32–33
ca. 1030 BC?	Samuel traveled back to Ramah and grieved over Saul.	1 Samuel 15:34–35
ca. 1029 BC Age 86	The Lord instructed Samuel to go to Bethlehem and anoint a new king—[David].	1 Samuel 16:1–13
	Samuel returned to Ramah.	1 Samuel 16:13
	David was brought to Saul to serve him.	1 Samuel 16:14–23
ca. 1026 BC	The challenge and death of Goliath at the hand of David.	1 Samuel 17:1–54
	Saul called for David.	1 Samuel 17:55–58
	Jonathan and David entered into a covenantal friendship.	1 Samuel 18:1–4
	David fought valiantly, but Saul despised him. David married Saul's daughter, Michal.	1 Samuel 18:5–30
	Jonathan defended David before Saul.	1 Samuel 19:1–7
	David battled with the Philistines, and Saul renewed his attacks against David, but he escaped.	1 Samuel 19:8–17
	David traveled to Samuel at Ramah, and they went to Naioth.	1 Samuel 19:18–24
	David and Jonathan entered into a covenant, and Jonathan agreed to protect David.	1 Samuel 20:1–29
	Saul's anger burned against Jonathan and David, but Jonathan still protected David.	1 Samuel 20:30–42
	David fled to Nob and received refuge and supplies.	1 Samuel 21:1–9
	David fled to Achish, king of Gath.	1 Samuel 21:10–15
	David went to the cave of Adullam, and four hundred men joined him.	1 Samuel 22:1–2
	David went to Mizpah of Moab and sought protection for his parents there.	1 Samuel 22:3–4
	David went to the stronghold and then to the forest of Hereth.	1 Samuel 22:4–5
	At Saul's command the priests of Nob were slain by Doeg the Edomite.	1 Samuel 22:6–23
	David had victory over the Philistines at Keilah.	1 Samuel 23:1–5
	Saul pursued David at Keilah, then in the wilderness of Ziph.	1 Samuel 23:6–14
	Jonathan encouraged David.	1 Samuel 23:15–18
	Saul still pursued David.	1 Samuel 23:19–28
	David fled to Engedi where Saul pursued him. David refused to kill Saul when he had the opportunity.	1 Samuel 23:29; 24:1–22
	Samuel died and was buried in Ramah. *"All Israel gathered together and mourned for him."*	1 Samuel 25:1
ca. 1011 BC	Saul sought advice from Samuel through a medium/spiritist.	1 Samuel 28:3–25

The Kingdoms of Israel and Judah
0 10 20 30 40 miles
0 10 20 30 40 kilometers
Beirut
Sidon
Tyre
PHOENICIA
Litani R.
Abana R.
Damascus
Mt. Hermon
Pharpar R.
Dan
ARAM
Kedesh
Hazor
J. Jarmuk
Acco
Sea of Galilee
Mt. Carmel
Mt. Tabor
Kishon R.
Ashtaroth
Yarmuk R.
Edrei
Mediterranean Sea
Megiddo
Mt. Moreh
Taanach
Beth-shan
Ramoth-gilead
Ibleam
Mt. Gilboa
Jordan R.
Jabesh-gilead?
Tirzah
Samaria
Mt. Ebal
Succoth?
Penuel?
Mahanaim?
Yarkon R.
Schechem
Jabbok R.
Mt. Gerizim
Aphek
Joppa
Shiloh
ISRAEL
Rabbah (Amman)
Bethel
AMMON
Gezer
Jericho
Ashdod
Aijalon
Jerusalem
Mt. Nebo
Heshbon
Medeba
Gath
Bethlehem
Ashkelon
Mareshah
Hebron
Dibon
Gaza
Dead Sea
Arnon R.
Gerar
Besor Br.
JUDAH
Raphia
Beersheba
MOAB
Kir-hareseth
PHILISTIA
Zered Br.
W. el-Arish
WILDERNESS
Region periodically contested by Judah and Edom
Bozrah
EDOM
Kadesh-barnea
WILDERNESS
© 1999 MapQuest.com, Inc

Notes

Notes

Following God When Those Around You Do not

Elijah came onto the scene at a critical juncture in Israel's history. Let's go back in time a little bit to present a review of the events that led up to the time of Elijah. Solomon replaced David as king. In his latter years Solomon's wives turned his heart away from God, and he *"did what was evil in the sight of the LORD, and did not follow the LORD fully, as David his father had done"* (1 Kings 11:6). As a result Israel split into two kingdoms. The northern ten tribes followed Jeroboam, Solomon's slave master, and were led into false worship complete with idols, pagan altars, false priests, and even false feasts. The Northern Kingdom languished through a series of wicked kings from Jeroboam to his son, Nadab, who followed in his sinful footsteps (1 Kings 15:26), and then to Baasha who did likewise (15:34). Baasha was succeeded by the drunken king, Elah, who was assassinated by Zimri, his commander. Zimri's reign lasted only seven days, but he is characterized as walking in the sinful ways of Jeroboam (16:19). Zimri was replaced by Omri, the most wicked king yet (16:25–26). The stage is now set for Ahab, the reigning king during the prophetic ministry of Elijah.

Elijah was called of God to minister to the northern ten tribes of Israel during the early years of the divided kingdom.

WHEN DID HE PROPHESY?

1050	1000	950	900	850
SAMUEL Judge and Prophet GAD	NATHAN	SHEMAIAH IDDO ODED	Hanani the Seer AZARIAH Jahaziel the Levite	OBADIAH JOEL
		Rehoboam **931–913** **Asa** **911–870** **Abijam** **913–911**	**Jehoshaphat** **873–848** **Jehoram (Joram)** **853–841**	**Ahaziah** **841** **Athaliah** **841–835** **Joash** **835–796**
Saul **1051–1011** **David** **1011–971**	**Solomon** **971–931**			
Ishbosheth ruled over Israel 1011–1004 David ruled over Judah from Hebron 1011–1004 David ruled over all Israel and Judah from Jerusalem 1004–971	960—Temple finished	**Jeroboam I** **931–910** **Nadab** **910–909** **Baasha** **909–886**	**Elah** **886–885** **Zimri** **885** **Tibni** **885–880** **Omri** **885–874** **Ahab** **874–853** **Ahaziah** **853–852** **Jehoram (Joram)** **852–841**	**Jehu** **841–814**
		AHIJAH the Shilonite "A man of God from Judah" A prophet from Samaria in Bethel	JEHU, son of Hanani MICAIAH ELIJAH	ELISHA
	Hiram I of Tyre 981–947		Benhadad I of Syria 900–860 Benhadad II of Syria 860–841	

Elijah DAY ONE

THE WORD OF THE LORD

Like a diamond against a backdrop of black velvet, the wickedness of Elijah's day highlights the workings of God through Elijah, and causes the full beauty of what God was doing to be seen. Today we will see that the *"word of the Lord"* (1 Kings 17:1ff.) coming to Elijah was Jehovah's gracious intervention to turn Israel away from their wickedness and back to following God. It was God who took the initiative. Even the drought Elijah prophesied, although an indication of judgment, is an evidence of God's grace. He is unwilling to leave us when we stray from Him. He always calls us back. Since the Northern Kingdom (the northern ten tribes of Israel) split from Judah and the kingly line of David, they had given themselves to idols. King after king followed the wicked example of Jeroboam in worshiping the Canaanite gods. Judah meanwhile was enjoying revival under Asa and Hezekiah. But God had not forgotten His people in the Northern Kingdom. He faithfully sent truth to them through the prophet Elijah.

ELIJAH, THE TISHBITE

Elijah bursts on the scene suddenly during the reign of Ahab, the most wicked king Israel had ever known. His past is as mysterious as his future. We know nothing of him before his prophetic ministry began, except that he is called "the Tishbite." Most scholars believe that Elijah was raised in the wild but beautiful mountain district of Gilead, the highlands of Palestine on the eastern side of the Jordan River. Unlike many of the other prophets, we know nothing of his parentage. The Scripture record tells us that he did not taste death, but instead was caught up to heaven with a chariot of fire and a whirlwind as his pupil and successor, Elisha, watched.

📖 To appreciate Elijah we must understand the context by which his life is framed. Read 1 Kings 16:29–34, and write what you learn about the reign of king Ahab.

____

____

____

____

____

Ahab became king of Israel (the northern ten tribes) during the time that Asa was king of Judah (the southern two tribes). Ahab did more evil before the Lord than did all the kings before him. The sins of Jeroboam (see 14:8–9) were trivial compared to Ahab's. He took a pagan wife, and she led him into Baal worship. He also erected the "Asherah" (wooden idols of a female deity).

As if all of Ahab's wickedness weren't enough, verse 34 indicates that during his reign, he allowed Jericho to be rebuilt despite the prohibition of God through Joshua when Israel first came to the promised land. At the culmination of the fall of Jericho, God led Joshua to require the victorious Israelites to take an oath that the man who dared to rebuild Jericho would be cursed of the Lord. This prophecy also claimed that the one who would lay the foundation for the reconstruction of Jericho would do so with the loss of his first-born and would set up the gates with the loss of his youngest son (see Joshua 6:26). It was a pagan custom to dedicate the gates and walls of a new city by burying children inside the foundations. As we see here, all that God promised came to pass. These events set the stage for the new prophet, Elijah.

📖 What, according to 1 Kings 17:1, is Elijah's prophecy regarding Israel?

____

____

____

____

Elijah began by saying, *"As the Lord, the God of Israel lives. . . ."* Everything that was going to happen was to give evidence to prodigal Israel, that the God of their fathers still lives. Elijah prophesied that there would be *"neither rain nor dew"* in the land for a long, long time except by his word. James 5:17 reminds us that this drought lasted for three years and six months.

Doctrine

PRAYER

James identifies Elijah as a fitting example of his premise that *"... the effective prayer of a righteous man can accomplish much"* (See James 5:16–18). The prayers he lists in his example are Elijah's prayer for the drought (which Scripture does not record) and his prayer on Mount Carmel for the drought to come to an end. We see from 1 Kings 18:42-45 that this second prayer lasted only a few minutes, and consisted of Elijah asking God to do what He had already told Elijah He would do in 1 Kings 18:1. It is not the length of our prayers that makes them effective, but that they align with the will of God.

📖 Read through 1 Kings 17, and mark every reference to *"the word of the Lord"* and what you learn about it.

____

____

____

____

____

The phrase appears five times in this chapter (vv. 2, 5, 8, 16, and 24). In verse 2 we see it as direct communication to Elijah from God. In verse 5 we see that Elijah obeyed the word of the Lord. In verse 8 we see it again as direct communication from the Lord. In verse 16 we see that it was fulfilled, and that it was spoken through Elijah. In verse 24 we see the widow of Zarephath affirming that the word of the Lord was in Elijah's mouth and that the word was true. In addition to these direct references, it is implied in verse 8 that the word of the Lord had already come to the widow of Zarephath *("... I have commanded a widow there ...")* about providing for him. Though verse 14 doesn't use the phrase, it is obvious God is speaking a word through Elijah *("... thus says the Lord")*. Verse 15 speaks of *"the word of Elijah"* which he told us in verse 14 was *"thus says the Lord."*

Based on what you observed about the *"word of the Lord,"* what would you conclude about the origin of the prophecy concerning the drought?

____

____

____

It would seem apparent that Elijah was a prophet accustomed to hearing from God and that he simply reported what God had told him. The idea of the drought originated with God, not Elijah.

What do you think God taught Elijah through the situations with the ravens and the widow?

____

____

____

____

____

In both situations God's supernatural provision met Elijah's needs. As Elijah was obedient, he enjoyed God's provision, first through the ravens and then through the widow's oil and flour. Following God had placed Elijah in great need, but God was faithful to meet those needs. Even if he didn't follow God, Elijah still would have had the same needs (because of the drought), but if he had not followed God, he would not have experienced God's provision. It is worth noting that the brook Cherith dried up before the word of the Lord came to Elijah about the widow of Zarephath. In the situation with the widow's son, we see Elijah's faith being built by answered prayer.

Elijah DAY TWO

A "GOD-INITIATED" MINISTRY

True ministry is initiated by God, which means that it is **received**, not achieved. In Acts 20:24 Paul says, *"But I do not consider my life of any account as dear to myself, in order that I may finish my course, and the ministry which I received from the Lord Jesus, to testify solemnly of the gospel of the grace of God."* You see, Paul recognized that his ministry was something he received from the Lord, not something he achieved on his own. In fact, the ministry he was trying to achieve went opposite to the one he would receive. We see this same idea reflected in Colossians 4:17 where Archippus is instructed, *"Take heed to the ministry which you have received in the Lord, that you may fulfill it."* A received ministry means that we are doing God's work, not just good works. This truth is clearly seen in 1 Peter 4:10 where we read, *"As each one has received a special gift, employ it in serving one another, as good stewards of the manifold grace of God."* One of the clearest manifestations of a received ministry is our spiritual giftedness. We had no say in the gifts God gave us. We did nothing to earn or achieve them. We received them from the Lord. A God-initiated ministry comes only through following God in a relationship of dependence. It begins with Him and requires that we hear from Him, and to do so, we must walk in fellowship with Him. That is what following God is all about. We see this principle illustrated beautifully in Elijah's challenge to the prophets of Baal.

RECEIVED MINISTRY

In Colossians 4:17 Archippus is instructed, *"Take heed to the ministry which you have received in the Lord, that you may fulfill it."* A received ministry means that we are doing God's work, the work He has called us to, not just good works.

Read 1 Kings 18. Now, looking at verse 1, why did Elijah go to Ahab?

____

____

____

____

____

The obvious truth here is that going to meet with Ahab was not Elijah's idea; it was God's. Elijah was simply obeying the *"word of the Lord."*

Look through chapter 18 again, and write down the details of Elijah's proposal to Ahab and Israel.

____

____

____

____

Elijah challenged Ahab to assemble for a showdown between God and Baal. Elijah called for an assembly of the whole nation along with the 850 false prophets (450 prophets of Baal and 400 prophets of the Asherah [v.19]) and there suggested the idea of a contest to see which god was strongest. He proposed that oxen be sacrificed and placed on an altar, and that each side would be allowed to call on their God to answer with fire.

📖 What is the result of this proposal?

____

____

____

____

Baal's prophets called out to their god all day with no response, and then it was Elijah's turn. He called the people near and repaired the altar of the Lord. He had water poured on the offering and then prayed a short prayer. Then *"the fire of the Lord"* fell and consumed the sacrifice. In the end the people fell on their faces and declared, *"The Lord, He is God."* After years of decline, the nation of Israel turned back to the Lord.

The next question is a key one when we look at this issue of a "received" ministry. According to verse 36, did the idea for this challenge to the prophets of Baal come from Elijah or from God?

____

____

____

Verse 36 makes it clear that Elijah did all of these things *". . . at* **Thy** *word."* As we have seen over and over again, Elijah was not thinking up ideas and asking God to bless them. He was walking in a relationship with God, following Him, and simply obeying what the Lord told him to do.

📖 Compare Elijah's prayer of verses 41–46 with verse 1 of chapter 18 and also James 5:16–18, and write your observations.

____

____

____

____

____

We see in James 5 that Elijah's prayer was identified as *"effective prayer."* It is noteworthy that he was not asking God to perform some uncertain task, but rather as 1 Kings 18:1 reveals, he was simply asking God to do what He had already intended to do. Effective prayer is not us coming up with an idea and asking God to fulfill it, but us trusting God to do what He has said He will do. This underscores what Jesus says in John 15:7–8 that before you can *"ask whatever you wish, and it shall be done for you,"* you must abide in Him and allow His words (Scripture) to abide in you.

Did You Know?

WORSHIP OF THE ASHERAH

The 400 prophets of the "Asherah" mentioned here in addition to the prophets of Baal, are associated with a Canaanite goddess who was purported to be the mother of some seventy different pagan deities including Baal. Worship of the Asherah usually involved erecting an altar next to a sacred tree or a carved wooden pole which functioned as an idol and may have looked much like the "totem" poles of the Northwestern Indians of the Americas.

"O Lord, the God of Abraham, Isaac and Israel, today let it be known that Thou art God in Israel, and that I am Thy servant, and that I have done all these things at Thy Word."

I Kings 18:36

Elijah DAY THREE

"HIGHS" AND "LOWS" OF FOLLOWING GOD

When we follow God into a received ministry, whatever that ministry may be, one of the things we must realize is that just because it is God-initiated, that doesn't mean it will always be easy. In a God-initiated ministry there will be high places where we see God move and work in miraculous ways. But there will also be low places. And quite often the low places follow on the heels of the high places. Elijah's encounter with the prophets of Baal on Mount Carmel was definitely a high place, but as we will see today, he did not stay there.

Just because a ministry is God-initiated, that doesn't mean it will always be easy. Second Timothy 3:12 promises, "...indeed, all who desire to live godly in Christ Jesus will be persecuted."

📖 Read 1 Kings 19:1–8, and looking specifically at verses 1–2, write down a summary of the circumstances which immediately follow the "high place" events of Mount Carmel.

____

____

____

____

____

____

Elijah was allowed no time to "rest on his laurels." When Jezebel heard the report of what Elijah did on Mount Carmel and of the execution of all the prophets, she vowed her own death if she had not killed Elijah within twenty-four hours.

📖 What, according to verses 3–4, was Elijah's response to Jezebel's threat?

____

____

____

____

We know Elijah was a man of faith and a model of effective prayer. What exactly is the request of verse 4, and does God answer it or honor it?

____

____

____

____

____

Did You Know?

JUNIPER TREE

A juniper tree is really not much of a tree but is a desert shrub, also called a "broom tree." It can grow up to ten feet high and is found in all of the deserts of Egypt, Sinai, and the Holy Land. The shrub gives poor protection from the hot desert sun, but is often the only shade to be found in the barren area to which Elijah wandered.

Clearly Elijah's response was not one of faith. He became afraid and fled for his life. He then wandered a day's journey into the wilderness to hide himself, and then sat down dejectedly under a juniper tree. Elijah says in verse four, *"It is enough,"* basically meaning, "I give up." Then in that same verse Elijah asks the Lord to take his life. It is significant that there is no "word of the Lord" in response to Elijah's request. Obviously God did not respect his request, for He did not take Elijah's life.

Think of all Elijah had seen the Lord do. He had seen the Lord sustain him miraculously through a three-and-a-half-year drought. He had watched God humble the nation of Israel and humiliate the pagan prophets by sending fire from heaven. Elijah had experienced a direct and immediate answer to his prayers in the form of a heavy shower bringing the drought to an end. He had even witnessed the Lord supernaturally enable him to outrun Ahab's chariot the seventeen miles from Carmel to Jezreel. Yet now we see him running for his life at the threat of one angry woman. We watch him wandering in the wilderness in a sea of depression and giving up under a tree, lamenting his own existence. What a difference a day makes! The profound truth revealed here is that we cannot live today's trials on yesterday's faith. This story also reveals the likelihood that our spiritual highs will be followed by spiritual lows. I believe there are spiritual, emotional, and physical reasons why this is so. In a spiritual "high place" there is usually a sense of euphoria that drains one emotionally and physically as well. This reality is accompanied by the fact that spiritual highs can move our focus onto the miracles and workings of God themselves instead of on the God who gave them. This leaves us spiritually vulnerable.

Look at verses 5–8, and identify all that God did to restore Elijah.

____

____

____

____

____

First, He allowed him to rest. Then He provided Elijah with a hot meal and allowed him to rest again. This was followed by another meal and the admonition that the journey ahead was too great. Even though the text does not say that God told Elijah to go to Horeb, that is the implication, for we know Elijah had no previous plans to go anywhere, and the angel spoke of his impending journey. Horeb is another name for Mount Sinai, the mountain of God, and is not a forty day journey from Beersheba, so apparently Elijah had to travel in a covert, roundabout manner.

APPLY What conclusions would you draw from Elijah's experience about managing your own travels from spiritual highs to spiritual lows?

____

____

____

____

____

One obvious principle here is that sometimes the most spiritual thing you can do is to have a good meal and get a good night's sleep. We cannot spiritualize physical needs. A second principle is that we shouldn't rely too heavily on our judgment when we are in a low place. Elijah thought that the best escape would come through his death, but God knew better. A third principle is that once we have rested, we need to meet with God, for this was the purpose of Horeb (Sinai), the place where Moses met with God.

Did You Know?

MOUNT HOREB

Horeb is another name for Mount Sinai, which is sometimes called "The Mountain of God." It was on this mountain that Moses met with God and received the tablets of the ten commandments along with detailed revelations about the tabernacle and priesthood which would become vehicles for the worship of God. It was a sacred place because of this history, and the fact that it was there God manifested Himself to the people in a cloud of glory. Moses entered into this cloud, which appeared as a consuming fire (Exodus 24:16). So holy was this place, the people were not even allowed to touch the mountain.

"I Alone Am Left..."

What an adventure this has been! After three-and-a-half years of drought where Elijah hid from Ahab and was miraculously provided for, then came the great showdown on Mount Carmel. Elijah saw God do the things that only God can do. Fire fell from heaven and consumed the sacrifice. Revival broke out among the people. In answer to a brief prayer, the drought finally came to an end. But then events seemingly took a sour turn for Elijah. Jezebel vowed his death. Elijah was devastated, despondent, and an attitude of hopelessness pervaded him. Then God sent help to him and fed him, but his depression did not immediately subside. He spent the next forty days slinking around from Beersheeba to Horeb. Elijah had recovered somewhat from his spiritual valley, yet he still needed to meet with God and begin to see things from His perspective.

Look at 1 Kings 19:9–10, and identify Elijah's perspective on the situation and what you think is wrong with it.

____

____

____

____

Put Yourself In Their Shoes

WE ARE NOT ALONE

Because of the difficulties and persecution he experienced, Elijah believed he was the only one left who followed God. Yet, in fact, there were 7,000 others who had not worshiped Baal. We must be careful of believing the lie that no one is as serious about God as we are, or that we are alone. Even if there were not 7,000 others, Elijah was not alone, for God is ever with His servants.

Elijah began by contrasting his own zeal for God with that of the nation of Israel, who had abandoned the Lord. He reminded God that all the other prophets had been killed, and then he says in verse 10, *"I alone am left; and they seek my life. . . ."* It almost seems that Elijah was saying, "God, I'm all you have left and they're about to kill me too!" Elijah's focus is on himself instead of the Lord, and the implication is that God needed Elijah's help.

What does God do in verses 11 and 12 to alter Elijah's perspective, and according to verse 14, did it work?

____

____

____

____

God manifested Himself to Elijah and demonstrated His power. It would seem that the manifestations of the *"great and strong wind,"* the earthquake, the fire, and the gentle breeze served to give Elijah a higher view of God, yet as we see in verse 14, his perspective had not changed any from verse 10.

Looking at verses 15–18, identify what God did next and how that might relate to Elijah's view that he was the only one left who followed God.

____

____

____

____

God gave Elijah the assignment of anointing Hazael, Jehu, and Elisha, and indicated that in addition to them, He had seven thousand who had not bowed to Baal. What a far cry from Elijah's prideful view that he was all that God had left. Rather than bluntly saying, "Elijah, you are wrong," God tactfully brought to the forefront all the others in Israel (Northern Kingdom) who stood for God.

We must always guard against the prideful notion that just because we follow God, He needs our help.

As you will see in the rest of Elijah's life and ministry, Elisha was a gift from God to him—a friend, a disciple, and the one who would continue his ministry when Elijah was gone. Sometimes when we follow God in the midst of those who are antagonistic toward the gospel, we become ensnared in the trap of pride, believing that God needs us because we follow when others don't. But God is totally self-sufficient. Like a loving father, He allows us to join Him in His work, but He **does not need** our help. As Mordecai told Queen Esther when she struggled with interceding with the king for Israel, "*. . . if you remain silent at this time, relief and deliverance will arise for the Jews from another place and you and your father's house will perish.*" In other words, "Don't think you are indispensable, for if you don't help us, God will provide relief from somewhere else, but you and your family won't get to have a part in it." We must always guard against the prideful notion that just because we follow God, He needs our help.

For Me to Follow God

It has been said that, "You are the only Bible some people will ever read." That statement presents to us an awesome responsibility. Yet it should be considered an awesome privilege. We must all be quick to recognize that our walk with God has an effect on those around us. More is at stake in our relationship with God than just our own walk, for if we live yielded to Him, then He can minister to others through us. James says an interesting thing about Elijah. In James 5:17 he says, *"Elijah was a man* **with a nature like ours . . ."** (emphasis mine). When we look at Elijah and what God did through him, we are tempted to place him into a separate category of super saints. But he was a man **like us**! As such, he is an example of how God wants to use us as agents of revival in our day. However, for that to happen, our study of Elijah must go beyond a mere collection of information. We must take the truths of God's word we have seen this week and put them into application.

One of the lessons we learn from Elijah is that following God means doing **His** work, not our own work. Elijah's ministry was **received**, not achieved. He didn't try to make a ministry happen on his own. He met with God and then responded to His leading. An achieved ministry, one that is initiated by man instead of by God, is of no consequence in eternity—and is also much more difficult to maintain. When we cease to do His work, the work gets burdensome because we are trying to perform tasks without the grace that only God can give.

Can you see any examples in your own life or those around you of ministry that is **achieved** (man-initiated) instead of **received** (initiated by God)?

To have a received ministry, we must hear from God before we act. The oft-repeated refrain of Elijah's life was "*. . . the word of the Lord came to him.*" What this makes clear is that the Word must come before the work. We need a regular diet of God's Word if we want to see Him minister through us to others.

Put Yourself In Their Shoes
FOLLOWING GOD

Three important lessons from Elijah:

- Following God means doing **His** work, not ours.
- Following God means drawing on **His** life, not ours.
- Following God means focusing on **Him**, not ourselves.

Looking at the list below, check every area where you currently receive biblical input.

❑ Sermons at church	❑ Sunday school	❑ Christian radio
❑ Religious TV	❑ Books	❑ Tapes
❑ Conferences	❑ Magazines	❑ Counselor
❑ Bible study group	❑ Study workbooks such as this one	
❑ Personal Bible reading	❑ Other________________	

Now, take a moment to look back through each of the places you marked and ask yourself, "Does that source take me to what the Word of God has to say, or does it merely take me to what man has to say about God?"

Are there any changes toward which the Lord is prompting you in this area?

Another key principle we see in the life of Elijah is that following God means drawing on **His** life, not ours. When Elijah wandered out into the wilderness to die, it was clear that he was no longer drawing on the resources of God's strength, but was walking in his own strength. When we cease to draw on the life of God, ministry becomes a fearful thing. We find Elijah running for his life from Jezebel, even though a few hours before, he single-handedly faced down the prophets of Baal. There is an important lesson here: **We cannot face today's trials with yesterday's faith or experiences.**

When Elijah wanted to die, God had two solutions to his despondency—rest and revelation. First, Elijah needed physical rejuvenation. We cannot spiritualize physical needs. Sometimes the most spiritual thing we can do is to eat a good meal and to get a good night's rest.

APPLY If you are depressed or despondent, are you taking care of your physical body?

What do you need to do differently?

While we cannot overlook the physical, we cannot look only there either. Once the physical was taken care of, Elijah still had a need. So God called him to Horeb (Sinai), the mountain of God. Are you facing fears and obstacles? Perhaps you need to get alone with God. Make time to do this.

To draw on the life of God, we must be surrendered to Him. He must be in control of our hearts. When He is in control, we never lack power for the tasks He gives us. Is every area of your heart yielded to Him? If not, take time to do that now.

A third principle we see in Elijah is that following God means focusing on **Him**, not ourselves. When Elijah came to Horeb to meet with God, his prayer was filled with self-pity and self-focus. He said, "**I** *have been zealous...* " and "**I** *alone am left. . . .*" Even after God revealed Himself to Elijah in a majestic way, his prayer was repeated unchanged. In essence, he said, "God, You'd better do something because I'm all You have left and they're trying to kill me."

Elijah's problem really was a math problem. He had not learned the truth of the equation listed below:

God + Elijah = God - Elijah

God chooses to use us, but He does not need us. He is complete—He has no needs. The Scriptures teach us that if we do not preach the gospel, the rocks and trees will cry out (see Luke 19:40). Yet as a loving Father, though He does not require our help, He desires our help. He invites us to join Him in His work. He does not want us working on our own, independent of Him, and He will not bless such labor.

God does not require our help, but He does desire our help.

Take a moment to reflect honestly on your service to the Lord. Have you seen any evidences in your heart of thinking God needed your help and was blessed to have you on His team? If so, confess that sin of pride to Him.

Not only did Elijah so focus on himself as to think that God could not do without him, but he also had so focused on himself as to think that he was all God had. Yet immediately God sent him to anoint three servants and made him aware of the 7,000 others of whom Elijah didn't even know.

Have you ever prayed, "I alone am left"?

Ask God to show you the other faithful servants around you that you haven't seen before. If we lose our focus on Him, ministry (and life) becomes a lonely place. If there are evidences of Elijah at Horeb in your heart, you need to stop focusing on yourself and start focusing on Him.

Let's spend some time in prayer to the Lord right now.

Lord, thank You for this very human example of Elijah. I thank You for the ministry I have received from You. Help me to be faithful to the tasks You have given me. Guard me from trying to achieve something else. Make me quick to listen for You and patient to wait for "the Word of the Lord" to come, so that I am doing YOUR work and not just good works. I long to draw on Your life, to walk in Your strength and not my own. Show me quickly when I am not doing that. Give me faith for today, and help me to focus on You and not me. I confess that You don't require my help, and I praise You that You still desire it. Thank You for inviting me into Your work. Help me to be faithful. Amen.

Prayer of Application . . .

As we close our lesson this week, take to heart any areas the Lord has singled out to you, and express them in prayer to Him.

Notes

Notes

lesson 3

Putting Down the Idols In Our Lives

In the midst of dark days, God sent to the kingdom of Israel (Northern Kingdom) a flaming prophet named Elijah the Tishbite. He appeared like a bolt of lightning, thundering the Word of God to a rebellious king and a deceived people. His life and message can be summed up in the challenge he delivered on Mount Carmel, *"How long will you hesitate between two opinions?* **If the Lord is God, follow Him;** *but if Baal, follow him"* (1 Kings 18:21). After the confrontation on Mount Carmel, the people acknowledged God for a time but returned to their idolatrous ways. Ahab and Jezebel remained in power over Israel, and the influence of their corrupt leadership continued to spread. The progressive moral decay grieved and angered the heart of God, as His covenant people continued moving further and further away from Him and His Word. He would deal with them and their sin, especially with the leaders of Israel. It was at this time that Elisha was born in the town of Abel Meholah, where he grew up working on the family farm. Like Elijah before him, he would play a critical role in the battle against Baal.

During the ministry of Elijah in Israel, the Lord instructed him to anoint Elisha as his successor. By his influence and instruction Elijah had a ministry **to** Elisha, and then, in passing his "mantle" to him, had a ministry **through**

Elisha's Ministry

Elisha ministered in the Kingdom of Israel (Northern Kingdom) during all or part of the reigns of Ahab, Ahaziah, Jehoram (Joram), Jehu, Jehoahaz and Joash (Jehoash). His contemporaries included Elijah and Micaiah in Israel and Obadiah and Joel in Judah. His ministry covered the period around 858 to 797.

When Did He Prophesy?

1050	1000	950	900	850
SAMUEL Judge and Prophet; GAD	NATHAN	SHEMAIAH	IDDO; ODED; Hanani the Seer; AZARIAH	Jahaziel the Levite; OBADIAH; JOEL
		Rehoboam 931–913	**Asa 911–870**; **Abijam 913–911**	**Jehoshaphat 873–848**; **Jehoram (Joram) 853–841**; **Ahaziah 841**; **Athaliah 841–835**; **Joash 835–796**
Saul 1051–1011	**David 1011–971**	**Solomon 971–931**		
	Ishbosheth ruled over Israel 1011–1004	960—Temple finished; **Jeroboam I 931–910**	**Nadab 910–909**; **Baasha 909–886**; **Elah 886–885**; **Zimri 885**; **Tibni 885–880**; **Omri 885–874**; **Ahab 874–853**	**Ahaziah 853–852**; **Jehoram (Joram) 852–841**; **Jehu 841–814**
	David ruled over Judah from Hebron 1011–1004	AHIJAH the Shilonite; "A man of God from Judah"; A prophet from Samaria in Bethel	ELIJAH; JEHU, son of Hanani; MICAIAH	ELISHA
	David ruled over all Israel and Judah from Jerusalem 1004–971			
	Hiram I of Tyre 981–947		Benhadad I of Syria 900–860	Benhadad II of Syria 860–841

to Elisha, and then, in passing his "mantle" to him, had a ministry **through** Elisha. God used Elisha in the continual battle against Baal worship ever seeking to eradicate that cancer from among the people of God. Elisha can teach us some things about the corrupting influence of the idols in our lives, and He can show us what it means to follow the true and living God.

Elisha DAY ONE

FOLLOWING THE TRUE GOD

Since the days of Moses, the Lord had warned again and again to guard against the lure of idolatry by the nations surrounding Canaan. Over the years there was a continual spiritual battle for the soul of Israel. Solomon compromised and went after many false gods, offering incense to their detestable idols. Jeroboam, the first king of the Northern Kingdom, lowered Israel to a new depth of depravity through the worship of the golden calves at Dan and Bethel. The kings after him only grew worse. King Omri came to the throne of Israel and was worse than all those before him (1 Kings 16:25), and when his son Ahab began to rule, God was forgotten in the flood of idolatry. Around 862 BC, God sent Elijah to confront Ahab's sin and to challenge the worship of Baal. Through Elijah, the Lord began working as a skilled surgeon to purge Israel of this deadly cancer of idolatry. After challenging and slaying the prophets of Baal on Mount Carmel, Elijah ran from the death threats of Jezebel (1 Kings 18). Finally at Mount Horeb resting in a cave, Elijah received instructions from the Lord

Did You Know?

OMRI AND AHAB

Just as David established Jerusalem as the capital of united Israel, so Omri built and established Samaria as the capital of the northern kingdom of the divided Israel, making it a well fortified city which prospered in its location on the North-South trade routes. Under the Lord's direction, David's son, Solomon built the Temple to the true Lord, while Omri's son, Ahab, built the temple to the false "lord," Baal. (Baal means "lord," "owner," or "husband.") He also paid the priests and prophets of Baal, thus helping establish Baal worship in Samaria.

Read 1 Kings 19:9–18. According to verses 15–17, whom would the Lord use in His continuing purge of the wickedness of Baal worship?

____

____

____

What encouragement did the Lord give Elijah (19:18)?

____

____

____

God told Elijah that He wanted Jehu anointed as king in Israel, Hazael anointed as king in Syria, and Elisha anointed as his spiritual successor. God was not finished working through Elijah nor was He finished dealing with the sins of Israel. In the midst of Elijah's days of discouragement over the battles he had faced, God encouraged him that there were 7,000 people who had not bowed the knee to Baal nor kissed the image set up to Baal.

What do you find out about Elisha and his surrender to God's call in 1 Kings 19:19–21?

____

____

____

Elisha was plowing with his yoke of oxen when Elijah approached him and threw his mantle on him, a symbol of investing one with the office of a prophet. How would Elisha respond and face this call? Elisha quickly ran to say farewell to his family and friends. His surrender to the call of God through Elijah was seen in the slaughter of the oxen and the use of the plow as firewood. There he held a feast and afterward began following Elijah as his servant. This occurred around 858 BC.

TWELVE YOKE OF OXEN

The reference to Elisha plowing with the twelfth yoke of oxen has been interpreted two ways. If Elisha's family farm had twelve yoke of oxen for plowing, this would indicate that the family owned significant acreage to need that many oxen to complete the task—with Elisha using the twelfth yoke. The phrasing could also refer to the size of the land—a "twelve yoke land" would indicate that the family farm was divided into twelve parcels of land, with Elijah covering the twelfth part or yoke. Either interpretation implies that Elisha's family possessed considerable land holdings.

For the next five or six years (858–852 BC), Elisha served as Elijah's servant. In 1 Kings 20:1–34 we find the account of Israel's war with Syria (which lasted around two years) followed by three years of peace between Israel and Syria (1 Kings 22:1). During those three years Ahab joined forces with Ben Hadad of Syria to fight against Assyria, only to later engage Syria in battle again.

As prophesied by Micaiah, Ahab died in battle (1 Kings 22:1–38). His son Ahaziah came to the throne following in the footsteps of his father and mother through his idolatry and evil ways (1 Kings 22:51–53). According to the word of the Lord spoken through Elijah, Ahaziah died soon after taking the throne of Israel (2 Kings 1:1–18).

After the death of Ahaziah, it was time for the Lord to take Elijah to heaven. We find Elisha with him as he had been for the past five or six years.

📖 Read 2 Kings 2:1–8, and answer the questions below.

What do you discover about the relationship between Elijah and Elisha in 2 Kings 2:1–8?

____

____

____

____

What is significant in the repetition in verses 2, 4, and 6?

____

____

____

____

What does this tell you about Elisha?

____

____

____

____

____

Put Yourself In Their Shoes

THE PLACING OF THE MANTLE

To place a mantle on someone's shoulder was used as a symbol of investing one with the office of a prophet, and it was also used of adopting one as a son. Elisha got the message. His request to kiss his father and mother was met with Elijah's *"Go back again, for what have I done to you?"* It was appropriate to say farewell, but Elijah's emphasis on the call of God to Elisha was clear. *"What have I done to you?"* In essence, Elijah told Elisha to recognize what it meant to assume the role of God's prophet and to take it seriously. Only God can call a man to serve as His prophet.

Elijah and Elisha left Gilgal, where one of the schools of the prophets was located. Elijah told Elisha that he could stay in Gilgal, apparently giving him the option of staying or going with him. The relationship between Elijah and Elisha appears to be exceptionally close, like a father to a son. At each point Elijah gave Elisha permission to stay behind, but Elisha considered it first priority that he stay with Elijah—*"As the LORD lives and as your soul lives, I will not leave you!"* (NKJV). This statement of total surrender meant that Elisha would remain faithful to the living Lord, to God's call on his life, and to the prophet through whom God taught him. Elisha was available and teachable throughout his time with Elijah. He did not want to miss anything the Lord might do or say through Elijah, especially in light of Elijah's imminent departure, a truth that Elisha knew through revelation either from Elijah or from the Lord Himself. Elijah told Elisha the Lord was sending him (Elijah) to Bethel, a location of another school of the prophets. From Jericho both Elijah and Elisha crossed the Jordan on dry ground as they walked toward Elijah's appointment with the Lord and the chariot of Israel with its horsemen. There Elijah asked Elisha what he would request of him.

Did You Know?

THE REQUEST OF THE FIRSTBORN

Deuteronomy 21:17 makes provision for the firstborn, *"But he shall acknowledge the firstborn . . . by giving him a double portion of all that he has, for he is the beginning of his strength; to him belongs the right of the firstborn."* Elisha was one of the "sons of the prophets" and had been chosen by God as Elijah's successor. He served Elijah as a "son" and requested the double portion of the firstborn.

According to 2 Kings 2:9–10, what was Elisha's request of Elijah (2:9)?

____

____

____

____

What was Elijah's reply (2:10)?

____

____

____

Elisha requested a double portion of Elijah's spirit, implying that as a "son" to Elijah he would request the blessing of the firstborn and receive a double portion of the inheritance (Deuteronomy 21:17). Elijah had no earthly wealth to give, and what Elisha wanted could not be carried in wagons or bags because he desired the spiritual power and authority that Elijah possessed. The request for a double portion of Elijah's spirit was indeed a difficult request to honor, and one that Elijah could not guarantee. Only God could give this spiritual blessing, and He apparently revealed to Elijah that He would honor this request if Elisha would be present when He came for Elijah. Then the Lord came in the whirlwind and took Elijah, and his mantle fell to the ground at Elisha's feet, a symbol of the office and authority of Elijah. Having witnessed Elijah's supernatural departure, Elisha returned to the Jordan.

Did You Know?

THE SCHOOLS OF THE PROPHETS

The Schools of the Prophets located at Gilgal, Bethel, and Jericho were centers where the "sons of the prophets" received instruction from a prophet. Samuel had schools at Gibeath (1 Samuel 10:5, 10) and Naioth (19:18–20). The fifty prophets Obadiah hid and fed could have been students at one of the schools (1 Kings 18:3–4). These pupils often shared living quarters, ate together, and received instruction together (2 Kings 4:38–44; 6:1–4). The ministry of Elijah and Elisha was to faithfully proclaim God's Word personally, as well as in and through these schools. This was particularly important in the midst of the idolatry and apostasy of the day. It is significant that the Lord sent Elijah to visit these schools before his translation to heaven.

📖 Read Elisha's question in 2 Kings 2:14. What was this question, and what kind of test was this for Elisha?

____

____

____

What was Elisha's concern?

____

____

____

Elijah's question focused on God's presence with him as He had been with Elijah. Rolling the mantle up like a rod as Elijah had done (and reminiscent of the rod of God that Moses carried), Elisha faced his greatest test thus far. Would the Lord invest His supernatural power in him as He had in Elijah? By faith Elisha struck the waters, and they parted. The men of the school of the prophets saw this first miracle of Elisha and honored him as the spiritual successor to Elijah (2:15). His next test came in dealing with the doubts of these men, for they believed that God had taken Elijah to some distant mountaintop. Their bothersome requests to go and search for the body of Elijah, in spite of Elisha's insistence that the search would prove futile, eventually persuaded him to let them go. When they returned, he gently chided them for their disbelief (2:16–18).

Read 2 Kings 2:19–22. The men of Jericho came to Elisha with a great need. This was yet another test in the early days of the prophet's ministry. What was the problem (2:19)?

___

___

___

What did Elisha do (2:20–22)? What was the source of the miracle according to verse 21?

___

___

___

___

The waters of Jericho were greatly polluted. It appears that the waters affected the crops and even caused the women and the livestock to be barren or to miscarry. By the word of the Lord, Elisha threw salt into the spring, and the Lord healed the waters. Elisha's spring, as it is called today, still provides fresh, clean water to the area of Jericho.

Elisha faced yet another test from some young men at Bethel, home of one of the two altars to the golden calf built by Jeroboam I. These were not children but most likely young men in their twenties. When Elisha looked at them the word of the Lord came to him and he cursed them by that word. God spoke a word of judgment because He knew their hearts and the evident disrespect they had for Elijah and Elisha, for the message they proclaimed, and for the Lord Himself.

As Elisha began his ministry he went through a time of testing, his first test coming from Elijah as to his desires and his determination to go where God sent the prophet Elijah. He chose to go. The tests did not stop at Bethel nor Jericho. Once over the Jordan, Elisha faced the test of his desires for the future—what did he want as a "son" of the prophet—a "firstborn" in essence? The tests of the sons of the prophets continued as they insisted that they look for Elijah's body, then tested the Lord's power over the barren waters of Jericho, and finally, tested Elisha's authority as prophet in place of Elijah. In each case Elisha faced the test with a desire to follow God. After Elijah's translation into heaven, he walked in the authority and power of a prophet sent from God. What would God do through him in the days ahead? We will begin to see in Day Two.

Word Study

TWO NAMES—ONE MESSAGE

"Elijah" means "my God is Yah/LORD," and reveals both his name and his mission—to proclaim the LORD as the one and only God, and to stand against any who sought to replace Him with a false god or "lord." "Elisha" means "my God is salvation" and also carries his message to the nation—there is salvation in no other.

Did You Know?

ELIJAH'S MANTLE

Elijah's mantle was a cloak used in a number of ways. It was used mostly as a covering from the sun, rain, or cold, but could also be folded and used as a chair or pillow, spread out and used as a blanket at night, or used as a bag to carry things. One's cloak was considered very valuable and could even be used as a down payment on a debt.

FOLLOWING THE LIVING GOD

Elisha came to prominence in a day when the God of the Word and the Word of God were held in disrespect by many in Israel. Many were deceived into believing that Baal brought rain and crops and the blessing of children. God used Elisha as He had used Elijah to show that *"the LORD, He is God"* (1 Kings 18:39), and He alone should be followed and obeyed. We know how the Lord revealed Himself in fire on Mount Carmel in the showdown with the prophets of Baal, but how did God manifest Himself in the life and ministry of Elisha?

When Ahab died, Mesha, the king of Moab, who had been paying tribute to Ahab, rebelled against the new king, Ahaziah, and then against king Jehoram. Jehoram mustered the men of Israel as well as Jehoshaphat of Judah and the king of Edom to fight Mesha and his Moabite army. Jehoram's troops traveled south of the Dead Sea to enter Moab at a more strategically beneficial location, but after seven days they began to run short of water, the one essential element for an army on the march. Jehoram despaired for the lives of the three kings and their armies. Then Jehoshaphat wisely asked, *"Is there not a prophet of the LORD here, that we may inquire of the LORD by him?"* (3:11).

Put Yourself In Their Shoes

"THE MAN OF GOD"

"The Man of God" was a term first used of Moses and then of several prophets after him. It was used of Elisha 29 times in 2 Kings, and points to his close walk with God and his ministry of speaking the messages that God had for His people.

📖 Read 2 Kings 3:11–25, and answer the questions that follow.

What do you find in verses 11–12?

____

____

____

____

____

What was Elisha's response to the king of Israel (3:13) and to Jehoshaphat of Judah (3:14)?

____

____

____

____

Elisha was nearby, perhaps even traveling with the army. He was recognized as Elijah's servant, and Jehoshaphat knew of him as one through whom the Lord spoke. The three kings (Jehoram, Jehoshaphat, and the king of Edom) went to Elisha to seek a word from the Lord. Elisha quickly confronted the king of Israel for his unbelief and for his continued association with the prophets of Baal that Ahab and Jezebel had honored. Jehoram felt that he was in trouble, thinking that the Lord had brought them all to judgment at the hand of the Moabites. Because of his favorable opinion of Jehoshaphat, Elisha was willing to listen to the request of these three kings. They wanted Elisha to seek a word from the Lord regarding this problem with the Moabites.

Looking at 3:15–19, what did Elisha prophesy?

What did the Lord do (3:20–25)?

Elisha instructed them to dig trenches that the Lord would fill with water, though they would neither see nor hear any wind or rain. This was *"a simple matter"* (NKJV) or *"a slight thing in the sight of the Lord"* (3:18). Their need for water would be satisfied, and the Lord would also deliver the Moabites into their hands. The next morning they saw the water coming from Edom filling the trenches, probably from rain storms which filled the wadis (canyons) with water that flowed from Edom to their camp. When the Moabites saw the red reflection of the morning sun on the water, they thought they saw blood, signifying to them that the three enemy armies had fought and massacred one another. They attacked and found the armies waiting. The Moabites were ambushed and almost totally overcome. However, when Mesha sacrificed his own son on the wall, and the armies saw this repulsive deed, they dispersed. Still, the people of Israel and Judah knew that the living God had given them water for their own lives and the lives of their animals. Once again, Jehovah manifested His power and separated Himself from the powerless idols of Canaan.

Doctrine

GOD'S TIMING

Some of the ways God revealed Himself centered on the timing of certain events such as the appearance of the water in the trenches the troops dug near Edom. In 2 Kings 8 the timing of the arrival of the Shunemite woman just as Gehazi told the king that Elisha had raised her son from the dead assured her of the king's assistance in getting back her land after the famine (2 Kings 8:1–6). The timing of the living Lord is always at work to accomplish His purposes and bring His provision.

Read 2 Kings 4:1–37. The questions throughout the remainder of the Day Two discussion relate to this passage of Scripture.

In another incident, the Lord showed Himself as the living God who sustains those who call on Him. What do you discover in 2 Kings 4:1?

A widow of one of the sons of the prophets came to Elisha with a great need. Elisha had known her husband to be a godly man who feared the Lord. His death forced her to raise their two children alone, but she could not meet all the financial needs and found herself in debt. Apparently there was one person to whom she owed an immense debt, and this creditor could have taken her children as slaves to pay the debt until the Year of Jubilee according to Leviticus 25:39–41. Certainly, this woman was in a desperate situation.

What was Elisha's solution (4:2–7)?

What principles do you see in this incident?

Elisha asked her what she had in her house to eat, and all she could present was a small jar or flask of oil, the kind used to anoint the body. Elisha instructed her to take that jar of oil and begin filling all the vessels she could find or borrow. As she did she found the flow of oil sufficient to fill every vessel she had, the implication being that if she had possessed more vessels the oil would have continued to flow. Elisha instructed her to take what she had, sell it, pay the debt, and live on the rest, a clear and unmistakable picture of the living Lord caring for one of His own and revealing His ability to pour forth all the provision a widow would need. In a land where many were looking to Baal or a similar god to provide crops and provision this widow's testimony revealed the true and living God who was ever faithful to His covenant people.

ELIJAH AND THE OIL FOR THE WIDOW

When there was a God-ordered famine in the land of Israel, the Lord told Elijah to go to Zarephath to a widow who would provide for him. Through Elijah she discovered the power of God to provide flour and oil throughout the famine, thus taking care of her, her son, and Elijah (1 Kings 17:8–16). In a somewhat different circumstance, Elisha saw the Lord provide enough oil in one day to fully take care of a debt as well as provide for the future (2 Kings 4:1–7).

Elisha traveled about Israel ministering the word of the Lord and seeking to bring the people back to worship the one true God. One of the places he visited was Shunem, where a prominent woman and her husband often hosted Elisha. Eventually they built a small room for him to stay in when he passed through Shunem. Elisha wanted to show his appreciation to them. However, when Gehazi, Elisha's servant, asked her what they could do for her, her response revealed her contentment. She said that she needed nothing, though Gehazi mentioned that she had no son (she had the stigma of barrenness), and that her husband was old. If her husband died, she would have no one to care for her—and no one to carry on the family name and receive the inheritance (2 Kings 4:8–14).

What did Elisha prophesy concerning the woman of Shunem (4:14–16), and what was the result? (4:17)?

What problem arose (4:18–20)? What did the woman do (4:21–28)?

ELISHA AND JESUS CHRIST

God performed some of the same miracles through Elisha that we see in the ministry of Jesus. Jesus healed many lepers and Elisha saw Naaman healed. Jesus raised the dead and Elisha saw a boy come to life. Jesus multiplied the loaves and Elisha saw the Lord work in a similar way. Some have also compared the gentle and kind spirit of Elisha to be much like that of Jesus. The miracles performed by both brought encouragement and comfort to many.

Elisha prophesied that the woman would have a son within a year's time, and so it happened. The child grew and worked with his father in the fields. During one of the harvests, the child became ill with what appears to have been sunstroke. When the child was brought to his mother she cared for him until noon, and then he died. Though it was neither New Moon nor Sabbath (times of special observance when one would more likely seek the prophet), she immediately set out for Mount Carmel to seek the aid of Elisha. Her reply to her husband that *"It will be well"* revealed her faith in

Elisha's God. When she reached him she cried out to Elisha from the very depths of her soul. She knew him to be the chosen prophet of the living God and that God could work through him.

What was Elisha's response? What did he do (4:26–37)?

____

____

____

What do you see about the living God in this incident?

____

____

____

Look at the incident in 2 Kings 6:1–7 and note how the Lord continued to reveal Himself as the provider for His people. How would this encourage the sons of the prophets?

Elisha recognized that God was working in a unique way in this situation having hidden the problem from him. He was prepared to go with her and seek the Lord on behalf of the child. When they arrived at the house Elisha began to call on the Lord and even stretched himself out on the child apparently at the prompting of the Spirit of God. After doing this two times the child arose, and Elisha presented him to his mother. Again the Lord revealed Himself as the living God who gives life. He is the Lord who can give a child to the barren, and the Lord who can give life to the dead. No idol could do these things.

The Lord continued to manifest Himself in many ways as Elisha traveled about the country teaching in various schools of the prophets and ministering to the people. During a time of famine, Elisha came to the school of the prophets at Gilgal, and while there discovered that he and the students had eaten some poisonous stew because of some wild gourds that were inadvertently placed in the stew. Elisha instructed them to add flour to the stew—and all was made well! Yet the flour itself did not make the stew wholesome. It was the gentle touch of the Spirit of the living God that purified the stew, making it wholesome and healthy (4:38–41). At this same place, someone brought a firstfruits offering of barley bread, but it was not enough for the one hundred men there. Therefore, Elisha proclaimed a word from the Lord. The Lord's message was thus: *"They shall eat and have some left over,"* and they did (4:43–44). The miraculous taming of the poisonous stew and the expansion of the barley bread are two examples of the work of God in the midst of famine, bringing to the forefront the life-giving nature of the living God versus the wicked ways of Baal.

THE LORD OF THE NATIONS

The power of the Lord was revealed in Israel. How did He manifest Himself in the nations around Israel? We see an example of this in the nation of Syria where a testimony about Elisha caught the attention of Captain Naaman, a leper. His Israeli maidservant assured him that he could be cured if he went to the prophet in Israel. Naaman went first to the king of Israel, who worried that this was a challenge from the king of

Syria. Elisha called on the king to send Naaman to him that he (Naaman) might *"know that there is a prophet in Israel,"* implying a prophet of the true and living God (5:1–8).

📖 Read 2 Kings 5:1–13, and answer the questions that follow.

What was Naaman's first reaction (5:11–12)? What do you see about his heart attitude?

___

___

___

___

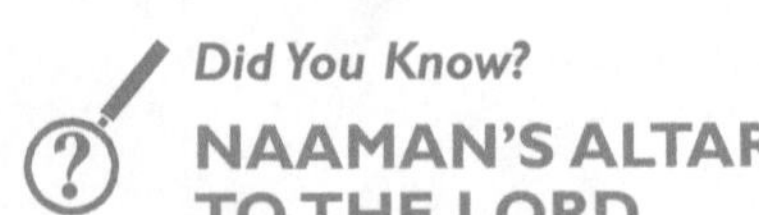

Did You Know?

NAAMAN'S ALTAR TO THE LORD

In Naaman's day many believed one could only worship God at the place (territory) of that God. Taking Israelite soil back to Damascus was Naaman's way of seeking to follow the one true God.

Naaman expected special treatment, something he assuredly received in Syria from his soldiers, the people, and the king's officials. He thought Elisha would come out, call on the Lord, and perhaps wave his hands in the air in some ceremonial way. But Elisha did not focus on himself. What he did, he did at the command of the Lord. The Lord wanted to focus Naaman's attention on Himself and what it meant to follow Him by faith. What the Lord required of Naaman was simple, even childlike, but it required him to act in faith.

What did Naaman have to change to heed the words of Elisha's servants and those of his own servants (5:13–14)?

___

___

Naaman had to humble himself before these servants and ultimately under the *"mighty hand of God,"* as 1 Peter 5:6 expresses it. God was dealing with far more than the external malady of leprosy. He was dealing with Naaman's proud heart, and Naaman found that when he humbled himself before the prophet of the Lord and obeyed his word, he experienced the healing touch of God—within and without!

📖 Looking at 2 Kings 5:15–18, what difference to you see in Naaman's attitude? What was his response to his healing?

___

___

___

___

How did Elisha respond to him (5:15–19)?

___

___

___

Naaman, a Syrian Gentile, acknowledged the Lord as the only God in Israel and in all the earth, and sought to give Elisha many gifts in gratitude for what the Lord had done. Elisha refused his gifts, wanting all attention, honor, and gratitude to be focused on Jehovah. Here is yet another example of how God revealed Himself as the true and living God to deceived Israelites who either still clung to Baal as a "lord" or diluted and polluted their worship by trying to worship the Lord **and** false gods. Naaman, a man who had worshiped many gods in Syria, now rejected all gods but the God of Israel, and even requested dirt from Israel to make an altar **on Israeli soil** back in Syria. While he erroneously thought he needed the Israeli soil for proper worship, his action revealed a clear surrender to the true God of Israel. Many Israelites could learn from this foreign captain. Naaman with his seeking heart also requested forgiveness for the outward religious ceremonial tasks required of him as the king's servant back in Damascus. Elisha understood his heart—*"Go in peace."*

Extra Mile

GEHAZI'S GREED

Read 2 Kings 5:20–27, the account of Gehazi's greed and deceit. What did he see in Naaman's silver (5:26)? What were the deceptions he practiced and the consequences he faced?

Another incident revealed the true and living God to Syria and Israel. The Syrian army often sought occasion to capture territory and goods from Israel. In 2 Kings 6:8–10 we find the account of such an occasion. It so happened that every time the king of Syria made a battle plan, Elisha knew it as though he had eavesdropped on the meeting, and he warned the king of Israel about the Syrian plans. The king of Syria was furious, wondering who in his forces was giving away military secrets. When he was informed that Elisha told the king of Israel every word that this Syrian king spoke in his own bedroom (6:12), he determined to deal with Elisha and sent chariots and horses and a sizable army to surround Elisha at Dothan (6:13–14).

Read 2 Kings 6:15–23.

What was Elisha's focus in this incident (vv. 15–17)?

____

____

____

What did Elisha do about the Syrian army threat (vv. 18–19)?

____

____

____

____

According to 2 Kings 6:20–23, what solution did Elisha have to deal with this army?

____

____

____

____

Extra Mile

THE LIVING GOD

For another example of how the Lord revealed Himself as the living God to Syria and to Israel read 2 Kings 6:24–33; 7:1–20.

Elisha stayed focused on the Lord. He knew the Lord had his protecting angels all around him. He prayed that his servant would **see** the greater army watching over them, the horses and chariots of fire put in place by God. He then prayed for the Lord to strike the Syrian army with blindness. After the Lord did that, Elisha led the army away to Samaria, where Elisha prayed that the Lord would open their eyes. When the Syrian army was allowed to see again, they saw where they were, and to their surprise were treated to a feast and sent back to Syria.

This incident with the Syrian army showed them that Elisha was indeed a prophet of the true God, and no power, no army, no battle strategy could capture him. The Lord opened the eyes of Elisha's servant to see the chariots of fire surrounding and protecting them. On the other hand the Lord blinded the eyes of the Syrian army that they too might come to see this same sovereign God as Lord not only over all Israel, but also over all the nations of the earth.

In these incidents selected from the life of Elisha we see the Lord continually manifesting Himself for all to see. Not only did the Lord want Israel to see Him as the one true God, but He also wanted the nations of the world to see and know that there was a true God, and that they too could know Him and follow Him.

Elisha DAY FOUR

GOD'S COVENANT FAITHFULNESS

When the Lord met with Elijah at Mount Horeb, Elijah was discouraged over the spiritual condition of the nation, thinking that he alone was left to serve the true God. God assured Elijah that He had a plan to deal with the idolatry and unfaithfulness of His people and furthermore, there were at least 7,000 who remained faithful to Him. He gave Elijah the assignment of anointing Hazael king of Syria, Jehu king of Israel, and Elisha as prophet in his place. With that the Lord also gave him a preview of the work of these men; it would be a work of covenant faithfulness, a work of judgment—*"whoever escapes the sword of Hazael, Jehu will kill; and whoever escapes the sword of Jehu, Elisha will kill"* (1 Kings 19:17). The purge of the cancer of Baal worship through Elijah would continue through Elisha. Today we will see how that worked out in the ministry of Elisha.

Doctrine

THE FAITHFULNESS OF GOD

In Romans 11:1–5, Paul used God's word to Elijah about the 7,000 faithful people to instruct his readers about God's faithfulness to His people. He will ever be faithful to us as well.

Sometime around 841 BC Elisha traveled to Damascus, Syria, where King Ben-Hadad II lay sick in bed. He heard that Elisha had come, and he asked his servant Hazael to take a present to him. Ben-Hadad also wanted Hazael to inquire of Elisha whether or not the king of Syria would survive this illness. Hazael obeyed and went to meet Elisha (2 Kings 8:7–9). Elisha stated that Ben-Hadad would recover from the illness, yet added that he would still die, for Elisha knew from the Lord that Ben-Hadad would die, but not from his sickness.

Read 2 Kings 8:7–15, and answer the questions below.

What made Elisha weep (8:11–12)?

____

____

____

What did Elisha tell Hazael (8:13)?

____

____

____

By the revelation of the Lord, Elisha knew that Hazael would be a ruthless king and bring God's disciplining hand on Israel. That made Elisha weep. The announcement to Hazael that he would be king fulfilled the word God spoke to Elijah several years before about anointing Hazael as king of Syria (1 Kings 19:15–18). Hazael would bring the sword to many in Israel because of the nation's unfaithfulness to its covenant Lord. God would deal with Israel's excursions into Baal worship. Hazael's attempts at aggression are first mentioned in 2 Kings 9:14–15 when he fought in Gilead against Ahab's son, Jehoram of Israel. In those battles Jehoram was wounded and had to retreat to Jezreel.

THE LORD'S KINDNESS

The Lord's kindness was shown to Israel many times and in many ways, seeking to bring them to repentance and back to Himself. The same is true in our lives. We must listen to the exhortation of Romans 2:4—*"Or do you think lightly of the riches of His kindness and forbearance and patience, not knowing that the kindness of God leads you to repentance?"*

📖 Hazael fought many other battles with Israel and Judah. What do you discover about Hazael of Syria in 2 Kings 10:32–33? What do you see about the Lord in these verses?

____

____

____

____

📖 What do you discover in 2 Kings 12:17–18 and 13:3, 22? Summarize the workings of Hazael in Israel.

____

____

____

____

Hazael conquered several portions of Israel's territory during the days of Jehu, particularly the areas east of the Jordan known as Gilead and Bashan. While Hazael was the human instrument, it was the hand of the Lord that wielded him (10:32). In His righteous anger (13:3), He used Hazael to deal with the idolatrous compromises of His people. Commissioned by God to deal with Israel, Hazael conquered territory not only in Gilead and Bashan, but also in the area of Gath south of Jerusalem. He inflicted judgment on Jerusalem and Judah, receiving great treasure from Joash, king of Judah (2 Kings 12:17–18; 2 Chronicles 24:17–25). In the reign of Jehu's son, Jehoahaz of Israel, Hazael continually oppressed Israel (13:3, 22), though the Lord did grant a measure of reprieve when Jehoahaz called on the Lord (13:4–5). God used Hazael as one of the *"rods of men"* to discipline His people just as He had warned that he would many times in the covenant and through His prophets (2 Samuel 7:14).

Hazael was not the only instrument in the hands of the Lord. In 841 BC, the same year Hazael became king of Syria, Elisha sent one of the sons of the prophets to anoint Jehu as king of Israel. The account is given in 2 Kings 9:1–6. What was to be Jehu's role in the nation of Israel (9:7–10)?

____

____

____

____

"... The army of Syria ... came to Judah and Jerusalem ... with a small company of men; but the LORD delivered a very great army into their hand, because they [Judah] had forsaken the LORD God of their fathers. So they executed judgment against Joash."
2 Chronicles 24:23, 24 (NKJV)

The Lord told Elijah He would use the sword of Jehu to deal with the worshipers of Baal. Elisha sent one of the sons of the prophets to Jehu in Ramoth-Gilead, and this "son" commissioned Jehu by the word of the Lord to *"strike down the house of Ahab"*—to avenge the blood of His prophets as well as the blood of His faithful servants such as Naboth. Jezebel was included in that judgment.

Jehu first dealt with Ahab's son, King Jehoram of Israel, who had just come out of a battle with Hazael of Syria. Jehu rode to Jezreel and there killed Jehoram. Here was an unmistakable picture of 1 Kings 19:17; Jehoram escaped the "sword" of Hazael but met the "sword" of Jehu (2 Kings 9:14–26). After that Jehu dealt the deathblow to Ahab's grandson, Ahaziah, king of Judah (9:27–28).

Jehu saw his call from God as a call to deal first with the wickedness of Ahab and Jezebel, then with the sons of Ahab, and then with all associated with Baal worship. In relation to the executions of Jehoram, Jezebel (9:22, 30–37), and the sons of Ahab (10:1–10), he knew he was acting according to *"the word of the LORD"* (9:26, 36; 10:10, 17). In addition to these, Jehu also slew Ahaziah's relatives at Beth-Eked and Ahab's entire family who were in Samaria (10:12–14, 17).

📖 Read 2 Kings 10:18–30, and answer the questions below.

What did Jehu do to the temple of Baal in Samaria and to the worshipers he found there (10:18–28)?

____

____

____

____

What do you see about Jehu's actions (10:30)?

____

____

Pretending to be a loyal follower of Baal, Jehu gathered all the priests and worshipers of Baal to the temple built by Ahab in Samaria. When they were all in place he ordered his men to slay every one of them. Then they tore down the sacred pillars of Baal, destroyed the temple, and made it a refuse dump. *"Thus Jehu destroyed Baal from Israel"* (10:28 NKJV). This same verse in the New American Standard Bible (NASB) says that Jehu "**eradicated**" Baal from the nation of Israel. The Lord honored Jehu for his faithfulness in destroying the godless line of Ahab and promised him that his sons would reign to the fourth generation.

As we consider the purge of Baal worship, we must not overlook Jerusalem, where this cancer had spread under the influence of Athaliah, daughter of Ahab and Jezebel. A temple to Baal had been erected and Mattan served as priest. When Joash was crowned king (835 BC), Queen Athaliah was slain, and the people went to that pagan temple of Baal and tore it down, including its altars and idols. They also executed Mattan. With the destruction of the pagan temple and the slaughter of the pagan leaders, the influence of Baal worship in Judah diminished significantly.

It is interesting that after the anointing of Jehu as king in 841 BC we do not hear of Elisha again until he was near death in 797. We know that his work with the "sons of the prophets" continued in the various schools, and the impact of Hazael and Jehu were certainly felt throughout the land. When we hear of Elisha again, Joash was king of Israel, and he went to visit Elisha on his deathbed. During that visit we see yet another revelation of the covenant faithfulness of God in dealing with His people.

"Thus Jehu eradicated Baal out of Israel."
2 Kings 10:28

📖 Looking at 2 Kings 13:14–19, what did the Lord promise Joash through Elisha?

____

____

____

Elisha promised Joash victory over Syria at Aphek by *"the LORD'S arrow of victory"* or *"the arrow of the Lord's deliverance"* (13:17 NKJV). Furthermore, Elisha commanded him to strike or shoot the ground with all the arrows he had, but Joash stopped at three arrows. The anger shown by Elisha implies that Joash practiced an incomplete obedience, apparently out of a limited faith in the Lord. He would win three victories over Syria, but could have had a final victory had he fully carried out Elisha's command.

📖 Looking at 2 Kings 13:24–25, what do you see about Jehoash (Joash) in his dealings with Syria?

____

____

____

How does this relate to Elisha's prophecy?

____

____

____

____

"But the LORD was gracious to them and had compassion on them and turned to them because of His covenant with Abraham, Isaac, and Jacob, and would not destroy them or cast them from His presence. . . ."
2 Kings 13:23

Joash experienced three victories over Ben-Hadad III of Syria, and recaptured several cities from him. This was in line with the prophecies that Elisha had made concerning Joash. God was faithful and compassionate toward His people.

Think of all that God did in Israel through seeking to bring His people back to the worship of the true and living God. What do you see about the covenant faithfulness of God in 2 Kings 13:22–23?

____

____

____

____

While the Lord raised up Hazael to discipline the wayward people of Israel and Judah, He did so with a perfect balance of His holiness and compassion.

The bedrock truth upon which His actions were based is seen in *"His covenant with Abraham, Isaac, and Jacob"* (13:23). He promised to be their God forever (Genesis 17:1–8), and He was fulfilling that promise.

God continued to reveal His faithfulness and work through Elisha even after Elisha's death. In the spring some Israelites were preparing to bury a man, when they spotted a band of Moabite raiders. Quickly, they put the man's body in Elisha's tomb. When the dead man's body touched the bones of Elisha he revived—another example of God using Elisha to show Israel that He alone was the true God, and that He had a special purpose for them as His covenant people. As Deuteronomy 30:20 (NKJV) states, *"that you may love the Lord your God, that you may obey His voice, and that you may cling to Him,* **for He is your life** *and the length of your days"* (emphasis mine). The God who was Israel's life wanted them to know and walk in that life, in a day-by-day living experience with Him—not in a diluted and polluted, superstitious worship of false gods like Baal which could never bring life to anyone. On the contrary, that deception would always lead to decay and death. God wanted to bring life to Israel and to show them that He was indeed the living God. This He did through Elijah and Elisha. He wants to do that through you and me as well.

"That you may love the Lord your God, that you may obey His voice, and that you may cling to Him, for He is your life and the length of your days." Deuteronomy 30:20 (NKJV)

Elisha DAY FIVE

FOR ME TO FOLLOW GOD

How important is health? Ask a sick man. How important is truth? Ask a businessman who has just signed a contract. Are the things we believe in important? Ask someone who has believed a lie for several years. Often in the "Pastoral Epistles"—1 and 2 Timothy and Titus—Paul speaks of the importance of "sound" doctrine. The Greek word for "sound" is *hugies* or *hugiaino* from which we get our word "hygiene." This word refers to that which promotes doctrinal, spiritual, and moral health. The ministries of Elijah and Elisha called the people to spiritual and moral health by putting away the deceptive idols and ways of Baal worship.

Times may have changed somewhat; the "isms" we deal with have different names, but the heart of man has not changed. He is still prone to wander like a sheep, grazing on anything he sees, oblivious to poisonous weeds and unhealthy plants. That's why sheep need a shepherd who understands the needs of sheep and what is best for them in terms of food, water, and shelter. Elisha was just such a shepherd for the nation of Israel, ever seeking to bring them back to the one true God and to feed them on healthy truth. Let's see what truths Paul can give us that can help us maintain our spiritual and moral health. (These truths affect us physically as well.)

How would you define *"sound doctrine"* or *"sound words"* according to 1 Timothy 6:3 and Titus 1:9?

____

____

What is *"contrary to sound teaching"* (1 Timothy 1:9–10)?

____

____

Sound doctrine includes all the words of our Lord Jesus Christ—His teachings, His words to the apostles, in essence all His revelation in Scripture. It is the *"faithful word"* handed down by the apostles that is used by the Holy Spirit to exhort, encourage, and build up as well as to convict of wrongdoing. First Timothy lists the following groups of people as being contrary to sound doctrine: the *lawless*, the *rebellious*, the *ungodly*, the *unholy and profane*, *murderers*, the *immoral*, *homosexuals*, *kidnappers*, *liars*, and *perjurers* among others (1:9–10).

What is the benefit of *"sound doctrine"* (1 Timothy 4:6–8 and Titus 1:9)?

____

____

____

____

Sound doctrine nourishes the person who listens and heeds. It builds one up in the faith and gives a person a clear path to follow, a path that leads to life and godliness, a walk that is *"profitable for all things, since it holds promise for the present life and also for the life to come."* Sound doctrine also allows one to exhort others so that their lives are built solidly on truth and grow with freedom that is from Christ. This *sound*, healthy truth applies to every age and every station in life (Titus 2:1–8; 2 Timothy 4:1–4).

". . .Discipline yourself for the purpose of godliness. . . . Godliness is profitable for all things since it holds promise for the present life and also for the life to come."
I Timothy 4:7, 8

There is a problem we may face in our acquisition of sound teaching. The very truths we hear can become ineffective or useless in our lives. How? The answer to this question is illustrated in Israel's participation in Baal worship in Elisha's day. Jesus illustrated this truth in a statement He made in the Sermon on the Mount in Matthew 5:13, *"You are the salt of the earth; but if the salt has become tasteless, how will it be made salty again? It is good for nothing anymore, except to be thrown out and trampled under foot by men."* What did Jesus mean? Salt doesn't spoil or go bad. How can salt lose its taste?

The salt used in New Testament times often came from an area around the Dead Sea. Sometimes the salt from that area was mixed with gypsum or some other mineral and thus diluted or polluted. As Christians we can mix truth with false seasonings that dilute, pollute, or even deaden our "saltiness." Consequently, our relationship with the Lord grows stale and our witness and effectiveness loses its appeal, its tastiness. That's what happened in Israel. They were mixing the word and worship of Jehovah with the falsehoods and the deceitful rituals, ceremonies and superstitions of Baal worship. Soon the lies of this false worship were so many that they overpowered the pure salt of God's Word, resulting in the spiritual and moral decay of the nation. Some of them were even deceived to the point that they sacrificed their children on the fires of Baal's altar.

Israel's relationship with the living God suffered. Like a leprous man who begins to lose feeling in his hands or feet, the people of Israel began to lose their sensitivity to the Lord. Their consciences became insensitive, hardened, and callous; their love for the Lord grew cold and stale; their walk became marked more by superstition than by revelation of truth, and their worship deteriorated into empty ritual at best and immoral, pagan rites at worst. In His love, God had to rescue them out of that diseased condition, even if it meant serious surgery. The problem of sin in Israel was serious to God, and this problem should be serious to us as well.

One of the greatest dangers a Christian faces in his devotion to God is mixing worldly opinions and philosophies with the Word of God.

Paul had words of caution for those he sought to bring to maturity in Christ. He told the Corinthians, *"But I am afraid, lest as the serpent deceived Eve by his craftiness, your minds should be led astray from the simplicity and purity of devotion to Christ"* (2 Corinthians 11:3). One of the greatest dangers a Christian faces in his devotion to God is mixing worldly opinions and philosophies with the Word of God. Christians today are bombarded from every angle of society with perspectives that radically differ from the teaching of God's Word. The battle is not won as we aggressively confront the lies, nor as we embrace the society in which we live and try to "fit in." The solution comes through immersing ourselves in the truth and then living that truth. When we are grounded in truth, the lies will be exposed for the solution-less counterfeits they are—but we will never "fit in!" So aptly it has been said, "if the world fits, then your faith is the wrong size."

In what ways are you receiving biblical input in an average week? How much time do you spend in each of the following areas?

	How Much Time?
☐ Worship service	____________
☐ Bible study group	____________
☐ Personal Bible study	____________
☐ Christian magazines/novels/books	____________
☐ Christian radio/TV/tapes	____________
☐ Other____________	____________

Baal worship focused on the physical (health, strength), the material (crops, business), and even the sensual. Some were willing to practice immoral rites as part of their "worship" or in conjunction with their offerings. Sometimes they went to the extreme of offering a child in the fires of the altar to Baal.

APPLY What do you find about the potential for idolatry in your life in the following verses? Write the obvious truths and any applications to your life.

Ephesians 5:5

____

____

"Little children, guard yourselves from idols."
I John 5:21

Colossians 3:5

____

____

1 Corinthians 10:5–14

____

____

1 John 5:21

____

____

Today are you focusing on the physical or the material or the sensual? How far does your idolatry take you?

____

Elisha, as Elijah before him, sought to lead the people to put down the idols of their lives and come back to following the true and living God. Their testimonies should lead us to do the same.

Spend some time in prayer. As you pray, consider where you stand in following the Lord. Commit yourself to tear down the idols that have come into your life.

Lord, I thank You for Your faithfulness to Your Word, to Your promises, to Your people, and to me personally. Thank You for faithfully convicting me of those times when I have "worshiped" an "idol," when I have relied on that "idol" to bring joy or peace or inner satisfaction rather than believing You and Your Word. Thank You for the loving discipline You have sent my way and for forgiving me of my foolish choices and willful ways. I praise You for the way You provide for me physically, materially, and spiritually. Thank You for not giving up on me, for leading me to humble myself before You, for showing me Your mercy and grace time and time again. May Your grace be multiplied to me that I might know You more fully, love You more deeply, and follow You more consistently. In Jesus' Name. Amen.

Express your prayer to the Lord, or write a journal entry concerning your walk with the Lord.

____

____

____

____

____

____

____

____

____

____

____

Notes

FOLLOWING GOD WHEN YOU DON'T WANT TO

Few biblical characters have enjoyed more secular fame than the prophet Jonah. His story of being swallowed by a great fish and taking a three-day, all-expense-paid Mediterranean cruise is known almost everywhere. Did Jonah really exist? Some have argued that the book of Jonah is not an historical book, but a Jewish allegory of Israel going through the Babylonian captivity. This view, however, runs opposite the evidence. The book itself is written as a straightforward historical account. We know from the Assyrian inscriptions that during the reign of Adad-nirari III there was a swing toward monotheism. In 2 Kings 14:25, Jonah is identified both as a real person and as an accredited prophet from Gath-hepher, near Nazareth. Further, Jesus calls Jonah by name, treating him as a historical person and his encounter with the "great fish" as factual (Matthew 12:39–41). Perhaps the most outstanding feature of the book of Jonah is its honest representation of human nature. Jonah's weaknesses are clearly visible as his "feet of clay" muddy the reputation of Israel. He was given a ministry he did not want to a people he did not like, and his response was far from spiritual. As we seek to learn from him what it means to follow God, the greatest lessons are in how God dealt with his rebellion.

Jonah was a prophet to the Northern Kingdom of Israel from 793 BC to 753 BC during the reign of Jeroboam II. Little is known of him except the events recorded in the book of Jonah.

WHEN DID HE PROPHESY?

800 | 750 | 700 | 650 | 600

"A Prophet" (sent to Amaziah)
ISAIAH
MICAH
NAHUM ZEPHANIAH HABAKKUK
HULDAH (a prophetess)
JEREMIAH

Amaziah 796–767
Azariah(Uzziah) 790–739
Jotham 750–735
Ahaz 735–715
Hezekiah 715–686
Manasseh 697–642
Amon 642–640
Josiah 640–609
Jehoahaz 609
Jehoiakim 609–598
Jehoiachin (Jeconiah) 598–597
Zedekiah 597 586

Jehoahaz 814–798
Joash (Jehoash) 798–782
Jeroboam II 793–753
Zechariah 753–752
Menahem 752–742
Hoshea 732–722
Shallum 752
Pekahiah 742–740
Pekah 752–732

JONAH
AMOS
HOSEA
ODED

There are no more kings or prophets in the Northern Kingdom. Foreign peoples are resettled into the land.

605—1st Captivity
DANIEL
Hananiah
Mishael
Azariah
597—2d Captivity
EZEKIEL
Nebuchadnezzar 605–562

Tiglath-pileser I 745–727
722—Assyria takes Israel into captivity
Shalmaneser V 727–722
Sennacherib 705–681
612—Fall of Nineveh

Jonah DAY ONE

THE RELUCTANT PROPHET

Often we look at the biblical characters of the Old Testament and assume that their obedience was easy and their faith unwavering. We place them on a pedestal and believe that they are somehow closer to God than we could ever hope to be, and we lose our ability to relate with them. Yet, if we look closely and honestly at them we find our own struggles and stumbling mirrored in their lives. Today, as we begin looking at the life of Jonah, we will see that he was a very reluctant prophet. In 2 Kings 14:27 Jonah's ministry is connected with the reign of Jeroboam II of Israel (793–753 BC), a wicked but militarily successful king of that time. From history we know that the area of Nineveh experienced a plague in 765 BC, a solar eclipse in 763, and a second plague in 759. These events were regarded by the ancients as evidence of divine judgment, and may have been the Lord's way of preparing them to receive Jonah's message. The preaching of Jonah was the greatest evangelistic success recorded in the Old Testament—made even more amazing by the reality that Jonah didn't want to go. Although the name "Jonah" means "dove," he did not want to be an ambassador of peace to this wicked pagan nation.

Did You Know?

NINEVEH

Nineveh was the capital city of Assyria, the dominant world power of the day. Its name is a translation of the Assyrian word for the goddess "Ishtar." The city was located half of a mile east of the Tigris River. Its population numbered about a million people, and the perimeter of the metropolis took three days to traverse on foot (Jonah 3:3). The city was destroyed in 612 BC, approximately 150 years after Jonah prophesied.

📖 Read through Jonah 1:1–2, and identify the assignment God gave Jonah.

____

____

____

____

____

The *"word of the Lord"* came to Jonah, instructing him to go to the great city of Nineveh (then the capital of Assyria) and cry against its sin. Though we are not told how God spoke, what is significant is **that** God spoke. When God has a task for us, He assumes the responsibility of communicating that task in a way we can understand.

What was Jonah's response to this ministry he was receiving from the Lord (v. 3)?

____

____

____

____

____

Instead of obeying, Jonah made plans to flee to Tarshish, *"from the presence of the Lord."* Although Jonah's theology taught him that he could not flee from God's presence (see Psalm 139:7–12), he obviously believed that he could flee from God's purpose. The repetition of the statement, *"from the presence of the Lord,"* makes it clear that he was running away from God and his appointed task.

To fully appreciate Jonah's plan, one must understand the geography of it. Nineveh was located some five hundred miles east of Palestine, while the location of Tarshish is believed by most scholars to be two thousand miles due west of Palestine on the south coast of Spain near Gibraltar. He ran in the exact opposite direction, and he tried to get as far away as he possibly could, for in that time, the area of Spain was on the outer frontier of the known world.

Put Yourself In Their Shoes

RUNNING FROM GOD

Running from God is always a losing proposition. Look what Jonah lost when he ran from the Lord.

1) He lost his prayer life.

2) He lost his compassion.

3) He lost his testimony.

A Christian saying no to God is far more repulsive to the world than a pagan who lives an ungodly life.

📖 Once Jonah set his heart to run from God's purpose, everything kept going from bad to worse. Read verses 3–5, and notice every time the idea of going "down" is mentioned.

____

____

____

____

____

____

First, he went **down** to Joppa, and then he went **down** into the ship. Once the storm hit, he went **down** into the belly of the ship, and eventually we see him going lower still when he is thrown into the sea and taken into the *"deep"* (2:3) inside the belly of a great fish. This seems to be a symbolic picture of what happens when we run from God.

📖 Looking at verses 4–13, how did God deal with Jonah's rebellion?

____

____

____

____

Doctrine

ATTRIBUTES OF GOD

The infinite nature of God is primarily summarized in three main attributes. He is omnipotent, omniscient, and omnipresent. The prefix, "omni" means all. Omnipotent means "all-potent" or "all-powerful." Omniscient means "all knowing." And omnipresent means "all present." In Psalm 139:7–12 David asks the rhetorical question, *"where can I flee from Thy presence?"* The answer: nowhere. David says, *"If I go to heaven, You are there. If I go into hell, You are there. If I fly to the remotest part of the sea, You are there. Even in the darkest night, You are there."* How foolish Jonah was to think he could run from God.

The Lord hurled a great wind on the sea, sending a storm so severe that the ship was about to break apart. God's power was manifested in His command of nature, underscoring the futility of running from Him and His purpose. The fact that Jonah understood this is reflected in his statement of verse 9 that his God *"made the sea and the dry land."* Although in verse 4 the storm was so bad the ship neared breaking, verse 11 indicates it got worse from there, and verse 13 shows it got *"even stormier."*

This rich passage of Scripture shows both the futility of running from God and the consequences bad choices can bring to our lives and the lives of others. When he said no to God, the first thing Jonah had lost was his prayer life. It is significant that even the pagans were praying when faced with apparent death—but not Jonah. Next, we see that he had lost his compassion. Even though he was a prophet of God, he didn't seem to care for the precious lives of the crew. He simply looked for a place in the ship where he would not feel so much of the harsh effects of the storm. Jonah found temporary refuge in the "hold" or belly of the ship, the lowest place in the boat. The third thing Jonah lost by saying no to God was his testimony. He eventually had to explain to the men that he was running from God, to which they replied, "How could you do this?" A Christian saying no to God is far more repulsive to the world than a pagan who lives an ungodly life.

Repent Now, Not Later!

Jonah tried to run away from God. Have you ever tried to run from God? He knew what God called him to, but it wasn't what he wanted, for he hated the people of Nineveh. Their wicked, tyrannical rule had made life hard for Israel, and the last thing he wanted to do was preach to them. God called Jonah east to Nineveh, but he ran west to Tarshish. Somehow in his foolishness, he thought that by running from God's will he could run from God. But God is omnipresent. Every time we run from Him we run back into Him. God sent a storm to get Jonah's attention, but Jonah still wouldn't respond. But as Jonah was about to learn, when we refuse to listen to God, we just invite Him to speak louder. The lesson here for all of us is, "If you don't get right when God sends the storm, you **will** get right when troubles grow far worse!"

What was Jonah's plan for resolving the dilemma (1:12), and what was revealed about his attitude?

____

____

____

____

____

Jonah's plan was to commit suicide, for he instructed them to throw him into the sea. The most significant thing revealed here is not what Jonah said, but what he did not say. There was no evidence of repentance or even remorse. Though he confessed to the men that he was running from God, he never fulfilled their request to *"call on his god"* (v. 6).

Jonah hated the Ninevites and had no desire to see them repent. It seems as if Jonah had it figured that if he killed himself, he wouldn't have to go to Nineveh and they wouldn't repent. Though God hemmed Jonah in through this tumultuous storm, he refused to repent. Even these pagan sailors exhibited a far more honorable response than Jonah did, as verse 16 indicates that once the sea stopped raging, they *"feared the Lord greatly,"* and *"offered a sacrifice to the Lord and made vows."*

God would not allow Jonah's selfish plan to succeed. It was not chance that was in control here, for **the Lord appointed** a great fish to swallow Jonah. Though we traditionally view this fish as a whale, the Hebrew word is not specific. It may have been a large shark for all we know, but that is not the point. The point is that God intervened in Jonah's rebellion.

📖 Read through Jonah's prayer (2:1–9), and record what stands out to you.

____

____

____

____

____

WHY DID JONAH HATE THE NINEVITES?

Nineveh was the capitol of Assyria, the dominant world kingdom. They were the Nazis of their day. Cruel and powerful, they had earned the fear of other nations because of their barbarism. Historical records indicate such atrocities as building a pyramid of human heads, blinding their enemies, cutting off limbs, tearing captives' tongues out, impaling victims on poles, even flaying victims alive and spreading their skin out on the walls of the city. Not only were they cruel and wicked, but prophets such as Isaiah, Hosea, and Amos prophesied that they would eventually destroy Israel. Jonah had good reason not to want them to experience God's mercy.

It seems obvious that Jonah had experienced a change of heart while sitting in the belly of this monstrous fish. Verse 4 denotes that he looked *"toward Thy holy temple,"* the place of seeking God. In verse 7 we see that while his life appeared to be slipping away, he remembered the Lord and prayed. We may deduce from verse 9 that his repentance was complete, and that he was now ready to obey God's direction.

Did You Know?

CAN A HUMAN LIVE INSIDE A FISH?

In the December, 1992 issue of *National Geographic* magazine, University of Maryland marine biologist Eugenie Clark, who has studied whale sharks extensively, confirms in detail nearly every aspect of the Jonah story. Professor Clark writes: "The whale shark's unusual digestive anatomy lends itself to Jonah stories. It is easy to imagine yourself being inadvertently sucked into a whale shark's mouth" The Jonah story concludes when the great fish *"vomited out Jonah"* (Jonah 2:10). Professor Clark: "Sharks have a nonviolent way of getting rid of large objects of dubious digestibility they swallow accidentally. In a process known as gastric eversion, a shark can slowly empty its cardiac stomach by turning it inside out and pushing it through the mouth."

📖 Read verse 3, and notice every reference Jonah made to God's control of the circumstances.

____

____

____

Look at Jonah's commentary on who was in control of the situation. He said, **"Thou** *hadst cast me into the deep,"* and again, **"Thy** *breakers and billows. . . ."* Jonah recognized that God was the one doing all these things. He made the connection between the circumstances of his life and God's sovereignty.

📖 Read the entire chapter one more time, noticing the occurrences of the word, **"then."** Briefly explain the significance of each instance this word is used.

____

____

____

____

____

The first instance of the word, *"then,"* is found in verse 1. It is only after Jonah was in the fish that he prayed. The second occurrence is not until the end of the chapter. It was not until after Jonah's repentance was complete that the Lord commanded the fish to vomit Jonah up on dry land. When God brings calamity upon us for our rebellion, He will not relent until we repent.

The Results of Repentance

DAY THREE

One of the most encouraging realities of following God is that even when we fail, God allows fresh starts. All that is required is repentance. Jonah failed miserably, but the Lord brought him right back to where he started and again invited him to be a part of the purpose of God. His job assignment did not change! The Hebrew word translated "repent" in the Old Testament *(shuwb)* paints a beautiful picture of what Jonah did. It literally means, "to turn back." In the King James Version it is often translated "turn" or "return." Like its Greek counterpart in the New Testament *(metanoeo)*, it has the idea of a change of thinking which results in a change of direction. Today we will see the results of the change in Jonah's thought processes.

Read the entire chapter of Jonah 3. Look at Jonah's response in verse 3, and compare it with 1:3.

This time Jonah got it right. Instead of rising up to flee, he rose up to obey. James 4:17 says, *". . . to one who knows the right thing to do, and does not do it, to him it is sin."* Failing to do what God directs is just as serious a sin as doing what He instructs us not to do. When God, by His Spirit, prompts us to a task, we must obey!

What is the essence of Jonah's message according to verse 4?

Jonah's message was simple: "Judgment is coming." There was no arm twisting or playing on the people's emotions. Often today we place too much emphasis on the persuasion of a message, but Jonah's trust was simply in God being the source of the message. As a result, there was no doubt that the people were responding to God, not to Jonah. It is a good example of what Paul described in 1 Corinthians 2:4–5, *"And my message and my preaching were not in persuasive words of wisdom, but in demonstration of the Spirit and of power, that your faith should not rest on the wisdom of men, but on the power of God."*

How did the people of Nineveh respond?

GREATEST MIRACLE?

The greatest miracle in the book of Jonah is not the prophet being swallowed by large fish, but the entire pagan city of Nineveh repenting at the one sentence sermon of Jonah. It is the single greatest evangelistic success recorded in Scripture—far greater than any event in the book of Acts. As noteworthy Bible expositor, G. Campbell Morgan, once said, "Men have been looking so hard at the great fish that they have failed to see the great God."

Verse 5 tells us they "believed God." Everything else recorded flows out of this one truth. The Ninevites were exhibiting faith in its purest form, for true faith is simply taking God at His word—believing that He will do what He says He will do and responding rightly to that. Because they believed God would do what He said, they repented in sackcloth, began fasting, called on God earnestly, and turned from their sins.

According to verse 10, how did God respond to their repentance?

"When they turned from their wicked way, then God relented concerning the calamity. . . ." God does not chasten to exact revenge or to punish, but to turn us back to Himself. How much easier it is on us when we turn back quickly. Even when judgment was pronounced, we find example after example in the Scriptures of that judgment being lessened when repentance is evident.

📖 Read Matthew 12:41, and write your observations on Nineveh's repentance.

____

____

____

____

____

Throughout Israel's history they have struggled by thinking they deserved God's favor no matter how they responded to Him. Jesus said that Nineveh would condemn faithless Israel at the judgment because the people of Nineveh repented when a very flawed and reluctant Jonah spoke to them, while Israel did not repent when the perfect Lord, Jesus Christ Himself came to them (see Matthew 12:41; Luke 11:32).

PRIDE AND PREJUDICE

DAY FOUR

Jonah was a prophet of God, but that does not mean he was always godly. Chapter 4 brings the story of Jonah to a bittersweet end. It underscores the fact that although God can make us do what He desires even when we don't want to, we still must choose to follow God. Obedience by fear is not the same thing as walking in a relationship with God. Jonah finally obeyed God after nearly dying in a storm and then spending three days in the belly of a great fish, but his heart attitude toward the Ninevites was still unchanged.

📖 Read through verses 1–5, and identify Jonah's desire for the Ninevites.

____

____

____

____

____

____

Still wanting the Ninevites to be destroyed, Jonah was *"greatly displeased"* at their repentance. Verse 2 reveals that from the beginning he did not want Nineveh to repent and experience God's mercy, and even now he prayed God would not relent in His punishment. He even went so far as to say that he'd rather die than watch God bless Nineveh. Jonah went out to the east of the city to wait and see if God would destroy it.

GO WEST YOUNG MAN!

In Jonah chapter 4 we see the prophet going out to the east of the city to wait and see if Nineveh will be destroyed. It is significant that in the Old Testament, to go west is a picture of moving toward God, while to go east pictures moving away from God. When the priest entered the temple or tabernacle from the only entrance (always on the east side) he would be moving west as he headed toward the altar and the holy place. Conversely, to go east consistently pictures moving away from God as Adam and Eve did when they left Eden.

Why didn't Jonah want Nineveh to repent? Why did he hate them so? Why did he not have the same compassion on them that God had? One of Jonah's problems (and Israel's as well) was that he interpreted the Jewish status of being God's chosen people to mean that the Jews were better than everyone else was because they possessed the Law. In truth, this only meant that they were more accountable than everyone else. Though they knew the Law, they were no better at obeying it than the pagan nations who had no law. Jonah did not realize that Israel was given the message of God to share, not to hoard. Also woven into Jonah's prejudice, many scholars believe, was a realization from prophecy that God was going to use the Ninevites (Assyrians) to chasten Israel. Jonah probably thought that he loved Israel more than God loved the nation, and in his foolishness was trying to protect Israel from the very thing that would move them back to God. He lost sight of the very attributes of God he mentions in verse 2; that God is *". . . a gracious and compassionate God, slow to anger and abundant in lovingkindness, and one who relents concerning calamity."* Jonah could not trust God to manifest these same attributes in dealing with Israel.

"And he prayed to the LORD and said, 'Please LORD, was not this what I said while I was still in my own country? Therefore, in order to forestall this I fled to Tarshish, for I knew that Thou art a gracious and compassionate God, slow to anger and abundant in lovingkindness, and one who relents concerning calamity.'"

Jonah 4:2

What is the point of the plant that grew up over Jonah (vv. 6–11)?

____

____

____

____

____

God used the plant as an object lesson to instruct Jonah. His point was that if Jonah was correct in having compassion on a temporal shrub that he neither planted nor cultivated, then certainly God was right in having compassion on the more than half a million Ninevites He created, whose eternal destiny hung in the balance. The 120,000 people God referred to in verse eleven refers to very young children who had not yet reached the so-called "age of accountability" (see also Hebrews 5:13, 14). This verse teaches so clearly that the Lord is God of all the nations, not just Israel. Jonah represents so many others in Israel who forgot this lesson. Later, prophets like Isaiah tried to expand the people's vision by looking forward to the day when God's message would reach out to all nations, and Jesus' great commission assured that this would indeed take place (Matthew 28:19–20; Mark 16:15; Luke 24:46–47).

The Hebrew word for the plant that covered Jonah means "nauseous to the taste" and seems to reflect Jonah's attitude. It was probably a castor oil tree—a very large bush that grows to ten feet high with very broad leaves. It is a very temperamental plant that wilts and withers with very slight handling.

What do you see reflected in Jonah's suicidal attitude reflected in verses 8–9?

____

____

____

____

Suicide is one of the most selfish acts man can ever choose. It was Jonah's only measure of control left, and control is the god of those who refuse to surrender. As we have seen throughout the whole book, Jonah would rather have died than to be used of God in a plan he did not agree with. He had elevated his own opinions and refused to trust God's sovereignty.

For Me to Follow God

The book of Jonah ends with a lot of unanswered questions. Jonah may have repented of his attitude, but there is no record of it. We should remember though, that he is the one who wrote this record of his failings with all its brutal honesty. There is no blaming of anyone else in his account. It would seem that he had taken full responsibility for his failings—a sign of a repentant heart. Though Jonah doesn't tell us, we know from history that God did not destroy the Ninevites at this time, but used them later on to chasten His people. Readers of this book often lose a bit of respect for Jonah; however, there are worldly reasons to think good of him. He experienced a great miracle in the fish, and finally obeyed the instructions of God. He experienced tremendous ministry results. But if you look closely at each of these bright spots in this prophet's life, none of these occasions actually say anything positive about the man, Jonah. The miracle of the fish was God's work, not Jonah's. The obedience of Jonah was reluctant and incomplete, based on his fear of what God might do, instead of a compassionate love for the people of Nineveh. The ministry results were of God, not Jonah, and Jonah even wished they could be undone! In the end, for all of us, the only thing really worthy of respect is a heart that follows God in loving obedience, and that is missing in Jonah. This portrait of following God that we see in Jonah is stained and smudged by flesh. But lest we jump to judging Jonah, we must realize that this same flesh is in each of us, and in big and small ways each of us reflects the same rebellions of Jonah.

APPLY Can you think of an example of running from God's will in your own life or in the life of someone you know?

____

____

____

What were (are) the reasons for wanting to run from God's will?

____

____

____

____

How did God deal with the situation?

____

____

____

"... and you have forgotten the exhortation which is addressed to you as sons, 'My son, do not regard lightly the discipline of the Lord, Nor faint when you are reproved by Him; For those whom the Lord loves He disciplines, And He scourges every son whom He receives.'"
Hebrews 12:5–6

Lest we draw the wrong conclusion, it is important that we see God's good intent in not letting us succeed in running away from Him. The Lord is not a cosmic bully, making people do whatever He likes for no good reason. God's discipline is a sign of His love for us.

📖 Read Hebrews 12:5–11, and answer the questions that follow.

What does God's discipline of us say about our relationship to Him (vv. 5–6)?

___

___

___

What would the indication be if we never experienced the Lord's discipline (vv. 7–8)?

___

___

___

What should we do when the Lord disciplines us (v. 9)?

___

___

___

What is God's motive for disciplining us (v. 10)?

___

___

___

What is the result (v. 11)?

___

___

___

That God disciplines us is evidence of His love for us. If we never experience His discipline when we sin, that may be an indication that we are not true sons of His. But how does God discipline us? Often, as with Jonah, God's chastening hand is seen in the difficult circumstances He brings into our lives. It was the Lord who sent a storm Jonah's way, and again, it was the Lord who brought the great fish. When God sends a storm, it is not to punish us. It is an act of grace to call a straying lamb back to Himself. If we do not respond to His chastening, we are inviting more difficulties. Because we are His children, when we stray, God will keep pursuing us until we return. He wants us to share in His holiness so we can experience the "peaceful fruit of righteousness."

Sadly, one of the reasons for Jonah's disobedience was his own prejudice against the people of Nineveh. While it is true they were an ungodly people, that should have motivated Jonah to seek their repentance rather than to rejoice in their judgment. Look below, and identify any categories of people who you hold prejudice against and have a hard time reaching out to.

___ Blacks
___ Whites
___ Native Americans
___ Jews
___ Hispanics
___ Arabs
___ Orientals
___ Other________________________
___ Homosexuals
___ Homeless
___ Uneducated

While we cannot change ourselves, we must look to the Lord to change areas that are not pleasing to Him, especially wrong attitudes toward people based on superficial reasoning. Man has a human tendency to focus on outward characteristics, but God looks at the heart (1 Samuel 16:7). Second Corinthians 5:16 teaches us, *". . . from now on we recognize no man according to the flesh. . . ."* We cannot walk with God and continue to view people through the lenses of the old sinful nature.

APPLY As you close out this week, confess to the Lord any areas of prejudice of which He has convicted you, and yield those areas to Him afresh. Ask Him to change your heart toward people to be like His compassionate heart. We cannot hold the hand of God while holding on to our prejudice.

Let's spend some time in prayer to the Lord right now.

Lord, thank You for this powerful reminder that You love me too much to allow me to succeed in running away from You and Your will. Give me a heart that runs to You instead of from You. Help me to trust that Your will is always best. Help me to hear, when You are using the circumstances of life to get my attention. Give me grace to lay aside my prejudices and reach out to those You want to minister to through me. Help me to rejoice in Your compassion to others, knowing how needy I am of that same compassion. Make me quick to repent when I stray from You. I may never be called to so great a task as Jonah, but help me to ever be diligent toward those things that are right in the promotion of Your kingdom. Amen.

Prayer of Application . . .

As we close our lesson this week, take to heart any areas the Lord has singled out to you, and express them in prayer to Him.

____
____
____
____
____
____
____
____
____
____
____

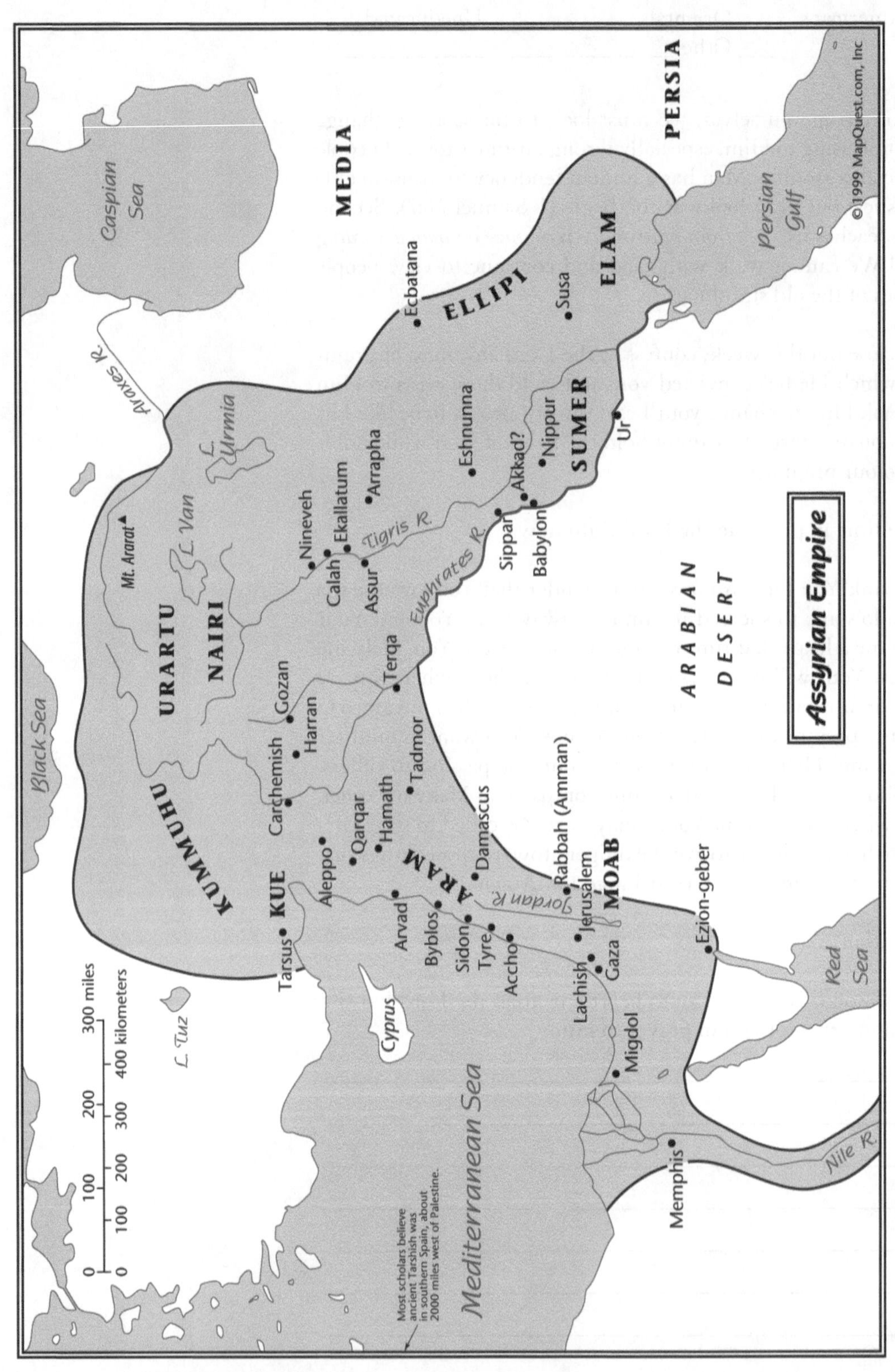
Assyrian Empire
Caspian Sea
Black Sea
Mediterranean Sea
Persian Gulf
Red Sea
MEDIA
PERSIA
ELLIPI
ELAM
SUMER
URARTU
NAIRI
KUMMUHU
KUE
ARAM
MOAB
ARABIAN DESERT
Araxes R.
L. Urmia
L. Van
Mt. Ararat
L. Tuz
Cyprus
Tigris R.
Euphrates R.
Jordan R.
Nile R.
Ecbatana
Susa
Eshnunna
Nippur
Ur
Akkad?
Sippar
Babylon
Arrapha
Nineveh
Ekallatum
Calah
Assur
Terqa
Gozan
Harran
Carchemish
Tadmor
Aleppo
Qarqar
Hamath
Damascus
Rabbah (Amman)
Jerusalem
Arvad
Byblos
Sidon
Tyre
Accho
Lachish
Gaza
Tarsus
Migdol
Memphis
Ezion-geber
0 100 200 300 miles
0 100 200 300 400 kilometers
Most scholars believe ancient Tarshish was in southern Spain, about 2000 miles west of Palestine.
©1999 MapQuest.com, Inc

Notes

Notes

lesson 5

RETURNING TO THE LORD

After the death of Solomon, his son Rehoboam made many foolish choices as king. The most tragic consequence of Rehoboam's behavior was the division of Israel into two kingdoms. Rehoboam reigned over the kingdom of Judah (the southern tribes of Judah and Benjamin), and Jeroboam reigned over the kingdom of Israel or "Ephraim" (the ten northern tribes). Fearful that any of the people might return to Jerusalem for worship, Jeroboam placed golden calves at Bethel and Dan, leading the ten northern tribes into idolatry. This newfound religion was a mixture of Jewish ritual and pagan idolatry consummated with rampant immorality, and the people loved it. God called Hosea to minister to this Northern Kingdom from around 760 to 720 BC. Israel was prospering as a nation, but Hosea could see the nation's sin and their total disregard for God, and he warned of imminent judgment. Hosea was faithful to preach the truth, but his warnings went unheeded, and in 722 BC the downward spiral of Israel culminated in its capitulation to the Assyrian Empire. Intermarriage with the Assyrians resulted in the mixed race known as the Samaritans. Although Israel didn't listen to the message of Hosea, we can listen and learn from Israel's mistakes.

Hosea's ministry spanned the last six kings of the Northern Kingdom of Israel (760 to 720 BC), and he witnessed the defeat and capture of the Northern Kingdom by the Assyrians in 722 BC.

WHEN DID HE PROPHESY?

800	750	700	650	600
"A Prophet" (sent to Amaziah)	ISAIAH MICAH		NAHUM ZEPHANIAH JEREMIAH	HABAKKUK HULDAH (a prophetess)
Amaziah 796–767 **Azariah(Uzziah) 790–739**	**Jotham 750–735** **Ahaz 735–715**	**Hezekiah 715–686** **Manasseh 697–642**	**Amon 642–640** **Josiah 640–609**	**Jehoahaz 609** **Jehoiakim 609–598** **Jehoiachin (Jeconiah) 598–597** **Zedekiah 597–586**
Jehoahaz 814–798 **Joash (Jehoash) 798–782** **Jeroboam II 793–753** JONAH	**Zechariah 753–752** **Shallum 752** **Menahem 752–742** **Pekahiah 742–740** **Pekah 752–732** **Hoshea 732–722** AMOS HOSEA ODED	There are no more kings or prophets in the Northern Kingdom. Foreign peoples are resettled into the land.		605—1st Captivity DANIEL Hananiah Mishael Azariah 597—2d Captivity EZEKIEL
	Tiglath-pileser I 745–727 722—Assyria takes Israel into captivity Shalmaneser V 727–722	Sennacherib 705–681		Nebuchadnezzar 605–562 612—Fall of Nineveh

Hosea DAY ONE

A Hard Sermon to Preach

God sometimes calls His messengers to take extreme measures to make sure that their message is received and understood. For several years Isaiah embarrassed his countrymen by walking around dressed as a prisoner of war. Jeremiah carried a yoke on his shoulders for a time, and once bought a farm from a relative even though the farm was in land held by the enemy. However, of the aforementioned prophets, none could match the apparent peculiarity of Hosea. God called him to confront the unfaithfulness of Israel to their God. As the apostle Paul said in 2 Corinthians 11:2–3, *"For I am jealous for you with a godly jealousy; for I betrothed you to one husband, that to Christ I might present you as a pure virgin. But I am afraid, lest as the serpent deceived Eve by his craftiness, your minds should be led astray from the simplicity and purity of devotion to Christ."* As Paul was called to confront those in the New Testament era, Hosea was called to confront Israel as a spiritually unfaithful bride. But God gave him a unique way to appreciate His point of view. Today we will see how Hosea lived his message.

"For I am jealous for you with a godly jealousy; for I betrothed you to one husband, that to Christ I might present you as a pure virgin. But I am afraid, lest as the serpent deceived Eve by his craftiness, your minds should be led astray from the simplicity and purity of devotion to Christ."
2 Corinthians 11:2-3

📖 Read Hosea 1:2.

What was God's appointed purpose for Hosea?

___

___

___

Why did God tell him to do this?

___

___

___

___

"When the Lord first spoke through Hosea . . ."—in other words, at the beginning of his prophetic ministry. God instructed Hosea to take for himself a wife of harlotry (prostitution) and have children of harlotry. Some take this to mean his wife was at one time pure, then became a harlot, but more likely the parallel indicates she had been a harlot since the earliest days of her womanhood. God intended for this harlot to serve as a picture in Hosea's life of the idolatry and unfaithfulness of Israel to the Lord. God gave Hosea a way to faithfully communicate His heart to His people.

📖 Looking at Hosea 1:3–9, identify each of Hosea's children and the message God spoke through the names He called Hosea to give them.

___

___

___

___

___

___

God called Hosea to name his first child, Jezreel, after a prominent valley in northern Israel whose name means "God sows" or "God scatters." It was in this valley that Jehu murdered the sons of Ahab in order to seize the throne. The prophecy is that God would *"put an end to the kingdom of the house of Israel."* Hosea's daughter was named Lo-ruhamah ("unpitied"), symbolizing the plight of Israel. The third child was a son named Lo-ammi, which means "not my people," symbolizing the rejection of Israel. Since these were the children of harlotry there is some question if Hosea was even the father of the last two.

HOSEA'S SUFFERING

"Hosea saw to the heart of the great subjects of which he treated, and he did so because in his training for the prophetic ministry his own heart was wrung with anguish. He who has much to teach must suffer much; and he alone can speak of the deepest things in the economy of God who has sooner or later entered into fellowship with the suffering of God. Hosea passed into fellowship in that suffering through his own suffering, and out of that fellowship in suffering spoke to his age. That, I think, is the key to all that is so appealing and powerful in this wonderful prophecy."

—G. Campbell Morgan

Now look at Hosea 1:10—2:1. Though Hosea preached a message of judgment, he also spoke of the future with hope. Look at these verses, and identify what the future holds.

____

____

____

Here we begin to see the grace of God. Though Israel did not repent, the negative prophecies of the names of Hosea's children would one day be changed. The "Jezreel" of scattering would become a place of sowing. Those who were called *"not my people"* would be called *"sons of the living God."* Clearly the "unpitied" would find the pity of God. Whom the Lord loves, He reproves. But He will not forget His covenant. Even when we are faithless, He remains faithful, for He cannot deny Himself (2 Timothy 2:13).

God has established complete integrity between the messenger and his message. Every time Hosea thought of his own unfaithful wife, he was reminded of Israel's unfaithfulness to the Lord. He could feel God's pains over Israel in a unique way. Now Hosea could passionately speak to Israel's unfaithfulness and accurately relate God's heart.

THE SINS OF ISRAEL

Hosea DAY TWO

One responsibility that was given to Hosea and all of the prophets was that of confronting the sins of God's people. It was an unpleasant but necessary task. Israel had been unfaithful to the Lord, their husband, and had gone after other gods as a harlot goes after lovers. We saw yesterday that Hosea could appreciate first-hand the sins Israel had committed against their God. God gave him a harlot as a wife so he could preach from God's heart against Israel's unfaithfulness. Today we want to begin looking at chapter 2 to see more specifically what those sins were.

Read Hosea 2:2–5 as well as 4:11–19, and summarize in your own words the sin Israel is accused of here, and that is pictured in Gomer's sin.

____

____

____

____

Like Gomer's unfaithfulness to Hosea, Israel was being unfaithful to the Lord. Every time they consulted wooden idols (4:12), made sacrifices on pagan altars (4:13), or joined in sinful worship with temple prostitutes (4:14) they were committing spiritual adultery. Israel was an unfaithful spouse to the Lord, her husband. As 13:4 says, *"Yet I have been the LORD your God since the land of Egypt; And you were not to know any god except Me, For there is no savior besides Me."* Harlotry and related words appear twenty-six times in Hosea.

"Yet I have been the LORD your God since the land of Egypt; And you were not to know any god except Me, For there is no savior besides Me."
Hosea 13:4

📖 Read Hosea 2:5b–9 along with 13:4–11, and (in your own words) briefly describe the sin of Israel that is depicted in Gomer's sin.

____

____

____

____

____

In 2:5b–9 we see that Gomer went to look for her provision from her lover instead of her husband. She failed to recognize that the abundant goodness in her life had come from Hosea. In the same way, Hosea 13:4–11 shows us that Israel was guilty of forgetting God and looking for another savior (13:4). Israel found herself actually fighting against God who was their help (13:9); consequently, God would take away her blessing so she would realize where it came from. One of the first steps toward rebellion and spiritual adultery comes when we refuse to give Him thanks for the mercies He showers upon us daily (Romans 1:21).

📖 Read Hosea 2:10–13 along with 6:6 and 7:13–16, and (in your own words) briefly describe another sin of Israel that is addressed through the picture of Gomer's sin.

____

____

____

____

These verses portray Israel's worship as mundane ritual laden with hypocrisy. They made sacrifices, but showed no loyalty to God (6:6). Yes, they cried to Him, but not from the heart (7:14). They assembled to ask for grain and wine, yet turned away from the Provider of those things (2:11; 7:14). Through their empty, mindless repetitions they honored God with their lips, but their hearts were far from Him (Matthew 15:8).

Hosea DAY THREE

THE CALL TO RETURN TO THE LORD

"*All we like sheep have gone astray . . ."*(Isaiah 53:6). With these words, Isaiah penned a powerful statement representative of all human nature, for indeed, our tendency to wander is much like that of sheep. In the pastoral culture of the land of Israel where shepherds were plentiful, people quickly connected this analogy and saw the application to their own lives. A sheep who had wandered from his shepherd's protective care was always in danger of being consumed by ravenous beasts. Because of the ever-present dangers, a shepherd of the Middle East was always quick to seek out straying sheep. In Matthew 18, in the context of His discussion on church discipline, Jesus told the parable of the shepherd who leaves the ninety-nine sheep in the fold to go out and search for the one lost sheep. If a particular lamb were prone to wandering, sometimes the shepherd would have to break that lamb's leg so it could not stray. During the period of convalescence while the bone mended, the shepherd would carry the lamb, reestablishing the relationship so that once he was healed the lamb would want to stay close. In Hosea we see God, the Good Shepherd, seeking out His wandering flock of Israel. He calls them to return to Him. This is the message He preaches through Hosea, but it is also the message He wanted Hosea to experience personally. Today we will look at the rest of the story concerning Hosea's family and the difficult object lesson God was teaching through this story.

"All of us like sheep have gone astray, Each of us has turned to his own way; But the LORD has caused the iniquity of us all to fall on Him."
Isaiah 53:6

📖 Read Hosea 3:1, and answer the questions that follow.

What was the course God called Hosea to follow?

____

____

____

Why?

____

____

____

After some time had passed, God called Hosea to find his wife and take her back. He said, *"Go again, love a woman who is loved by her husband. . . ."* The phrase *"loved by her husband"* does not refer to Hosea, or to what we think of a husband today, but perhaps could be better translated, "who is loved by an illicit lover." The same verse in the New International Version (NIV) reads, *"Go, show your love to your wife again, though she is loved by another and is an adulteress."* God wanted Hosea to mirror His love for unfaithful and idolatrous Israel.

📖 Take a few minutes to look at Hosea 3:2–5.

What did Hosea have to do to win back Gomer's love?

____

____

____

What does this say about Israel?

____

____

____

____

Word Study
HOSEA AND THE WORD "RETURN"

In Hosea we see God, the Good Shepherd, seeking out His wandering sheep, Israel. He calls them to return to Him. The key word in the book of Hosea is the word, "return." The Hebrew word (*shuwb*) appears twenty-two times in this prophecy. All of God's dealings with Israel have but one goal in mind—not their humiliation, but their returning to Him.

Hosea had to buy his wife back for fifteen shekels of silver and some barley. Though she was legally his wife, her harlotry had gotten her into such a mess that she ended up in the slave market. The usual price for a slave was 30 shekels of silver (Exodus 21:32), so she was on the "clearance table"—cheap goods with a reduced price for quick sale. Hosea paid the price of her redemption in a beautiful Old Testament portrait of Christ's redemptive work on the cross, buying us back from the slavery of sin—though we already belonged to God, our Creator. She was now doubly Hosea's. But she had to be given time to come to her senses before she would become a faithful wife—a picture of the process of sanctification. In the same way, Israel would be restored, but there would first come a time of chastening via the Assyrian Empire.

🕮 Now look back at Hosea 2:14–23, and identify God's restoring work with Israel reflected in the *"I will . . ."* promises of these verses.

". . . do you think lightly of the riches of His kindness and forbearance and patience, not knowing that the kindness of God leads you to repentance?"
Romans 2:4

"I will allure . . ." (2:14)

____

____

____

God was going to woo His prodigal people back by bringing them to the wilderness (a place of barrenness) and then speaking kindly to them. Romans 2:4 instructs us that it is the kindness of God that leads us to repentance, for though He takes the initiative to pursue a relationship with us, the final decision is still left with us. God never forces His people to follow Him.

"I will give . . ." (2:15)

____

____

____

This promise was to restore the land *("vineyards")* and to make the Valley of Achor as a *"door of hope."* Achor was a place of judgment where Israel's army was defeated because of Achan's sin. Now it would become a place of hope.

"I will take away . . ." (2:16–17)

____

____

____

God vowed to take away their idolatry. *Ishi* means "my husband," and *Baali* means "my owner." God wants His people to walk with Him in a bond of love, not a bond of law.

"I will betroth . . ." (2:18–20)

____

____

____

In this passage of Scripture, God promises a new marriage based in righteousness, justice, lovingkindness, and compassion. Though Gomer's period of straying and abandonment foreshadows the Assyrian captivity of Israel, in a broader prophetic sense, it prefigures the rejection of Israel as a nation after Christ's first coming, and His reestablishment of Israel as a nation of prominence in the millennium after His second coming.

"I will respond . . ." (2:21–22)

____

____

____

God promises to speak to creation to produce bountifully. *"In that day . . ."* speaks of when this will occur: when Israel is betrothed to the Lord in faithfulness.

"I will sow . . ." (2:23)

____

____

____

The name Jezreel means "God sows," and here He promises to sow His people back in the land. The three components of this promise directly correspond to the names of Hosea's three children.

The key word in the book of Hosea is the word, "return." The Hebrew word (*shuwb*) appears twenty-two times in this prophecy. All of God's dealings with the people of Israel have but one goal in mind—not their humiliation, but their returning to Him. Like a Good Shepherd, God doesn't wait for us to seek Him, but comes seeking after us. Six times in this chapter God said, *"I will. . . ."* He will take the initiative with Israel, just as He does with us as well. We don't "find" God—He finds us, for as Romans 3:11 tells us, *"There is none who seeks for God."*

THE GOOD SHEPHERD

Like a Good Shepherd, God doesn't wait for us to seek Him, but comes seeking after us. Six times in this chapter God has said, *"I will. . . ."* He is going to take the initiative with Israel, just as He does with us. We don't "find" God—He finds us, for as Romans 3:11 tells us, *"There is none who seeks for God."*

Reasons to Return

Hosea DAY FOUR

Perhaps no single verse in all of Scripture cuts through the smoke and clouds of human confusion to the heart of following God than the simple statement of 1 John 4:19, *"We love, because He first loved us."* Though we, His prodigal people, are prone to straying, He is a God of lovingkindness, for it is not the judgment of God that calls us back to Him but His love. Hosea is a book awash with the love of God. The Hebrew word used in 2:19; 4:1; 6:4, 6; 10:12; and 12:6 is *chesed*, which means God's steadfast, loyal, covenant-keeping love—His faithful love for His unfaithful people. In the last chapter of Hosea, we see from God's own words the reasons we should return to Him.

Read Hosea 14:1–3, and identify the components of this suggested prayer.

"We love, because He first loved us."
I John 4:19

What heart attitudes do they reveal of what God desired in Israel?

Verse two communicates a powerful idea about returning to the Lord. We are told to *"take words with you. . . ."* In other words, be prepared to confess your wrongs. One might think that in returning to the Lord, we could say nothing, for He knows all that we have done. However, confession is not for God's benefit, but for ours. We need to take responsibility for the wrongs we have done. We also must repent—not simply turning **to** the Lord, but also turning **from** the other gods we have pursued. We cannot hold the hand of God while holding on to our sin.

Read Hosea 14:4, and write what the outcome will be when we return to Him with a right heart.

God says first of all that He will *"heal our apostasy."* It is important to realize that repentance is an attitude in our hearts that God must honor and empower us to fulfill. We cannot heal our own apostasy any more than we can pay for our own sins. We must turn to Him, and He will clean up our lives. Second, God promises to "love us freely." God never ceases to love us, but our sins can keep us from experiencing His love. The sun always shines, but the clouds can sometimes keep us from experiencing the benefits of the sun. In the parable of the prodigal son (Luke 15), the father never stopped loving the son, but when the son left home, he was no longer able to experience the benefits of that fatherly love.

Put Yourself In Their Shoes

A RETURNED HEART

How do we return to the Lord? There are two main components of a returning heart . . .

- Turning to God
- Turning from my sin

We cannot hold the hand of God while holding on to our sin.

Looking at Hosea 14:5–8, make note of each of the illustrations God gives of life after repentance.

The first illustration is of the *"dew,"* pointing to covering. Next, God speaks of *"blossoming," "taking root,"* and *"sprouting shoots."* Each of these illustrations speaks of the new life of spring following the death of winter. There is freshness in life when repentance is in the heart. This new life results in beauty, fragrance, produce, and renown. Repentance always brings blessing!

📖 Looking at Hosea 14:9, what choice did God give Israel?

____

____

____

____

____

Much like God's challenge through Moses as Israel prepared to enter the Promised Land, this challenge was to follow God. In Deuteronomy 30:19 we read, *"I call heaven and earth to witness against you today, that I have set before you life and death, the blessing and the curse. So choose life in order that you may live, you and your descendants."* Basically there are only two options in life—rebel against the Lord and continue to stumble, or return to Him and enjoy His blessings.

Hosea's advice to Israel was to *"break up your fallow ground."* The hearts of Israel had grown hard like ground that had not been plowed for years. No seed could be sown in such unplowed ground with any hope of producing fruit. In the same way, hearts must be plowed. It is the plowing of brokenness that prepares our hearts for the seed of God's Word. When we make the choice to return to Him, our hearts must become soft again. But fortunately, it is never too late to return to Him.

For Me to Follow God

Hosea DAY FIVE

If God sent one of His prophets of old to visit us today, what would his message be? What sin would he confront? What sin would he find? The messages of the prophets are timeless because man has not changed. Sin is still sin, and each of us constantly struggles with it. James, the brother of our Lord wrote, *". . . we all stumble in many ways"* (James 3:2). In other words, the road of life is littered with obstacles that cause us to stumble or stray. Every one of us, sooner or later, will hear the call from God to "return." But it is God's goodness that draws us back to Him. In the last verse of the great hymn, "Come Thou Fount of Every Blessing," we are reminded:

". . . we all stumble in many ways. . . ."
James 3:2

> O to grace how great a debtor daily I'm constrained to be!
> Let Thy goodness like a fetter, bind my wandering heart to Thee.
> Prone to wander, Lord I feel it, prone to leave the God I love.
> Here's my heart, O take and seal it.
> Seal it for Thy courts above.

Each of us has sung from the heart, "Prone to wander, Lord I feel it, prone to leave the God I love." But do we know how to return? Do we know how to come back to our first love?

APPLY When you look at your own relationship with God, are there any ways your walk with Him could be compared to an unfaithful spouse?

____

____

____

Have you ever thought about how your sin affects God?

____

____

____

Are there any areas of your life in which God has told you that you need to improve?

____

____

____

In Luke 15 Jesus tells the parable that has come to be known as the parable of "The Prodigal Son." Take a few minutes to read Luke 15:11–32, and answer the questions that follow.

What did the son do with the resources the father gave him (vv. 12–13)?

____

____

What was his life like once he had spent all the inheritance (vv.14–16)?

____

____

What made him want to "return" to the father (v. 17)?

____

____

"Remember therefore from where you have fallen, and repent and do the deeds you did at first. . . ."
Revelation 2:5

This son took the wealth given to him by his father and *"squandered his estate with loose living."* He wasted it all. Once the money was gone, times turned hard. There was a severe famine in the land, and he went from possessing great abundance to experiencing dire need. Times were so bad for this wayward son that the only job he could find was slopping pigs. It didn't take very long for this young man to realize that the pigs were eating better than he was. The climax of the whole story, though, comes when he remembered what it was like in his father's house. He suddenly came to his senses, and realized that even the servants back home had it better than he did right then. Returning to the Lord always begins with remembering. In Revelation 2, in Jesus' letter of rebuke to the church at Ephesus for leaving their first love, His solution reads like this: *"Remember therefore from where you have fallen, and repent and do the deeds you did at first . . ."* (Revelation 2:5). If your life is far from God right now, take some time to remind yourself of what it was like to be close to God, and write those things in the lines provided on the next page.

How did the son expect the father to receive him when he returned (vv. 18–19)?

How did the father take him back (vv. 20–24)?

When the prodigal son made up his mind to return to the father, he did what we often do with the Lord. He decided he would try to come back on "probation." He felt unworthy to be a son, so he offered to come back as a "hired hand." In other words, he wanted to work his way back to the father's favor by compensating for his sinful acts with good deeds. The problem with his plan is that this was not how he became a son in the first place, and this is not how a son should return. He said he was no longer worthy (v. 21), but **he never was worthy**. Worthiness has nothing to do with being a son. The father didn't even let him finish his humble speech. He had been grieving over his son while he was away and ran to him as soon as he was within sight. (The father saw him while he was a long way off, so he must have been looking for him.) He received him back not as a hired man, but as a son as He embraced and kissed him and threw a party to celebrate. The father treated him as if he had never strayed, giving him clean clothes and the family signet ring. The son did not have to do anything. He simply returned.

Put Yourself In Their Shoes

THE PRODIGAL SON

Lessons from the parable of the prodigal son . . .

- The Father will let us stray
- Straying will make us miserable
- The Father lets us come home

We learn from Jesus' story of the prodigal son that the Father will allow us to stray. He will search for us, but if we insist on wandering He will not stop us. We also learn that straying will make us miserable, for sin only brings pleasure for a season, then it brings famine. Yet the most important lesson from the parable of the prodigal son is that the Father will let us come back home. What we must do, first of all, is **remember** *("he came to his senses"* [Luke 15:17]), and then secondly, **return** *("I will get up and go to my father"* [Luke 15:18]). Maybe there is a lesson for you in this story of a straying son and his loving father.

Not only is the parable of the prodigal son a story that teaches us how to return when we stray, but it is also a story that teaches us what to do when others stray and then return. In the words of the father, *". . . we had to be merry and rejoice, for this brother of yours was dead and has begun to live, and was lost and has been found"* (Luke 15:32). In that same context Jesus taught, *"there will be more joy in heaven over one sinner who repents, than over ninety–nine righteous persons who need no repentance"* (Luke 15:7).

APPLY Is there someone in your life for whom you need to pray that they would return to God?

Is there anything you can do to call them back?

Is there anyone you know who has returned with whom you need to rejoice?

As we saw with Hosea, sometimes there is a greater purpose when those around us stray. God uses other people to teach us how sin affects Him. Through seeing others stray, God allows us to know how He feels when we veer off course. He continually works His message of **"return"** into our hearts. Understanding God's pain should give us grace to bear up under the pain and courage to reach out to other straying sheep.

Why not spend some time with the Lord in prayer right now?

Lord, thank you for revealing Yourself to me. I know that I did not seek You out. I only responded to what You revealed. Help me to see the vastness of my sins of which You have forgiven me. Help me to remember what it was like when I was closer to You. Give me a grateful heart for Your forgiveness of my sin, and guard me from judging the mistakes of others. When I see their sin, help me to remember what You feel when I sin. Make me an instrument of Your peace. Thank You for the new life You give me through Jesus Christ. Never let me take this new life for granted! Amen.

Prayer of Application

Take a few moments to write down a prayer of application from the things that you have learned this week.

Notes

Notes

Isaiah

SUBMISSIVE TO GOD'S PURPOSE

God has a plan for man. He created Adam and Eve with the purpose that they would reflect God's image, reproduce a godly heritage, and reign over God's creation—but sin stained all of that! After Adam fell, the image of God in man could no longer be clearly seen. Genesis 5:1 reminds us that man was created in the likeness of God, but in verse 3 we see that when Adam had children, they were *"... in his own likeness, according to his image."* In other words, instead of bearing the image of God, they bore the fallen image of their father, Adam. In order for God's purposes to be accomplished through man, there must be a re-creation. That is the whole point of Christian growth—once a person turns to Christ, the Lord wants to transform that person into the image of His Son. He desires to so change them, that they can become agents of His love to those who don't know the Lord. But before God can use us in the lives of others He must change us. He must do a work **in** man before He can do a work **through** man. Often we pray, "Lord, use me," yet we fail to realize that the more important prayer is "Lord, make me useable." We see this principle illustrated in the life of Isaiah. Before he could say, *"Here am I, send me"* (Isaiah 6:8), he had to come to the place where he confessed, *"Woe is me"* (Isaiah 6:5).

Isaiah ministered as a prophet for nearly sixty years from about 740 BC to approximately 681 BC. His prophetic service spanned the reigns of five different kings.

WHEN DID HE PROPHESY?

	800	750	700	650	600
	"A Prophet" (sent to Amaziah)	ISAIAH MICAH		NAHUM ZEPHANIAH HABAKKUK HULDAH (a prophetess) JEREMIAH	
	Amaziah 796–767 **Azariah(Uzziah) 790–739**	**Jotham 750–735** **Ahaz 735–715** **Hezekiah 715–686**	**Manasseh 697–642**	**Amon 642–640** **Josiah 640–609** **Jehoahaz 609** **Jehoiakim 609–598**	**Jehoiachin (Jeconiah) 598–597** **Zedekiah 597–586**
Jehoahaz 814–798	**Joash (Jehoash) 798–782** **Jeroboam II 793–753** **Zechariah 753–752**	**Menahem 752–742** **Hoshea 732–722** **Shallum 752** **Pekahiah 742–740** **Pekah 752–732**	There are no more kings or prophets in the Northern Kingdom. Foreign peoples are resettled into the land.		605—1st Captivity DANIEL Hananiah Mishael Azariah 597—2d Captivity EZEKIEL
	JONAH AMOS HOSEA	ODED			
		Tiglath-pileser I 745–727 Shalmaneser V 727–722 722—Assyria takes Israel into captivity	Sennacherib 705–681	612—Fall of Nineveh	Nebuchadnezzar 605–562

ISAIAH'S EARLY MESSAGE

Isaiah grew up in an influential, upper class family and was a close friend and counselor to King Uzziah. His book is one of the longest found in Scripture and some have called it "the Bible in miniature." The Holy Scriptures contain 66 books (39 in the Old Testament and 27 in the New Testament). The book of Isaiah contains 66 chapters. The first section of Isaiah (chapters 1—39) focuses on God's character and judgment. The second section (chapters 40—66, 27 chapters) reveal God's comfort and redemption, with special emphasis on the coming Messiah. Isaiah has more direct references to Christ than any other Old Testament book. One of the things we observe when we look closely at Isaiah's life and ministry, however, is a change in his message after the death of his friend, Uzziah.

Did You Know?

THE NAME, ISAIAH

The name Isaiah means "Jehovah is helper" or "Salvation is of the Lord." The meaning of Isaiah's name is practically synonymous with Joshua or Jesus and is symbolic of His message. He is identified as "the son of Amoz" who has been suggested to be the uncle of Uzziah, which if true, would make Isaiah the king's cousin. This may explain why Uzziah's death had such a profound impact on his life. His wife was identified as a prophetess (Isaiah 8:3), and she gave him two sons whose names fit in with the message God had given to him.

Isaiah's early message was one of "woe." Look up the references below, and identify the message and to whom it is directed.

*NOTE: In each of these passages Isaiah's message is directed towards the sins **of others.** The purpose to this exercise is to contrast Isaiah's early sentiments with the different direction he later takes in chapter 6, where he sees only **his own** sin. You don't need to spend too much time on this section.

Isaiah 3:8–9

___

___

___

___

This woe (at the end of verse 9) is directed to Jerusalem and Judah who have rebelled against the Lord with sin so blatant that they didn't even try to hide it.

Isaiah 3:11

___

___

___

This woe is directed to all the wicked, and we are reminded that they will get what they deserve.

Isaiah 5:8

___

___

___

This woe is directed to those who live luxuriously and selfishly without regard for the things of the Lord (verse 2 points to their fruitlessness).

Isaiah 5:11

This woe is directed at those who live for sensual pleasure and neglect the deeds of the Lord and His work.

Isaiah 5:18

This woe is for those who hold on to their sin and refuse to believe the judgment of God until they see it for themselves.

Isaiah 5:20

This woe is for those who have fallen into reprobation—their sin has inverted their values so much that they think evil is good and good is evil.

Isaiah 5:21

This woe is for the self-righteous who are consumed with pride.

Isaiah 5:22

This woe is for those who take pride in their sin and have no regard for righteousness.

In summary, what are the common denominators of Isaiah's early message?

THE OFFICE OF THE PROPHET

Filling the office of prophet was not usually a very popular job. Because their ministry involved confronting the people with God's truth about their sins, prophets were often disliked and even persecuted. Tradition holds that Isaiah was executed during the reign of the wicked king, Manasseh, by being placed inside a hollow tree and sawn in two. If this is true, then perhaps Isaiah is the one referred to in Hebrews 11:37, having been *"sawn in two."*

Isaiah focuses all his "woes" on those who are blatantly unrighteous, but as we will see later, the blatant sin of others keeps him from seeing that his sin is just as abominable to God.

Isaiah DAY TWO

KING UZZIAH'S DEATH

Isaiah chapter six begins with the statement, *"In the year of King Uzziah's death, I saw the Lord. . . ."* Why was this significant? What did the passing of the king have to do with Isaiah's encounter with God? The death of King Uzziah marked a turning point in the life and ministry of Isaiah. Uzziah had been Isaiah's best friend. In fact, many scholars believe that Amoz, Isaiah's father, was Uzziah's uncle which would make Isaiah and Uzziah cousins. Uzziah had been a godly king during the early years of his reign, but he came to a dismal end. Like so many kings before him, pride was his undoing. He trusted God and saw mighty deliverances, but his successes made him proud, and in his pride he forgot God.

📖 Read 2 Chronicles 26:1–23, and record what you learn about Uzziah.

____

____

____

____

Uzziah came to the throne at age 16 and reigned for 52 years. Seeking God and prospering marked his early reign. The promise of his reign was, *". . . as long as he sought the Lord, God prospered him."* (*NOTE: The Zechariah mentioned is not the post-exilic [after the period of exile] prophet whose book bears his name.) Uzziah built Judah into a military power. Unfortunately, the damage of pride and sin marked his later years.

What was the turning point in Uzziah's reign?

____

____

____

"But when he [Uzziah] became strong, his heart was so proud that he acted corruptly, and he was unfaithful to the Lord his God. . . ."
2 Chronicles 26:16

According to verse 15, Uzziah became famous because of the army he had built, and he reached a point of self-sufficiency. Verse 16 reveals that his heart became proud, which was his undoing. The resulting offense of usurping the priests' authority was merely a symptom of the deeper problem of his heart. When he refused to listen to the priests' rebuke, he was struck with leprosy.

Obviously Scripture doesn't fill in all the gaps and tell us everything about Uzziah and Isaiah, but, understanding human nature, what do you think was Isaiah's response to the failings of Uzziah?

____

____

____

Isaiah probably began by a self-righteous response of "I would never do that," but Isaiah's encounter with the Lord changed his perspective. Throughout his prophetic ministry he had pronounced "woes" on the sins of others. Perhaps watching the sinful decline of Uzziah had produced a righteous indignation in Isaiah that had subtly shifted into spiritual pride. With Uzziah out of the way though, now God wants Isaiah to see his own sin.

"I Saw the Lord"

Up until the death of Uzziah, the focus of Isaiah's message was on people: "woe is this person . . . woe is that person." After Uzziah is gone, God meets with Isaiah in a special way. What practical application to our lives can be found here! It is so easy to think of ourselves as righteous when we compare ourselves to those around us. Not only is it easy to find someone less godly to compare ourselves to, but scarce is the man who can weigh the faults of another without putting his thumb on the scales. We can easily focus on the most obvious flaws of others and compare them selectively, allowing our hearts to deceive us. But when we see the Lord, then we see ourselves as we truly are—sinners in need of a Savior.

"In the year of King Uzziah's death, I saw the Lord sitting on a throne, lofty and exalted, with the train of His robe filling the temple."
Isaiah 6:1

Read Isaiah 6:1–4, and summarize what Isaiah saw.

____

____

____

____

For quite some time Isaiah had seen the sins of the people and now the shortcomings of his friend Uzziah. But, in chapter 6, Isaiah sees the Lord in all His glory. He uses words like *"lofty"* and *"exalted"* to describe his view of God. The Hebrew word translated exalted is "*nasa*" (pronounced: *nawsaw*), and means "to lift up or separate away from." Isaiah already knew the Lord, but he did not have a high view of God until this encounter. The message of the seraphim (verse 3) reminded him of the holiness and glory of the Lord.

Where is his focus now?

____

____

____

____

Instead of having his focus on people or Uzziah or himself, now his focus is on God.

After Isaiah sees the Lord, what is his immediate response? (v. 5)

____

____

____

> "God is opposed to the proud, but gives grace to the humble."
> James 4:6

As soon as Isaiah saw the Lord, his whole view of himself changed. His message of "woe to this person" or "woe to that person" changed to *"woe is* **me**" [emphasis added]. His response is common to the saints (see also Job 42:5–6; Ezekiel 1:28; Daniel 10:8–11; Revelation 4:3).

📖 Until there is an awareness of our own sinfulness, we see no need for cleansing. Read James 4:6, and identify what is required to draw on God's empowering grace.

____

____

God is in opposition to the proud but gives grace to the humble (see also 1 Peter 5:5). The Greek grammatical structure here indicates that God stands in continual opposition to the proud. Pride is the death of grace. To draw on grace we must have the humility that recognizes its need.

What is the significance of the coal being applied to Isaiah's lips?

____

____

____

Doctrine THE SCAPEGOAT

The "scapegoat" was a term derived from the sacrificial practices of the Day of Atonement. Aaron was instructed to present two goats before the Lord at the doorway of the tent of meeting (Leviticus 16:7). A process of casting lots determined which animal would be sacrificed, and which would be offered to the Lord alive, and then released into the wilderness. The sacrificed goat was to picture the death which sin requires. The live goat wandering away was to picture our sins being carried away. This innocent goat carrying the sins of the guilty is the source of our modern use of the term "scapegoat."

A coal of fire, taken from the altar, was applied to Isaiah's lips. Remember, he said, *"I am a man of unclean lips, and I live among a people of unclean lips."* Isaiah was a prophet—his mouth was the tool of his trade (and perhaps the source of his pride). Fire has long been used to purify and cleanse. Even today, we use heat to sterilize things. This fire from the altar (either the altar of incense or the altar of burnt offerings) pictured the full significance of the Temple ritual of cleansing. God cannot use what He has not cleansed.

📖 What is the result according to Isaiah 6:7?

____

____

____

Isaiah's sin was both taken away and forgiven. The picture is of the sacrificial goats of the sin offering (Leviticus 16). One goat was slain to purchase forgiveness, and the other (the scapegoat) was sent into the wilderness, a portrayal of sins being carried away. The idea pictured here is a prophetic example of complete cleansing.

Isaiah DAY FOUR

"HERE AM I"

Isaiah had been in the presence of God and through seeing the Lord in His holiness, had also been given a new understanding of himself. Perhaps for the first time in his life, Isaiah saw himself as God saw him. If Isaiah is like the rest of us, he probably thought of himself as a good and godly man, especially when he compared himself to the likes of Uzziah. But in the presence of God, his message of woe to others became *"woe is me."*

The irony of this subject is that until we see ourselves as useless, we really aren't useable. Isaiah had to learn his need for cleansing.

What is the significance of when God asks, *"Whom shall I send"* (v. 8), in light of what happened to Isaiah in verse 7?

____

____

____

____

Once sin had been dealt with, notice the result in verse 8. Now Isaiah is useable and is invited to join the Lord in His work. We are not really useable as saints, only as dependent sinners. God has to do a work **in** us before He can do a work **through** us.

God has to do a work in us before He can do a work through us. He cannot use what He has not cleansed.

📖 Look at verses 9–10, and identify Isaiah's new task.

____

____

____

____

____

God gives Isaiah a message to which no one will listen. Jesus used these same words to explain why He taught in parables (Matthew 13:14–15; Mark 4:12; Luke 8:10). John also used them to explain why so few listened to Jesus' message (John 12:40), and Paul used them to explain why his ministry emphasis switched from the Jews to the Gentiles (Acts 28:26–27).

Why didn't God want to heal His people?

____

____

____

____

____

This is a difficult question to answer, and in the end we must trust the sovereign wisdom of God. Apparently, God's purposes required the coming judgment on Israel. In a sense, this message secured God's justice in judging, for the Israelites could not say that they had received no warning. This is also why the gospel must go out to the entire world, though many will not respond to its message of hope and salvation.

📖 How long, according to verses 11–13, would Isaiah preach a message to an unresponsive people?

____

____

____

____

Put Yourself In Their Shoes

SPIRITUAL FULFILLMENT

How do you judge the effectiveness of a ministry? Do you evaluate based on results or on faithfulness to God's calling regardless of results? Isaiah was given a message that no one would listen to. If he found fulfillment in results, there would be little fulfillment in his life. Instead, he had to be satisfied with the knowledge that he had done what God had asked. In evaluating her husband's death in ministry, Elisabeth Elliot writes, "Was it worth it? Does it make sense that five men with those kind of credentials and qualifications should die for the sake of 60 people? . . . Let's suppose for a moment that not one Auca [tribesman] got saved, that not one person ever heard the story of those five men, let alone was changed by it. Would it be worth it? YES! Why? Because the results of our obedience are the business of Almighty God who is sovereign. . . ."

Isaiah would continue to preach until the land was desolate and there was no one left to listen.

What is the significance of the remnant of verse 13?

____

____

____

____

____

There is always a remnant of people who will follow God. It is this remnant that insures the continuance of Israel as a nation and as a spiritual entity.

Isaiah DAY FIVE

FOR ME TO FOLLOW GOD

How would you evaluate the effectiveness of Isaiah's ministry? Obviously from the human yardstick of immediate results, his ministry was a doomed failure, for in his day no one listened. But the demand for immediate results is not the yardstick used in heaven. God measures our effectiveness by how our works align with His purpose. By this measure, the ministry of Isaiah was greatly effective, for he fulfilled the purpose of God for his life. Thousands of years later, we are still ministered to by the life and message of Isaiah. To reach the purpose of God, we must die to our own agendas and ambitions. Dying to self is a small sacrifice, for only the purpose of God brings eternal fruit—everything else is wood, hay and stubble (see Isaiah 5:24; 1 Corinthians 3:12–13). Use the following thoughts and questions to search your own heart as you look at your life and God's purpose for it.

To reach the purpose of God, we must die to our own agenda and ambition. But it is a small sacrifice, for only the purpose of God brings eternal fruit. Everything else is wood, hay, and stubble.

As we look at Isaiah, there are definite principles from his life with which we can relate. We acknowledge, first of all, how easy it is to evaluate ourselves by how we measure up against those around us. When sinful people surround us, sometimes it is difficult to see our own sin.

To what degree is that a struggle in your present experience?

____

____

Who are the Uzziahs in your life that you tend to look at and think of yourself as more godly than?

____

____

____

Another principle that shaped Isaiah into becoming useable was that he gained a high view of God. He saw the Lord *"high and lifted up."* We will never see ourselves accurately until we see the Lord accurately.

APPLY How is your view of God?

____

____

____

What can you do to move toward a higher view of God?

____

____

____

It is impossible to gain a high view of God without becoming aware of our own sinfulness. Honestly, do you really see yourself as sinful?

____

____

What do we do with sin when God reveals it? First of all, we don't need to look for sin. It is God's job to reveal sin. We will see as much of our own sinfulness as we can handle when our eyes are on Jesus. When He does reveal sin, we must remember that only He can take it away. We cannot pull ourselves up by our spiritual bootstraps, grit our teeth, and make a vow, "I'll never do that again!" That will not take sin away. Only when we **confess** our sins do we see God take them away. First John 1:9 promises, *"If we confess our sins, He is faithful and righteous to forgive us our sins and to cleanse us from all unrighteousness."*

A person can learn to change his behavior through various programs, but that doesn't mean his character (what is inside) is any different. The only way to know true freedom (being free from the power of sin) is to know the One who is willing and able to free you from slavery. You have a choice to handcuff yourself to sin, or to handcuff yourself to Christ. There is **hope** and it is found in Christ.

Victory is not you overcoming sin—victory is Jesus overcoming you!

Most of us know how we tend to handle sin. We're trying to make the right choices, but eventually we blow it, and the guilt hits us! We feel horrible, so we vow to God—"I'm sorry God. I will never do that again!" And then we try harder, but if our efforts could make us better we wouldn't need a Savior. Sooner or later we blow it again, and the cycle continues as we continually plead, "God, I will never, **never** do that again!" And then we try even harder!

SIN

GUILT

DOWNWARD SPIRAL OF SIN

TRY HARDER

VOW

But there is a way to break that cycle—it's called surrender! Surrender is giving the Holy Spirit complete access to your life. When faced with temptation, if we immediately surrender to God, rather than trying harder to resist the temptation, His power will carry us safely through.

Recognition of our own sinfulness is directly related to how much we see our need for God. If we are not living lives of dependence in our walk and ministry, we probably don't see our need. Meditate on this, and write your thoughts.

Let's spend some time in prayer to the Lord right now.

"Here am I. Send me!"
Isaiah 6:8

Lord, thank You for this very human example of Isaiah. I see myself in him. Forgive me for the many times I have judged my righteousness by comparing myself to others instead of to You. As Moses cried, *"I pray Thee, show me Thy glory"* (Exodus 33:18). Let me see your holiness. Make me dissatisfied with my self-righteousness. Cleanse me, Lord—make me useable! And call me to Your task. I will not shrink back. Here am I, send me. Whatever it is. Wherever it is. Whenever You want. Whatever the results. Here am I . . . send me. Amen.

Most believers, especially those involved in active ministry, do not struggle with being willing to be used of God. The greater difficulty comes when God puts us to a task with little or no apparent fruit. Are you willing to say to the purpose God has for you, "Here am I, send me," even if it is not significant in the eyes of man? If so, express that willingness below in the form of a prayer to Him.

Notes

Notes

Micah

WHAT DOES THE LORD REQUIRE OF YOU?

Have you ever wondered what it takes to please God? Not only does the prophet Micah ask the question, he gives God's answer as well. Through his ministry of confronting and reminding, he pulls open the curtains and sheds God's light on the world of his day. Speaking almost as a lawyer in a cosmic courtroom, he shows how far all of Israel and Judah had wandered from the Lord, and how they were headed toward judgment. They had lost sight of what God really requires of His people. Preaching to Samaria (the Northern Kingdom) and Jerusalem (Judah), he explains how the religious sinner is just as abhorrent to God as the rebellious one. He grieves over the state of his divided nation, saying, *"The godly person has perished from the land, and there is no upright person among men"* (Micah 7:2). Judah pointed the finger at Israel and their blatant idolatry. Somehow they thought that because they still kept the rituals of Jehovah, their sins of injustice, their lack of compassion, and their own practice of idolatry were not concerns to God. Since they were "religious" they saw themselves better than "rebellious" Israel. But sin is sin, and through Micah God promises judgment unless they repent. *"He has told you, O man, what is good; and what does the Lord require of you but to do justice, to love kindness, and to walk humbly with your God"* (Micah 6:8).

THE BOOK OF MICAH

The book of Micah consists of three messages (Micah 1:2—2:13; chaps. 3—5; chaps. 6—7), each beginning with the exhortation to "hear" or "listen" to what the Lord had to say to the nation. Though Micah talks about the destruction coming to the kingdom of Israel, he is mainly talking to the people of the kingdom of Judah. His three messages showed that Judah was just as guilty as Israel was. His warning was that if they did not repent, they too would be disciplined by God.

WHEN DID HE PROPHESY?

	800	750	700	650	600
	"A Prophet" (sent to Amaziah)	ISAIAH MICAH		NAHUM ZEPHANIAH HABAKKUK HULDAH (a prophetess) JEREMIAH	
	Amaziah **796–767** **Azariah(Uzziah)** **790–739**	**Jotham** **Ahaz** **750–735** **735–715** **Hezekiah** **715–686**	**Manasseh** **697–642**	**Amon** **642–640** **Josiah** **640–609** **Jehoahaz** **609** **Jehoiakim** **609–598**	**Jehoiachin** **(Jeconiah)** **598–597** **Zedekiah** **597–586**
Jehoahaz **814–798**	**Joash** **(Jehoash)** **798–782** **Jeroboam II** **793–753** **Zechariah** **753–752**	**Menahem** **Hoshea** **752–742** **732–722** **Shallum** **Pekahiah** **752** **742–740** **Pekah** **752–732**	There are no more kings or prophets in the Northern Kingdom. Foreign peoples are resettled into the land.		605—1st Captivity DANIEL Hananiah Mishael Azariah 597—2d Captivity EZEKIEL
	JONAH AMOS HOSEA	ODED			
		Tiglath-pileser I 745–727 722—Assyria takes Israel into captivity Shalmaneser V 727–722	Sennacherib 705–681	612—Fall of Nineveh	Nebuchadnezzar 605–562

Micah DAY ONE

THE MAKING OF THE MESSENGER

Micah achieved prophetic distinction in Judah during the days of Hosea and Isaiah. Little is known about him personally, but his ministry was one reason Judah lasted nearly a century and a half longer than the kingdom of Israel. His name, Micah, is a shortened form of the name Micaiah, which means "Who is like Yahweh?" Micah 1:1 tells us he was from Moresheth, a Judean town about 25 miles southwest of Jerusalem near the Philistine city of Gath (Micah 1:14). Just as his contemporary Isaiah had also prophesied, Micah described the future fall of the Northern Kingdom at the hands of Assyria, and the later defeat of the Southern Kingdom by Babylon. Micah's ministry was in the eighth century BC during the reigns of Jotham, Ahaz, and Hezekiah (Micah 1:1), and the revival of Hezekiah's day can be traced to Isaiah's and Micah's early efforts. Micah spoke of the judgment that was coming on the Northern Kingdom because of its idolatry and rebellion. At the same time, he confronted the sanctimonious orthodoxy of Judah. Their sin was not as blatant, covered as it was with the outward form of religion, but the people's hearts were just as far from God. The key question he raises and answers is *"What does the Lord require of you?"*

📖 Read Micah 1:1, and write down the details you learn of Micah and his ministry.

____

____

____

____

Did You Know?

JUDAH AND SAMARIA

Micah's message was *"concerning Samaria and Jerusalem."* When Israel split into two separate nations after the reign of Solomon, the descendants of David continued to reign over the Southern Kingdom (Judah). Jerusalem was the capital city and center of religious activity. Jeroboam, Solomon's slave-master, became king in Israel, and set up Samaria as the capitol of the Northern Kingdom. Although Micah's message was about Samaria and Jerusalem, clearly it is written to Judah, since theirs are the only kings mentioned. God wanted Judah to learn from Israel's mistakes and to be warned by Israel's destruction in 722 BC.

The one thing that distinguished prophets from other people was that the *"word of the Lord"* came to them. It was a "received" ministry, not an "achieved" one. God selected them to speak for Him. We are told here that this *"word of the Lord"* came to Micah of Moresheth. Verse 1 gives us the "when" of his ministry by linking it with the reigns of Jotham, Ahaz, and Hezekiah—all kings of Judah. The verse closes by imparting to us the focus of the message God had given him—to speak concerning Samaria and Jerusalem.

📖 To fully appreciate what Micah has to say, we must understand the day in which he lived and ministered. Look at 2 Kings 15:33–35 and 2 Chronicles 27:1–2. What were the people like during the reign of Jotham (the first king during Micah's ministry)?

____

____

____

____

____

Although Jotham was not a wicked king, he did not lead the people to righteousness. Second Chronicles 27:2 tells us the people *"continued acting corruptly."* In other words, his reign did not promote godliness or revival. In 2 Kings

15:33–35 we see more specifically that the "high places" with their false worship were still in the land. This tells us not only what the people were like, but that Micah's ministry was less than fruitful during Jotham's day.

🕮 Now look at 2 Chronicles 28:1–5 and 16–25. What was Judah like in the days of king Ahaz, the second king to reign during Micah's ministry?

____

____

____

____

The leadership of Ahaz proved to be a moral step down for Judah. At least Jotham was a good man, even though he did nothing to spur his people to follow God. Ahaz, however, was the embodiment of evil who, instead of following the godly example of his ancestor, David, followed after the sins and idolatry of the wicked kings in Israel. He instituted Baal worship, and even **sacrificed his own infant son** to the pagan gods of Canaan. As a consequence, God brought hard times upon Judah with invading armies, but instead of returning to the Lord and seeking His help, Ahaz made treaties with his pagan neighbors and followed their gods. During his days on the throne, Ahaz *"brought a lack of restraint in Judah, and was very unfaithful to the Lord"* (2 Chronicles 28:19).

AHAZ AND IDOLATRY

Ahaz followed the negative pattern established by the self-appointed kings of Israel (the Northern Kingdom). He made molten images (idols) for Baal worship. He burnt incense in the Valley of the Son of Hinnom, adopting the pagan practices of his northern neighbors. This valley was also known as "the place of burning" where Molech worship, including infant sacrifice, was practiced. He even went so far as to sacrifice one of his sons as a burnt offering to Molech, an Ammonite deity (2 Kings 16:3), thus resurrecting the pagan practices of the Canaanites who dwelled in the land before Israel. Every form of pagan ritual was brought back during the reign of Ahaz. He even locked the doors on the temple and began worshiping the gods of Damascus after that nation defeated him in battle.

🕮 Looking at 2 Kings 18:1–6, write what you learn from this summary of Hezekiah's reign.

____

____

____

____

Hezekiah was like a breath of fresh air for Judah, reversing many of the negative practices his father brought to Judah. The most important thing that is said about him is that he did right *"in the sight of the Lord."* He removed the high places Micah spoke of (Micah 1:3) and tore down all other objects of idol worship. He even destroyed the bronze serpent of Moses because it had also become an idol to the people. His life was characterized by trusting God, so much so that he is called the greatest king of Judah (2 Kings 18:5). Of course calling him the greatest king of Judah does not make him better than David, who was a king not just of Judah, but of all Israel. Obviously the preaching of Micah bore fruit during Hezekiah's day.

THE MESSAGE OF JUDGMENT

When American President Millard Fillmore's cabinet was in session on one occasion, several members were trying to draw Secretary of State Daniel Webster into the conversation. They asked Webster, "What is the most important thought you have ever had?" After a moment of silence he replied, "The most important thought I have ever had is that as a child of God, I am accountable to Him." He then proceeded to speak for twenty minutes on this subject. The cabinet session was over, and the members walked out in a hushed silence.

Because God is God we are accountable to Him. He created us, He redeemed us, and one day He will judge us. Like Daniel Webster to his day, and like so many prophets before him, Micah stood before the people of God and reminded them of their accountability to the Lord. Micah began his message with an abrupt reminder that God will judge His people. Israel was in a wretched state of malaise, and soon would cease to exist as a sovereign nation. Judah, Micah's main audience, had a front row seat to witness God's judgment of Israel. Yet Micah's message reminded the people of Judah that they were just as guilty as Israel, and would also be judged. Keep in mind that Micah's message was a call to accountability.

MICAH'S THREE MESSAGES

The book of Micah consists of three separate messages, each marked by the word "hear." The first message begins in 1:2 *("Hear, O people . . .")*, running through the end of chapter two, and is a message of judgment. The second message begins in 3:1 *("Hear now, heads of Jacob . . .")*, running through the end of chapter five, and focuses on God's promises to His people. It is a message of hope for the future. The third message begins in 6:1 *("Hear now what the Lord is saying. . .")*, running through the end of the book, and focuses on forgiveness.

📖 Look at Micah 1:2–7, and answer the questions that follow.

To what audience is Micah's first message directed (v. 2)?

____

____

In this "cosmic courtroom" who is the witness, and from where does He speak (v. 2)?

____

____

What will God do (vv. 3–4)?

____

____

Why will God's judgment come (vv. 5, 7b)?

____

____

____

Micah begins his first message by setting the stage for a "cosmic courtroom." The jury consists of all the earth's inhabitants as God Himself prepares to take the stand as a witness against His own people. It is significant that He would come from *"His holy temple."* What a contrast exists between God in His holiness and the wicked people who bear His name! He would leave His holy temple to come in judgment on Israel and Judah. He would one day *"tread on"* the high places of the land. This doesn't mean that He would go for a hike in the mountains. The "high places" were the shrines erected throughout Israel and Judah for the purpose of worshiping false gods, or, in some cases, for worshiping the true God in ways other than He had dictated. God was going to stamp out false worship and idolatry. He would judge Jacob's (Israel's) rebellion, expressed in its idolatry, which He equates with spiritual harlotry. This judgment on Israel was fulfilled in 722 BC (roughly 13 years after Micah began his ministry) when the nation fell to Assyria and was taken into captivity.

Look at 1:8–9, and then answer the following questions

What is Micah's response to his prophesy over Samaria (v. 8)?

What would be the outcome for Samaria relating to God's judgment (v. 9a)?

How do Israel's misfortunes relate to Judah (v. 9b)?

Micah grieves or "laments" over the judgment on Israel that was close at hand. In that time, being barefoot and naked was a sign of humility, and when accompanied with wailing, pointed to the cultural manifestations of grief. Micah had to carry the weight of knowing in advance that judgment was sure to come, and the "wound" of judgment was sadly incurable. There would be no last minute repentance to delay God's wrath. God would judge Samaria (Israel) partly because they had begun to pull Judah down with them. The idolatry of Israel had become a stumbling block, as Judah and Jerusalem began to follow Israel's example.

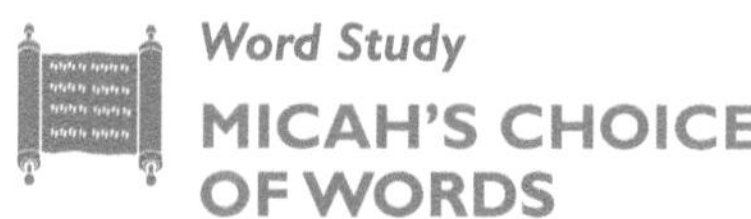

Word Study

MICAH'S CHOICE OF WORDS

In Micah 1:10–15 the prophet uses a series of plays on words to clarify his message of judgment. In our English translations the verse is not as clear as it would be to Micah's audience. Playing on the Hebrew meanings of the major cities, Micah expounds his message in poetic fashion. For example, in verse 10 he says, *"At Beth-le-aphrah* [the town's name means 'house of dust'] *roll yourself in the dust."* In verse 11 we are told, *"The inhabitant of Zaanan* [the town's name means 'going out'] *does not escape* [lit. 'go out']." Creatively, Micah makes his point.

Chapter 2 of Micah explains why God would bring judgment on His people. Read through the whole chapter; then look at the references listed below. Summarize what you learn from each verse about the moral and spiritual climate of the land.

2:1 –

2:2 –

2:6 –

2:8 –

2:9 –

2:11 –

In this disheartening chapter we see that God's people had sunk to such a vulgar state that injustice had become normal, and righteousness had become abnormal. People would lie awake at night dreaming of ways to cheat and steal (2:1–2). They took advantage of strangers who passed through the land and stole from helpless women (2:8, 9). Justice no longer prevailed in the land, nor a desire for it. People didn't want to hear the truth preached by God's prophets (2:6), but if anyone wanted to speak of wine and liquor, he would always have an audience (2:11). It is no wonder judgment lurked on the horizon for this degenerate people. Even today, judgment always comes first on God's people, for it is we who have received truth that have the higher accountability. The greater the revelation, the greater the responsibility to obey.

"For it is time for judgment to begin with the household of God; and if it begins with us first, what will be the outcome for those who do not obey the gospel of God?"
I Peter 4:17

Micah's first message was a severe one! Judgment is never a pleasant message either to preach or to hear, yet Micah's message was necessary. A fundamental law of the universe is that we reap what we sow. Micah's second message begins in chapter 3 by revealing why Israel would collapse as a nation, and why Judah would follow if its people did not repent.

📖 Read Micah 3:12, and summarize what would happen. Tell who Micah blames for this.

Micah prophesies in this verse that Zion would be as a plowed field. God would break their hard soil and turn them over to another empire. Jerusalem would become *"a heap of ruins."* Micah also says that the temple mount would become *"high places of a forest."* "High places" could refer to the places around Israel where incense and false worship were prevalent. More likely, the term implies that the temple mount would become a desolate place. The interesting thing about this judgment is the little statement at the beginning: *"Therefore, on account of you. . . ."* God's judgment is blamed on the people addressed in chapter 3.

Word Study

THE LOVE OF MONEY

When Micah speaks of those who served as leaders and priests, he indicates that they were doing the right job for the wrong motives. Leaders were supposed to pronounce judgment, and priests were supposed to instruct. Money, however, perverted the way they did their jobs. In contrast, when Micah speaks of those who served as prophets (the very office he himself held), he uses a word that did not characterize their responsibility, but rather what they were actually doing. He says that they *"divine"* for money. The Hebrew word indicates activity God had forbidden—sorcery and witchcraft. How low the office had fallen!

📖 Read Micah 3:1–11.

What sin did the political and civic rulers practice (vv. 2–4)?

Describe the sin of the religious leaders (v. 5).

Israel's *"heads"* (civic leaders) and *"princes"* (appointed leaders) knew exactly what justice meant. Yet they hated good and loved evil. They used their positions to take advantage of others and, in turn, serve themselves. They *"consumed"* people as food. But Israel's religious leaders were just as corrupt. They preached *"peace"* to those who fed them, and *"war"* to those who didn't. In other words they were crowd pleasers. Verse 11 tells us, *"Her leaders pronounce judgment for a bribe, her priests instruct for a price, and her prophets divine for money."* The politicians did not serve the people and the priests did not serve the Lord—they all simply served themselves. Even the ordinary citizens were guilty, for they were the ones giving bribes and supporting false prophets who told them what they wanted to hear. *"Therefore, on account of you,"* Micah said that judgment would indeed come. Often we want to blame all the ills of society on corrupt politicians and hypocritical preachers, but politicians have to be elected, and preachers have to be supported. As 2 Timothy 4:3 warns, *"For the time will come when they will not endure sound doctrine, but wanting to have their ears tickled,* **they will accumulate for themselves** *teachers in accordance with their own desires."*

THE MESSAGE OF PROMISE

It has been said that man can live three months without food, three days without water, and three minutes without air, but **no more than three seconds without hope!** One thing that sets the Christian apart in life is that he is never without hope. In Titus 2:13 we are told that the way we are to live in this present age is to look *"for the blessed hope and the appearing of the glory of our great God and Savior, Christ Jesus."* First Thessalonians 4:13 addresses how we ought to think about Christian loved ones who have died. The text instructs us that knowing our future is what keeps us from grieving *"as do the rest that have no hope."* Hope is a facade to those who don't know the Lord, but to the believer hope is as real as the Lord Himself, *"who is our hope"* (1 Timothy 1:1). If Micah had stopped preaching after prophesying the judgment that was to come, Israel and Judah would have slipped even deeper into a hopeless state. But Micah did not stop preaching, and as we will see today, although judgment was certain for Israel and would eventually come to Judah, all was not hopeless. God would not abandon His people. Though they were faithless, He would still be faithful to them. In a day yet to come, God will fulfill every promise He has ever made to Israel. As we move into chapter 4 of Micah, we will get a glimpse of the hope that is yet to come.

"But we do not want you to be uninformed, brethren, about those who are asleep, that you may not grieve, as do the rest who have no hope."
I Thessalonians 4:13

📖 Compare Micah 3:12 to 4:1–4.

What happens in 3:12?

____

____

What happens in 4:1–4?

____

____

When does each event happen?

Which of the promises in 4:1–4 are yet to be fulfilled?

What a stark contrast between Micah 3:12 and the beginning of chapter 4! We see that Micah speaks of a day to come when *"Zion will be as a plowed field, Jerusalem will become as a heap of ruins."* Those prophecies were fulfilled when Israel was destroyed in 722 BC and Judah and Jerusalem fell in 586 BC. Yet Micah 4:1 begins with the promise that *"in the last days,"* instead of a wasteland, Jerusalem will be the center of the world and a place where all will come to learn of the Lord and His ways. In that day, justice will reign with Him as supreme judge, and peace will prevail. Obviously much of what is said here has not yet been fulfilled, for mankind has not exactly changed their weapons of war into tools of agriculture, and there are still those who train for war. We have yet to see the day when people no longer have anyone to make them afraid. But all of these things **will** come to pass, for *"the mouth of the Lord of hosts has spoken."*

PROPHECY YET TO BE FULFILLED

Micah 4:3 prophesies of a day when wars will be no more, and the instruments of war will be converted to agricultural tools. *"Then they shall hammer their swords into plowshares, and their spears into pruning hooks"* (See also Isaiah 2:4). But that day has not yet come. In fact, Joel 3:10 speaks of a day that will come first when God will call to Israel, *"Beat your plowshares into swords, And your pruning hooks into spears."* Before the time of peace Micah speaks of, there will be a time of war such as the world has never known. Joel calls it *"the day of the Lord."*

📖 Look at Micah 4:5–13.

What does the immediate future hold for Zion and her people (vv. 9–11)?

What does the future ultimately hold (vv. 8, 13)?

Hard times were soon to be the norm for Israel and Judah. In fact, Israel may have already fallen to Assyria when Micah's second message was given. Micah 5:13 indicates the message is directed to Judah and Jerusalem (*"the city"*). Soon God's people would be forced to leave the city for a seventy year period of captivity in Babylon, but from there they would be redeemed. In the distant future a day will dawn when Israel will find her former glory and dominate the world from Jerusalem. God gave them hope to go with their hard times.

FULFILLED PROPHECIES

During the years of Micah's ministry, his prophecies about Samaria (Israel) were fulfilled as the nation was conquered by the Assyrians in 722 BC. Because of Micah's ministry and that of his contemporary, Isaiah, Judah repented during the reign of King Hezekiah, and judgment was delayed for them. Judah would last as a nation nearly 140 years longer because of its repentance. In 586 BC Judah finally fell to Babylon. Though this generation learned from the mistakes of Israel, they failed to pass on what they had learned to future generations.

📖 In Micah chapter 5 we see prophecies that specifically point to Christ. Look at Micah 5:2–5, and answer the questions that follow.

From where will the Messiah come (v. 2)?

What will be His purpose (v. 2)?

What does this verse say about His origin?

What kind of ruler will the Messiah be (v. 4)?

What will be the outcome of His reign (v. 5a)?

Seven hundred years before His birth, Micah accurately foretold exactly where the Messiah would be born (Bethlehem). God would raise Jesus up to be *"ruler in Israel."* Having all the revelation of Scripture, we can more easily understand that though Jesus would be born in Bethlehem, His origin is *"from the days of eternity."* Through Jesus, Israel will finally have a ruler who will be a faithful shepherd to them in the strength of the Lord. Christ will be *"great to the ends of the earth."* Perhaps the most powerful statement here is the phrase, *"this One will be our peace."* Jesus Christ is the blessed hope of Israel—and our only hope today!

God was not finished with Israel. Although He would judge them, it was for their own cleansing. The punishment was for their good to purify them and mold them into the vessels He wanted them to be.

Read Micah 5:10–14.

Make a list of all the things God would *"cut off"* from His people.

Why did God intend to do this (v.13)?

What is the meaning behind God cutting off their horses and chariots and tearing down their fortifications?

In the Hebrew Bible, Micah 5:2 is actually the first verse of the chapter, and 5:1 closes out chapter 4. This seems to be a more logical break. Matthew quotes this verse (Matthew 2:6) as the report given by the chief priests and scribes to King Herod when the Magi came looking for the Christ-child. These Magi were of an order of intellectuals who were placed under the prophet Daniel during his days in Babylon. The prophecies he taught them were passed down through the generations so that they knew of the coming of a King.

In this future day of promise and hope, God would cut off from His people horses and chariots and fortifications—all human hope of deliverance. Horses were the strength of Egypt in war, and chariots were the inventions of the Hittite and Canaanite kings. Likewise, fortified cities were an example of man trusting the work of his own hands to deliver and protect him. God would one day cut off sorceries, fortunetellers, and idols—anything that His people would place their trust in other than Him. With Him as their peace (5:5) they would need to trust nothing else.

"Some boast in chariots, and some in horses; But we will boast in the name of the Lord, our God." Psalm 20:7

What a contrast Micah offers in these chapters! He began his prophecies by unmasking and denouncing the false leaders of Israel and Judah. Now he unveils and proclaims the true Ruler—Jesus! The false leaders of Micah's day ruled for personal gain. The Messiah will rule in the strength and majesty of the name of God (5:4). Because of sin, judgment and war were coming on God's people. Righteousness will come through Christ, and peace will reign—*"And this One will be our peace."*

Micah DAY FOUR

THE MESSAGE OF FORGIVENESS

What does it take for guilty people to experience forgiveness? As Micah begins his third and final message, he asks and answers the question, *"What does the Lord require of you?"* Throughout countless generations, man has changed very little. Like Israel and Judah of days gone by, each of us stumbles in many ways. And like the people of God in Micah's environment, we are prone to deal with our wrongs in an inappropriate way. We try to ignore our sins, but God will not let us forget them. We try to compensate for our sins with religious activity, but it doesn't work. We make great sacrifices to try and pay God back for our sins, but none of this succeeds. Our works cannot compensate for our sin, and they never could! If our efforts could deal with our own sins, we wouldn't need a savior. Micah's messages are hard to swallow; they are as a bitter pill. Micah's messages are the bitter medicine of a cold, stark reality check—**we will not get away with our reckless disregard for God's law!** But Micah doesn't leave us hopeless. He closes by showing us the way to forgiveness. His message is timeless, for the people of Israel and Judah were not the first to sin, nor were they the last.

📖 Read Micah 6:1–3 where God was calling the mountains to hear *"the indictment of the Lord."* What was the *"case"* the Lord had against His people ?

___

___

___

___

In essence, the Lord asks Israel, "What wrong have I done to you for you to turn to other gods?" Notice He calls them, *"My people."* Even though Israel had abandoned the Lord, and had grown weary of Him, He still called them, *"My people."* After all God had done for Israel, delivering and protecting them as 6:4–5 gives evidence, they still turned away from Him.

📖 Look at Micah 6:6–7. How did the people of God attempt to make up for their sins?

___

___

___

Micah's indictment of the people was that even when they tried to return to the Lord, they did it the wrong way. They thought they could compensate for their sins with sacrifices. They even suggested offering more than was required (*"thousands of rams . . . ten thousand rivers of oil"*). *"Shall I present my first-born for the sin of my soul?"* they asked, *"the fruit of my body for the sin of my soul?"* In fact, Ahaz, king of the day, did just that. Following the pagan example of the Cannanites, he sacrificed his son as an offering to Molech, the god of Canaan (2 Kings 16:3). Instead of walking in a close relationship with their God, Israel's solution was to show religious penance.

"Has the LORD as much delight in burnt offerings and sacrifices as in obeying the voice of the LORD? Behold, to obey is better than sacrifice, and to heed than the fat of rams."
I Samuel 15:22

What did God want from His people (6:8)?

___

___

___

God is not interested in the outward form of religious activity. He longs to see changed hearts. He had already told them what He required, both through the giving of the Law, and through the many prophets He had sent them. What God desires of His people is that they do justice, love mercy, and walk humbly with Him. He wanted justice to reign instead of the corruption that marked their day. He wanted to see mercy, not the exploitation of the poor and helpless. Most of all, God wanted them to lay down their pride and walk humbly with Him.

What were the sins of God's people (7:1–6)?

___

___

___

___

Micah grieves that *"the godly person has perished from the land."* Astoundingly, there were no righteous people to be found. Everyone strived to take advantage of each other. Concerning evil, the people were ambidextrous—equally good with either hand (7:3). Even one's own spouse or family could not be trusted. The best among them was as a "briar" or a "thorn." What an evil day it was! Yet even to these people God offered forgiveness. If they would only repent (and history tells us Judah did for a time), God would forgive.

"Who is a God like Thee, who pardons iniquity and passes over the rebellious act of the remnant of His possession? He does not retain His anger forever, because He delights in unchanging love."
Micah 7:18

📖 Read Micah 7:18–20, and summarize what you learn about the forgiveness of God.

___

___

___

"Who is a God like Thee," Micah calls out to a nation flooded with idols, *"who pardons iniquity and passes over the rebellious acts of the remnant of His possession?"* What a powerful promise it is to know that God's anger toward His people does not last because *"He delights in unchanging love"*! Micah closes out this powerful book by reminding those he has warned of coming judgment, that a day will come when the Lord will again have compassion on His people. He will cast their sins into the sea of forgetfulness and place by its side a sign that says, "No Fishing." The most powerful message of all is that God will be faithful to His covenant with Israel in spite of the unfaithfulness of its inhabitants. *"Who is a God like Thee!"*

Micah DAY FIVE

FOR ME TO FOLLOW GOD

"What do you want from me?" a rebellious teenager screams at his parents. But the truth is the problem is not that he doesn't know what they want—it is that he doesn't want to do what his parents want him to do. The divided kingdoms of Israel and Judah are like God's child going through the teen years in rebellion. Judah, the good sibling, watches her older sister Israel rebel, and sees the awful consequences. Yet Judah ends up making the same mistakes. Someone once said, "There are two ways to learn every spiritual truth—**academically** (by studying the Word and the mistakes of others) and **vocationally** (by your own mistakes)." Through the book of Micah, God gives us the opportunity to learn from the mistakes of Israel so we don't have to make them ourselves. We dare not think that being children of God means that we have immunity from God's judgment if we walk in rebellion. No amount of religious activity can compensate for an unrepentant heart. *"He has told you, O man, what is good"* (Micah 6:8). God does not want us to merely show the form of religion. He wants us *"to do justice, to love kindness* [mercy]*, and to walk humbly"* with Him.

"He has told you, O man, what is good; And what does the LORD require of you But to do justice, to love kindness, And to walk humbly with your God?"
Micah 6:8

Israel was a rebellious child. Instead of seeking justice, every man dreamed of ways to get ahead by taking advantage of others. Instead of showing mercy, people evicted widows from their homes, essentially kicking them out in the street. The poor and disadvantaged were robbed. Instead of humbly walking with God, Israel chased after the pagan idols of Canaan. God's judgment was inevitable!

APPLY Is there an "Israel" in your life? Do you know someone who has been openly rebellious and has consequently experienced God's judgment?

____

____

____

What was their sin?

____

____

____

What were the consequences?

____

____

____

Have you been tempted to think of yourself as better than they are?

____

____

God wanted Judah (and us) to watch what He did with Israel. He wanted all to see that sin had to be judged. A fundamental law of the world God created is that you reap what you sow. God's chosen people had witnessed Him judge the nations of Canaan when He gave them the land. Somehow though, they thought that judgment would never come to them, even though they had committed every sin that those before them had committed. He had to teach Israel a lesson. But He would also teach Judah a lesson, for the sins of Israel had stained Judah as well (Micah 1:5). Judah's rebellion was not as overt as Israel's, masked as it was by their religious ritual. They still observed the Temple program, but their hearts were far from God, and their Sabbath religion had little effect on the rest of the week.

APPLY Is your relationship with God genuine and meaningful, or are you just "going through the motions"? Rank yourself on the scales below.

A right relationship with God ⟷ ReligiousRitual

Overt Rebellion ⟷ Hidden Rebellion

What are some of the religious activities that you participate in regularly?

___ Church attendance	___ Sunday school	___ Giving
___ Bible study	___ Witnessing	___ Deacon/Elder
___ Teaching	___ Quiet time	___ Prayer
___ Fasting	___ Worship music	___ Community service
___ Other ____________________		

Now, go back through the list and ask yourself, "Which of these am I doing out of a desire to know God, and which are done out of habit, guilt, or trying to compensate for my shortcomings?" Write your thoughts below.

____

____

____

____

____

What does the Lord require of you? It is not religious sacrifice that He desires. King David wrote, *"Thou dost not delight in sacrifice, otherwise I would give it; Thou art not pleased with burnt offerings. The sacrifices of God are a broken spirit; a broken and contrite heart, O God, Thou wilt not despise"* (Psalm 51:16–17).

"You shall love the Lord your God with all your heart, and with all your soul, and with all your mind. This is the great and foremost commandment. The second is like it, You shall love your neighbor as yourself. On these two commandments depend the whole Law and the Prophets."
Matthew 22:37–40

What does the Lord require of you? He requires you to do justice, to love mercy and to walk humbly with Him. These three ideals cover the three significant relationships in our lives. To do justice is how we relate to our own actions. We must examine our actions to see if they are just. To love mercy defines our relationship with others. Proverbs 19:11 tells us, *"A man's discretion makes him slow to anger, and it is his glory to overlook a transgression."* We should delight to show mercy. Yet this is the opposite of what we tend to do. When we judge, we often judge ourselves based on our intentions (what we meant to do), but we judge others based on their actions (what they actually did). Finally, to walk humbly defines our relationship with God. Humility comes through grasping as best we can God's greatness, and recognizing how far short we fall. When man walks in pride, he does not have a right view of himself or of God.

"Thou dost not delight in sacrifice, otherwise I would give it; Thou art not pleased with burnt offerings. The sacrifices of God are a broken spirit; a broken and contrite heart, O God, Thou wilt not despise."
Psalm 51:16-17

Relationship with Self

As you reflect on your relationship with God and how you live your life, is there any injustice of which the Lord is convicting you?

____

____

____

What do you need to do to make it right?

____

____

____

Relationship with Others

Is God calling you to have a heart of mercy towards someone in need or towards someone you feel has offended you? How can you learn to delight in being merciful towards them?

____

____

____

____

____

Are there some acts of mercy you have neglected?

____

____

____

Each of us stands before God always and only by grace. Yet so often we demand vengeance in our relationships with others. We hold others to a higher standard than we ourselves can live. The best place to start in developing a heart of mercy towards others is to reflect on your own need for God's grace and forgiveness.

Relationship with God

You are called to walk humbly *"with your God."* Are there any stains of pride of which the Lord is convicting you this week? Are there any idols that have shown up in your life?

Let's take some time to pray right now about this week's lesson.

Lord, I have failed to do justice, and I have not shown mercy. I have excused myself while judging others. Worst of all, I have walked before You in pride instead of humility. *"If Thou, Lord, shouldst mark iniquities, O Lord, who could stand? But there is forgiveness with Thee, that Thou mayest be feared"* (Psalms 130:3–4). Show me the justice that is lacking in my life. Grip me with Your grace and forgiveness so that I can be an agent of Your mercy to others. Let me see Your majesty and recognize my need for You. Thank You that You delight in unchanging love. *"Who is a God like Thee!"* Amen.

Prayer of Application

Now, write out your own prayer to the Lord based on what you have learned this week from the prophet Micah.

Jeremiah

Trusting in God When Life Looks Hopeless

The life of a prophet was not a pleasant one. Faithfully confronting spiritual unfaithfulness was not a way to win friends and influence people, as the prophet spoke the truth at his own expense. Shunned and embarrassed by his own family and friends, the prophet was no stranger to persecution. Often the ministry of the prophet was sealed with his own blood. But of all the Old Testament messengers, none is more lonely, none more maligned, none suffered the pains of his message more than the prophet Jeremiah. He was called as a youth to preach a message of coming doom. He was invited by Jehovah to feel His anguish over sin. Placed in his heart was a compassion for Judah that wept with the knowledge that they would have to be broken to be healed. Jeremiah lived in a seemingly hopeless day, but this "man of sorrows" of the Old Testament, also had glimpses of the Man to come (Jesus, the Messiah). Jeremiah's prophetic message is a foreshadowing of the Messiah, who would be broken for His people that He might make them again as a new vessel. This "prophet of the broken heart" preached God's word faithfully for over forty years, and in the end, punctuated his testimony with a martyr's death by stoning. He warned Judah that 70 years of captivity awaited them as judgment for their sins. And when he lay cold in the grave and that captivity had become reality, the prophet Daniel would pick up the

JEREMIAH

Jeremiah was born a priest, the son of Hilkiah of the priestly line of Abiathar (2 Chronicles 35:25; 36:12, 21-22; Jeremiah 1:1). Appointed as a prophet while still a teenager, he ministered in Judah about one hundred years after the prophet Isaiah. (Israel was no longer a nation.) Josiah, a good and godly king, had been on the throne for some thirteen years when Jeremiah first preached words of warning. Jeremiah's ministry would spread into five decades, and cover the reigns of four kings. His ministry ushered in the end of Judah and the beginning of their 70 years of captivity.

WHEN DID HE PROPHESY?

	800	750	700	650	600
	"A Prophet" (sent to Amaziah)	ISAIAH MICAH		NAHUM ZEPHANIAH HABAKKUK HULDAH (a prophetess) JEREMIAH	
	Amaziah 796–767 **Azariah(Uzziah) 790–739**	**Jotham 750–735** **Ahaz 735–715**	**Hezekiah 715–686** **Manasseh 697–642**	**Amon 642–640** **Josiah 640–609** **Jehoahaz 609** **Jehoiakim 609–598**	**Jehoiachin (Jeconiah) 598–597** **Zedekiah 597–586**
Jehoahaz 814–798	**Joash (Jehoash) 798–782** **Jeroboam II 793–753**	**Zechariah 753–752** **Menahem 752–742** **Hoshea 732–722** **Shallum 752** **Pekahiah 742–740** **Pekah 752–732**	There are no more kings or prophets in the Northern Kingdom. Foreign peoples are resettled into the land.		605—1st Captivity DANIEL Hananiah Mishael Azariah 597—2d Captivity EZEKIEL
	JONAH	AMOS HOSEA ODED			
		Tiglath-pileser I 745–727 722—Assyria takes Israel into captivity Shalmaneser V 727–722	Sennacherib 705–681		Nebuchadnezzar 605–562 612—Fall of Nineveh

and that captivity had become reality, the prophet Daniel would pick up the words of Jeremiah, and in them find hope. Though no one heeded Jeremiah's message while he lived, God has challenged every generation, believers and unbelievers, with his message. In his words we will see the promise that God judges our sin, the reality that God grieves over our sin, and the truth that God is willing and able to take away our sin and all its stains.

Jeremiah DAY ONE

JEREMIAH'S PREPARATION–LEARNING TO TRUST GOD'S PURPOSE

Jeremiah was born in Judah during the reign of the wicked king Manasseh, some one hundred years after the prophet Isaiah. He had, no doubt heard of Isaiah's successful efforts to save Jerusalem from Assyria. Jeremiah would spend his life during the reigns of the last five kings of Judah, preaching warnings in effort to save Jerusalem from Babylon. But Judah was spiritually too far gone, and Jeremiah would not succeed in leading the nation to revival. A.W. Streane introduces his commentary on the book of Jeremiah for the *Cambridge Bible for Schools and Colleges* with a remarkable quote from Lord Macauley:

> It is difficult to conceive any situation more painful than that of a great man, condemned to watch the lingering agony of an exhausted country, to tend it during the alternate fits of stupefaction and raving which precede its dissolution, and to see the symptoms of vitality disappear one by one, till nothing is left but coldness, darkness, and corruption.

Put Yourself In Their Shoes

JEREMIAH'S CONTEMPORARIES

Jeremiah was the leader among a brilliant cluster of prophets gathered around the destruction of Jerusalem. Ezekiel, somewhat younger than Jeremiah, was a fellow priest who preached in Babylon among the captives. He preached the same message Jeremiah voiced in Jerusalem. Daniel stood for God in the palace of Nebuchadnezzar. Habakkuk and Zephaniah helped Jeremiah in Jerusalem. Nahum and Obadiah were also contemporaries with messages to the surrounding nations. God sent many voices to His chosen people even though He knew they would not listen.

Macauley's assessment of Judah just prior to the period of exile aptly captures the hopeless situation that played out in the life of Jeremiah as he ministered to the nation at the end of the monarchy. Like the dying embers of an untended fire, he watched for approximately forty years as Judah received warning after warning but refused to repent of their wickedness. He saw the partial destruction of Jerusalem in 606 BC, and then the second wave of foreign invasion and deportation in 596 BC. He witnessed the flame flicker out in 586 BC when Jerusalem was burned and desolated. The glorious temple of Solomon lay in ruins, and the remnant of God's people were taken away to captivity. Judah was no more.

But what brought Jeremiah to this place? What events set the stage for this most discouraging of ministries? To appreciate Jeremiah and his ministry, we must first understand the circumstances of his day.

In 2 Kings 22 and 23 we see the death of Josiah, the last godly king of Judah. Although he personally experienced revival and led the nation in spiritual renewal, the people's devotion was to their godly king, and not to the God he served. Once Josiah was dead, the reforms of his reign were forgotten by most of the nation. Jeremiah began his ministry in the latter years of Josiah's reign. King Josiah was followed by four leaders of mediocrity who ruled over the demise of Judah. Let's look at the downward spiral of their days.

Look at 2 Kings 23:30—25:11, reading each portion and then summarizing the answers to the questions below.

How long did Jehoahaz reign, and what happened to Jerusalem during his rule (23:30–33)?

____

____

____

How long did Jehoiakim reign, and what happened to Jerusalem during his rule (23:34—24:7)?

____

____

____

How long did Jehoiachin reign, and what happened to Jerusalem during his rule (24:8–16)?

____

____

____

How long did Zedekiah reign, and what happened to Jerusalem during his rule (24:17—25:11)?

____

____

____

Jehoahaz reigned a very brief three months over Jerusalem, doing evil in the sight of the Lord. He was the people's choice, even though he was not Josiah's oldest son. His reign came to an end when Pharoah Necho deposed him and took him to Egypt in chains. His brother Jehoiakim, a godless puppet ruler for Egypt, replaced Jehoahaz, and heavy taxes were placed on the people. Three years later, Jehoiakim rebelled against Egypt, and one pagan tribe after another invaded Jerusalem. Jehoiakim was replaced by his son, Jehoiachin who also did evil in the sight of the Lord. Egypt was no longer a threat, having been conquered by Babylon at the battle of Carchemish (605 BC), but this did not make things any better for Jerusalem. Nebuchadnezzar, king of Babylon, placed Jerusalem under siege until Jehoiachin surrendered. Jehoiachin was taken captive, and the city was plundered. All of the king's wealth and the temple treasures were taken, and the most refined members of society were brought into exile in Babylon (including the prophet Daniel and his friends). Jehoiachin's uncle, Zedekiah, then became king with Babylon's approval, and like those before him, did evil in the sight of the Lord. When he rebelled against Babylon, the final siege of Jerusalem began, lasting a year and a half. As starvation drove the army to flee, Jerusalem collapsed and was overtaken by Nebuchadnezzar. Zedekiah saw his sons slaughtered and then saw no more because he was blinded and taken captive to Babylon. Jerusalem was burned to the ground, and the temple and city walls were destroyed. The people were taken away, and Judah, all that remained of the nation of Israel, came to an end.

In days of antiquity when military weapons were simple and hand-held, cities protected themselves from invasion by surrounding themselves within walls. The most effective way of attacking such a city, if one wanted to be conservative and minimize casualties, was through a "siege" method. Basically this meant that an army would surround the city, cutting off supply routes and simply waiting until the city ran out of food. While this took much longer than a direct invasion, it was very effective at producing surrender.

Indeed, Jeremiah lived through some dark days! His pain was even greater, for he knew in advance that the end was coming. He cried out warnings to the people, yet no one listened. What a disheartening situation to see the hand of God moving in judgment, but to be powerless to intercede! Yet God had a purpose in his life and message, and He has a purpose for us as well. In God's economy no one's life is meaningless. Our purpose, planned by Him, is not to be judged by immediate results, but by our obedience to Him and the ultimate fruit He brings. Let's look at God's calling of Jeremiah.

Take a look at Jeremiah 1:1–3, and list what details you find there about Jeremiah and his ministry.

____

____

____

____

____

Word Study

JEREMIAH'S CALLING

Jeremiah 1:5 uses three different Hebrew words to describe God's activity in Jeremiah's life before he was born. The first is the word "knew" *(yada)*. The Hebrew verb is in the perfect tense, indicating in this instance, that this knowledge was not the result of a process of learning or investigation. It means that before he was even born, God knew everything there was to know about Jeremiah. God knew Jeremiah's strengths and weaknesses, his failings, his fears—God even knew every mistake he would ever make. The second word is "consecrated" *(qadash)*. It means, "to cleanse, to set apart, to sanctify." God prepared Jeremiah for the work to which He called him. Third, we are told he was "appointed" *(nathan)*. This means, "to assign or appoint, to ordain." Before Jeremiah was born, God had already given his job description.

Jeremiah was a priest by birth. He would have learned from his earliest days the Law of God and the ways of worship. Raised in Anathoth, a small village three miles north of Jerusalem, his prophetic ministry began in the thirteenth year of Josiah's reign, and continued until after the destruction of Jerusalem under Zedekiah and the Babylonian captivity, which he predicted.

Now read Jeremiah 1:4–10, answering the questions that follow.

What three things did God do to Jeremiah, **before** He formed him in the womb to qualify him for his calling (v. 5)?

____

____

____

What was Jeremiah's concern (v. 6)?

____

____

____

How did God respond to this concern (vv. 7–8)?

____

____

____

What did God do to equip Jeremiah for his calling (vv. 9–10)?

____

____

____

In Jeremiah's call we see a splendid illustration of God's attending providence which accompanies His purpose for our lives. Before God formed

Jeremiah, He "knew" him. Second, God "consecrated" him, or set him apart. Third, God "appointed" him. Before God formed Jeremiah, He defined His purpose for him and set him apart to do that work. Like all of us, Jeremiah struggled with a sense of inadequacy for his God-given assignment. He said, "I'm too young! I don't know how to speak!" But God rebuked him and clarified his thinking about his call. The important thing was not his age or his qualifications, but his calling. God's calling of Jeremiah guaranteed that by God's grace he would be adequate for the task. The Lord gave him two important instructions: **first,** don't make excuses, and **second,** don't fear. God made Jeremiah adequate for his calling by putting His words in his mouth, and His calling on his life. Where God guides, He provides!

Jeremiah's Preaching—Obedient to God's Calling for Him

We saw in the discussion of Day One that God created Jeremiah for a purpose. That makes sense, for He is a purposeful God. One with all knowledge and all power would not waste His created people for a random existence. Not only is that significant to Jeremiah, but it is also significant to us. God created each of us with a purpose, and we will not find fulfillment nor satisfaction apart from walking in that purpose He has for us. You see, success is not based on the results of our obedience, but on the fact that we have done what God intended for us to do. If we have been obedient to His leading and calling, it doesn't matter what the results are, or how hopeless our task looks—we are a success! God gave Jeremiah a ministry—to preach His truth and call Judah to repentance. If Jeremiah had determined his success by how Judah responded, he would have despaired and seen himself as a dismal failure. But though he grieved over Judah's lack of repentance, he was able to find hope in the midst of an otherwise hopeless situation based on knowing that he had obeyed God. You see, God did not intend for his preaching to be only for the people of Judah in that day. Jeremiah preached to people such as the prophet Daniel, who would follow God in exile in Babylon. He preached to the Israel of the future—the remnant who would return to the land of promise seventy years later. His message was written down so that it could still speak to Israel six hundred years later when the Messiah would come, and Jeremiah's message was meant for us as well. Today we want to take a look at that message—those words of God that He placed in Jeremiah's mouth (1:9).

BROKEN CISTERNS

In the desert land of Palestine, water was a tremendously valuable commodity. To make the most of the water that was available, it was common to dig "cisterns" into the rock. These covered pits were used to collect and save rainwater as it fell. One can imagine how difficult and laborious it would be to carve such a pit out of solid rock. A cistern that would hold no water would be a continual mockery of that labor. The people of Judah were working hard to meet their own needs, but all their labor was wasted because they had rejected God.

The first component of Jeremiah's preaching was a rebuke of the sins of Judah. Look at Jeremiah 2:1–19 and answer the questions that follow.

Describe Judah's relationship with God in the beginning (vv. 2–3).

___

___

___

Describe how that relationship changed (vv. 5–8).

What was the essence of Judah's sin (vv. 12–13)?

What was God using to bring about their judgment (vv. 14–19, see especially v. 19a)?

"'Be appalled, O heavens, at this, And shudder, be very desolate,' declares the LORD. 'For My people have committed two evils: They have forsaken Me, The fountain of living waters, To hew for themselves cisterns, Broken cisterns, That can hold no water.'"
Jeremiah 2:12–13

In the beginning Israel's relationship with God was like a bride to her groom, characterized by love, devotion, and following (obedience). Israel was *"holy to the Lord,"* acceptable to Him, and any nation who rose up against Israel had to contend with God. But God's people began to stray. They forgot Him and *"walked after emptiness."* They didn't even miss their lost intimacy with God. No one, not even the priests were saying, *"Where is the Lord?"* (vv. 6a, 8a). The core of their sin could be characterized by two major problems: **1)** they had forsaken God, the source of the waters of life, and **2)** they had turned to the solutions of self. They had *"hewn for themselves"*—they had tried to find meaning, purpose and satisfaction their own way instead of God's way. But their solutions didn't satisfy. The cisterns they had hewn would hold no water. Because of these two evils, they were experiencing God's judgment.

Through Jeremiah, God gave two examples of His judgment. The first is found in verse 15: the land lay waste, the cities were destroyed, and the people were gone. This referred to the fact that the kingdom of Israel (Northern Kingdom) no longer existed. They had been conquered and scattered by Assyria in 722 BC. The second example of God's judgment is found in verse 16: the men of Memphis and Tahpanhes (cities of Egypt) had shaved their heads (a sign of being dominated and made subservient). God used Assyria to punish Israel, and now He would use Egypt to punish Judah. The amazing thing here is the way God implemented His judgment. God used the foolish choices of wandering Judah as their own rod of chastening. Judah had made alliances with Egypt instead of turning to God for support, and now they had to live with the consequences of that foolish choice. Sometimes God's clearest manifestation of wrath is giving us what we want. Notice the message of the Lord: *"Have you not done this to yourself. . . ?"* (v. 17); *"Your own wickedness will correct you"* (v. 19).

📖 The second component of Jeremiah's preaching was a call to repentance. Read Jeremiah 3:6–15, and answer the questions that follow.

What example had Judah seen in Israel, the northern ten tribes (6–8a)?

What lessons did Judah learn from God's judging of Israel (8b–11)?

What promise did God offer if they would return (v. 12)?

What effect would this have on leadership in Judah (v. 15)?

Judah had watched as their northern neighbors followed after the pagan gods of Canaan. They saw Israel's lack of repentance and how that culminated in their being given over to captivity to the Assyrians. Yet Judah did not learn from Israel's mistakes. Instead they committed the same evils for which they had seen God judge Israel. The big difference between Israel and Judah was not their sin, but that Judah put up a facade of repentance. Israel's sin was blatant, but at least Israel's people were honest about it. Judah's sin was covered over with religious-looking actions that belied a wandering heart. God promised that if they would return, He would not vent His anger. They only needed to come to the place of acknowledging from their hearts their sins against God. If they would do this, they would no longer have to deal with the despicable kings they had been enduring. God would give them leaders with a heart after His heart.

Did You Know?

ISRAEL AND JUDAH

The nation of Israel came into existence when God changed Jacob's name to Israel. The families of his twelve sons grew into the twelve tribes of Israel. The nation remained identified by the name Israel until the reign of King Solomon. His divided heart resulted in a division of the nation after he died, as Israel became two separate nations. The ten northern tribes (still referred to as Israel) followed Solomon's slavemaster, Jeroboam. The two southern tribes came to be known as Judah, and were ruled by the descendants of David. At the time Jeremiah ministered, the Northern Kingdom had ceased to exist because of its idolatry.

The third main component of Jeremiah's preaching was a prediction of judgment. Read Jeremiah 4:1–8, and answer the questions that follow.

To what kind of repentance was God calling Judah, and what *"detested things"* were they to put away (v. 1)?

If they did not repent, what was going to happen (vv. 6–7)?

God was calling Judah to a true and total repentance. He did not want them calling out to Him when they were desperate while still holding on to their idols. In essence, He said, "If you are going to repent, then make sure you really mean business and come back to Me. Don't just give lip service to repentance." This is His point in verse 3 where we read, *". . . do not sow among thorns."* In other words, pull the weeds before you plant! Make sure your hearts are really ready to return. Often we cry out to God from remorse for the consequences of our sins, without truly being repentant. This was also Judah's problem. In verse seven we see what would happen if Judah did not repent. Already a lion was on the move toward them, bent on destruction, for Babylon was coming!

Confronting sin is never easy, yet Jeremiah faithfully preached the message God gave him. Even persecution could not silence him, as Jeremiah would be shunned and shamed; he would be mocked and berated—he would even be imprisoned and eventually martyred. Judah was not willing to repent. A willing heart receives correction, but an unrepentant heart makes an enemy of the messenger.

Jeremiah DAY THREE

JEREMIAH'S PAIN—COPING WITH THE LACK OF CHANGE

What would you do if you were a pastor of a church, and no one listened to your preaching? In fact, instead of applying God's truth through you, they berated you for your messages. They mocked you and persecuted you. What if your congregation had you thrown in jail because they didn't want to hear that their lives were sinful? What if they never turned, never repented? What if you knew that judgment was coming, and you warned and warned but you could see that they were not going to respond? Would you be discouraged? Would you keep preaching, or would you give up, calling your ministry hopeless? For forty years Jeremiah remained faithful to his calling with no encouraging results. Jeremiah knew the truth—he knew what Judah needed to do, and he knew that they would not turn before judgment came. This recognition of Judah's plight brought him immense pain. Today we will take a closer look at how Jeremiah's message was received.

"Is there no balm in Gilead? Is there no physician there?"
Jeremiah 8:22

📖 Look at Jeremiah 8:21—9:1, and summarize in your own words the anguish of the prophet over the judgment he saw coming to his own people.

____

____

____

____

Jeremiah had so identified with Judah and Jerusalem that their pain was his own. *"Is there no balm in Gilead?"* he asks. In other words, "Is there no way to heal this pain?" The only solution Jeremiah sees is found in chapter 9, verse 1, where he says, *"Oh that my head were waters, and mine eyes a fountain of tears, that I might weep day and night for the slain of the daughter of my people!"* Although a chapter break appears here in the English Bible, verse 1 of chapter 9 is actually the last verse of chapter 8 in the Hebrew Bible. The thoughts in these verses are intertwined.

Sadly, people did not see Jeremiah's compassionate heart for them. Instead, all they could hear were the negative words he spoke about their future. Though he loved them, they persecuted him.

In the beginning of his ministry, God had Jeremiah go through all the cities of Judah to challenge the people to repent of the way they had broken their covenant with God.

🕮 Look at Jeremiah 11:21. What was the attitude of the young men in Anathoth toward him?

____

____

____

Jeremiah grew up in Anathoth, a small village only three miles north of Jerusalem. Anathoth was close enough to enjoy all the benefits the metropolis of Jerusalem had to offer. But it also had all the aspects of small-town life. Jeremiah was well known there, and sadly, once his ministry began, the young men of his hometown wanted to kill him. God would not let their plans succeed, however (11:22–23).

🕮 In Jeremiah 26 we see a message Jeremiah preached shortly after the death of Josiah when Jehoiakim was on the throne. Read Jeremiah 26, and answer the questions that follow.

What was main point of his message (vv. 4–6)?

____

____

____

How did the crowd respond (vv. 7–8, 11)?

____

____

____

Early on in his ministry, Jeremiah prophesied that if God's people would not repent, judgment would surely come upon Jerusalem. The priests, the prophets, and the people gathered at the temple seized Jeremiah, wanting him put to death. God providentially protected him through one of the city elders named Ahikam (26:24). Yet another fellow prophet named Uriah was not so fortunate, for as King Jehoiakim sought to put him to death for his sobering prophecies, Uriah fled to Egypt, only to be hunted down by the king's men and assassinated (26:20–23).

Later on during the reign of Jehoiakim, Jeremiah was instructed to write down on a scroll all of his prophecies going back to the days of King Josiah.

THE PROPHETS

In addition to good and godly prophets who ministered alongside of Jeremiah, such as Habakkuk, Nahum and Obadiah, there were also during this day a number of false prophets who were people-pleasers, not speaking for God. In Jeremiah 14 we are told of Jeremiah's struggle when he encountered these men who preached that there would be no sword nor famine—the opposite of Jeremiah's message. God made it clear that these men did not speak for Him (see Jeremiah 14:13-22).

As this scroll was passed and read, it became a catalyst for repentance for some, but when word of this mini-revival reached the king, he was not the least bit enthused.

📖 Look at Jeremiah 36:21–26. How did King Jehoiakim respond to Jeremiah's scroll?

___

___

___

Showing how little he feared God, Jehoiakim cut the scroll in two and then threw it into the fire. Neither he, nor those with him paid attention to the warnings of Jeremiah's message. They did not "rend their garments" which would have been a sign of repentance. Instead, Jehoiakim gave orders for Jeremiah and the scribe who copied his words to be arrested, but God protected them. Jehoiakim's reign didn't last much longer, and his son Jehoiachin's reign was over almost before it started. When Nebuchadnezzar invaded Jerusalem, he took Jehoiachin back to Babylon in chains and put Zedekiah, another descendant of Josiah, on the throne. However, this change of command would hardly make things any easier for Jeremiah.

📖 Look at Jeremiah 20:1–2. How did Pashhur, the priest in charge of the temple, treat Jeremiah during the reign of Zedekiah?

___

___

___

Pashhur didn't like Jeremiah's words of doom about the temple of which he was in charge, so he had Jeremiah beaten, and then placed him in the stocks to shame him before the people. What a tragedy to see someone who was supposed to be in the service of the Lord, persecuting His messenger! Yet we should not be surprised, for it was the so-called religious people of Jesus' day who put Him to death.

The book of Lamentations, which Jeremiah authored, takes its name from a Greek verb that means "to cry aloud." This accurately describes the contents of this short but powerful book, which consists of five poems expressing Jeremiah's grief over the destruction of Jerusalem. Tradition holds that it was composed in a place just outside the North wall of Jerusalem. This cave is under the knoll that is now called "Golgotha," the same hill where Jesus is believed to have been crucified. If so, then the suffering prophet wept where later the suffering Savior died.

📖 Look at Jeremiah 38:1–6. What did the king's officials do to Jeremiah during Nebuchadnezzar's seige?

___

___

___

Jeremiah's messages were especially unpopular with the political and military brass, for he encouraged all to surrender themselves to Nebuchadnezzar and Babylon. This fractured the ranks of the soldiers who were supposed to be preparing for war. These officers of the king took Jeremiah and threw him into an empty cistern, presumably to starve him to death. Ironically, the cistern contained no water, housing only mud. This empty cistern was one more sign that the words of Jeremiah were about to come true. Again, God would protect Jeremiah, and he would be rescued and placed under house arrest at the court of the guards (38:13).

To the very end of Jerusalem's sovereign existence, Jeremiah was faithful to preach the truth even though few listened, and still fewer obeyed. As we reflect on Jeremiah's persecution, we must understand that the physical torture, mocking, and imprisonment were not the cause of his greatest pain. Following the book of Jeremiah is Lamentations—the record of Jeremiah's words after Jerusalem fell. In this short book we see his broken heart over the nation that was no more, and the city he loved. *"How lonely sits the city that was full of people,"* he writes. *"She has become like a widow who was once great among the nations!"* (Lamentations 1:1). Jeremiah's greatest pain came from the grief of a broken heart. But in the middle of this book of mourning, the message suddenly turns as Jeremiah remembers the Lord and His promises. As we will see tomorrow, though His people were faithless, God would remain faithful, and though Jeremiah wouldn't live to see the end of the seventy years of captivity, through the eyes of faith he could see a better day coming. After all the wicked kings he had seen come and go, God gave him glimpses of a King to come (Jesus Christ) who would bring back the glory!

Jeremiah's Prospect–Trusting God with the Future

DAY FOUR

Jeremiah had every reason to despair. He had been faithful to preach the truth God had given him, but an overwhelming majority rejected his message. If they had only repented, Jerusalem would have been spared. But now it lay in ruins. The once glorious temple of Solomon became a pile of charred rubble, and the precious temple treasures that had served for worship since Moses' day were in pagan hands. Many of the people of Judah were dead, as some had starved to death, while others died by the sword. Those who survived were headed to captivity. It looked like a hopeless situation, but over and over Jeremiah called Jehovah *"the hope of Israel."* He understood that Judah's hope was not in its circumstances but in its God. Most of us will never see our houses or our city destroyed. Most of us will never be taken into captivity by a foreign army. But all of us have seen "hopeless" situations, and many of us have survived them. Some of us are in the middle of desperate circumstances, but our solution, like Jeremiah's, is to look beyond our circumstances to our God. That is the only cure for despair. Whatever is hopeless for man is not hopeless for God. What hangs over our heads is under His feet. Today let's examine Jeremiah's hope, and find some of our own.

"I would have despaired unless I had believed that I would see the goodness of the Lord in the land of the living. Wait for the Lord; be strong, and let your heart take courage; yes, wait for the Lord."
Psalm 27:13-14

In the darkest days, just before the fall of Jerusalem, a unique thing happened in Jeremiah's life. Babylon had Jerusalem surrounded. The rest of Judah was already in enemy hands. Nebuchadnezzar had cut off all supply routes, and the city was starved into submission. Jeremiah was imprisoned because the king was tired of his message of doom (Jeremiah 32:1–5). At this unlikely moment, his cousin came to him with an amazing proposal.

Read Jeremiah 32:6–15, and answer the questions that follow.

What was Hanamel's proposal to Jeremiah (vv. 7–8)?

____

____

What did Jeremiah do (vv. 9–10)?

Who all witnessed the purchase (vv. 11–12)?

> **"Ah Lord GOD! Behold, Thou hast made the heavens and the earth by Thy great power and by Thine outstretched arm! Nothing is too difficult for Thee."**
> **Jeremiah 32:17**

What explanation for his actions did Jeremiah offer to those who witnessed his purchase (vv. 13–15)?

While he was imprisoned, Jeremiah received a visit from his cousin, Hanamel, who wanted to sell him a piece of family land in their hometown of Anathoth. It was a foolish request, for the land he offered to sell was already in the control of the Chaldeans (Babylon), and even if the land were available, Jeremiah was in prison for treason and had no ability to use it. But Jeremiah bought the farm anyway. God gave him an opportunity to put actions to his trust. He had been preaching that God was going to bring His people back to this land after seventy years. His actions here show that he truly believed the message God had given him to preach. The text doesn't tell us the identity of all the witnesses, but the indication is that there were many of them. To the crowd present, Jeremiah explained that *"houses and fields and vineyards shall again be bought in this land."*

Immediately following Jeremiah's act of faith before the people, he went to the Lord in prayer. As we look closely at this prayer, we surmise that Jeremiah's trust was perhaps a bit more fragile than he allowed others to see. He began his prayer by saying, *"Ah, Lord God!"*

📖 In Hebrew, the word used here (*ahah*) is an interjection, a sigh of worry often associated with great fear. Read Jeremiah's prayer with this in mind (Jeremiah 32:17–27).

> **"Behold, I am the LORD, the God of all flesh; is anything too difficult for Me?"**
> **Jeremiah 32:27**

What did Jeremiah remember at the beginning of his prayer (v. 17)?

On what did he focus at the very end of his prayer (v. 25)?

How did God answer his doubt (v. 27)?

____

____

____

Jeremiah obeyed God, but then after everyone was gone he began to doubt. He experienced "buyer's remorse." He asked himself, "What in the world have I done? I've bought a farm I can't use." Jeremiah's remorse is comparable to buying a deed to a car that has been stolen. He ends his prayer, not by focusing on God's power, but on the fact that God asked him to buy a piece of land that had already been conquered by the Chaldeans. Jeremiah was honest with God, and God met with him. Verse 26 begins with the word, *"then."* After Jeremiah leveled with God, the Lord spoke to him. Notice what God says in verse 27—it is exactly what Jeremiah said in verse 17. He didn't tell Jeremiah anything he didn't already know. He just reminds him of truth in the midst of his doubting. The great theologian, John Calvin, said it well: "The heart is never so established and the mind so enlightened that there remain no vestiges of doubt." It is so easy to doubt, especially when our circumstances look hopeless. Often we are like the father who brought his demon-possessed boy to Christ—*"I do believe; help my unbelief"* (Mark 9:24). What a comfort to know that God meets us at our unbelief!

"This I recall to mind, therefore I have hope. The Lord's lovingkindnesses indeed never cease, for His compassions never fail. They are new every morning; great is Thy faithfulness." Lamentations 3:21-23

Jeremiah's message of judgment was softened with a suggestion of mercy. Though he prophesied of the day when Judah would end, and Jerusalem would be destroyed, he also foretold a message of a better day.

📖 Look at Jeremiah 23:5–6, and write what you learn there about what God would do for Judah and Israel in the future.

____

____

____

"Behold, the days are coming," Jeremiah promises. God allowed him to see that somewhere in the future a new descendant of David, *"a righteous branch,"* would come to rule as King over Israel and Judah. While this promise certainly pointed to Jesus' first coming, it finds its ultimate fulfillment in His Second Coming. It is only then that Israel will finally *"dwell securely."*

📖 Look at Jeremiah 30:1–10, and answer the questions that follow.

What does God promise for the future of Israel and Judah (v. 3)?

____

____

____

What negative things are going to happen first (v. 7)?

____

____

____

What will the end of Jacob's (Israel's) distress be (vv. 7b–10)?

____

____

____

We are told once again, *". . . behold, days are coming,"* when God is going to restore the fortunes not only of Judah, but of Israel as well. He promised to bring them back to the land, but before that happens, there will be a time of *"Jacob's distress."* While this promise found partial fulfillment in the difficulties of Jeremiah's day, ultimately this distress points to *"the day of the Lord,"* that seven year period of difficulties of which Daniel foretold (Daniel 9:27). The final outcome of those days will be that the yoke of slavery will be forever broken from Israel. Although Israel returned to the land after seventy years in Babylon, they remained under foreign domination at Christ's first coming. It is at His Second Coming that Israel will serve God and their King, David (meaning David's Descendant, pointing to Christ [Jeremiah 30:9]). In those days, Jacob (Israel) *"shall return and shall be quiet and at ease, and no one shall make him afraid."*

Jeremiah DAY FIVE

FOR ME TO FOLLOW GOD

Jeremiah lived through some hopeless days. Though these dark times were not a result of any wrong he did, he still sympathized with the nation's pain. He had to live with the consequences of the rebellion of others, but in the midst of those days, he found hope in God. Jeremiah also found hope in the future God planned for His people. We can learn an important lesson from Jeremiah—no situation is truly hopeless, for Jehovah is the God of hope. The words, *"Behold, days are coming"* speak to each of us. Wherever we are, and for whatever reason we are there, our situation is never hopeless. The present may look dark, but our future is always bright in the Lord.

"Before I formed you in the womb I knew you, And before you were born I consecrated you; I have appointed you a prophet to the nations."
Jeremiah 1:5

In order for Jeremiah to cope through such trying times, he first had to come to a place of trust in God's sovereignty. He had to trust that God created him with purpose. Each of us must make such an acknowledgment if we are to navigate the trials of life, for trials will certainly come as sure as rain falls from heaven. If we are to trust God with our trials, it starts with trusting God with ourselves.

Take a look again at Jeremiah 1:5. What were those three things that God did in Jeremiah's life before he was born?

____

____

____

In Day One we saw that Jeremiah was knitted in his mother's womb by Jehovah. God **knew** him, God **consecrated** him, and God **appointed** him. God knew him inside and out, perfectly and completely. He knew every one of his days before even one of them had passed. He knew every victory and every defeat, every strength and every weakness, every friend and every foe. Not only did God know Jeremiah, but He also **consecrated** him. God prepared him for the path his life would take. And finally, God **appointed** him. God gave him assignments in life. But, how does God's special relationship with Jeremiah affect you?

Everything that was true of Jeremiah is true of you! Before you were born, God knew you, God consecrated you, and God appointed you. Take a few moments to reflect on what each of those mean to you personally.

God **knew** you—

____

____

____

God **consecrated** (prepared) you—

____

____

____

God **appointed** you—

____

____

____

Have you surrendered your hopeless situation to God and accepted what He has appointed you for?

____

____

____

📖 Take a look at 1 Corinthians 10:13. What does this verse tell you about which trials are allowed to come into your life and which ones are not?

____

____

____

____

We have the sure promise of God that He will not allow us to be tempted beyond what we are able to bear. It is important to understand that the Greek word (*peirasmos*) translated *"tempted"* here is the same Greek word translated *"trial"* in James 1:2 (*"Consider it all joy, my brethren, when you encounter various trials"*). God's faithfulness to us guarantees that no trial will come our way that has not first passed His test. If He in His infinite wisdom determines that we are able by His grace to endure trials, He allows them to come. But if He determines that a particular trial is more than we can bear, He will not allow it. This is both good news and bad. The good news is that we don't

"No temptation has overtaken you but such as is common to man; and God is faithful, who will not allow you to be tempted beyond what you are able, but with the temptation will provide the way of escape also, that you may be able to endure it."
1 Corinthians 10:13

have to fear that He will put more on us than we can bear. The bad news is if we don't endure, we can't blame the trial, for God has already determined that we were able to bear it before He allowed it to come our way.

"For we are His workmanship, created in Christ Jesus for good works, which God prepared beforehand, that we should walk in them."
Ephesians 2:10

God lets us suffer through hopeless looking situations only if He determines that by drawing on His grace we can handle it. He knew what we could handle before we were born. He consecrated us for what He would allow to come our way, and He appointed tasks for us in those trials. He prepared a ministry for us. Ephesians 2:10 tells us, *"For we are His workmanship, created in Christ Jesus for good works, which God prepared beforehand, that we should walk in them."* God prepared our good works before we were born. He mapped out His will for our lives before He knitted us in our mother's womb.

One of Jeremiah's struggles was that he did not feel adequate for the ministry to which God had called him. In Jeremiah 1:6 he replied, *"Alas, Lord GOD! Behold, I do not know how to speak, Because I am a youth."* His fear was that he didn't know what to say. He thought that he was too young, too inexperienced.

APPLY Have you ever struggled with a sense of inadequacy for the tasks God has given you?

____

____

____

What difference does knowing these truths make to your situation?

____

____

____

____

What ministry has God given you?

___ Parent	___ Counselor	___ Sunday School teacher
___ Pastor	___ Friend	___ Mate
___ Employer	___ Leader	___ Discipler
___ Other ______________________		

Are there any in your sphere of influence to whom God has called you to give a message of truth?

____

____

____

Have you spoken to them what God wants you to say?

____

____

____

Are they responding?

Maybe you can relate with Jeremiah, who was called to speak truth to people who would not listen. If God has given you a message to deliver, you can't judge success by how others respond. You can only evaluate success by whether or not you did what God wanted you to do with a right heart. I have learned that confronting someone else's sin is never easy. But it is very easy for me to get in the way of them responding in the right fashion. If I am looking forward to confrontation then my heart is not right or ready. If I am dreading confrontation, but I have a sense of compulsion before God to speak the truth in love (Ephesians 4:15), then my attitude is probably right. If God has given you such compulsion, do not neglect obedience even if you think the person is not going to respond. The person might not respond at first, but God will honor our obedience some day in some way.

You can only evaluate success by whether or not you did what God wanted you to do with a right heart.

When our situation looks bleak, as Jeremiah's did, we have to be able to look beyond the present to the future. No trial lasts forever, for there are no trials in heaven. Hebrews 11:24–26 says, *"By faith, Moses . . . refused to be called the son of Pharaoh's daughter; choosing rather to endure ill-treatment with the people of God, than to enjoy the passing pleasures of sin; considering the reproach of Christ, greater riches than the treasures of Egypt; for he was looking to the reward."* We can never make our choices based on immediate results—we must look to the ultimate result. It is always worthwhile to do the right thing, and it is never worthwhile to do the wrong thing. Jeremiah's heart changed when he took his eyes off of his hopeless situation and focused them back on God. This change of attitude is reflected in his message recorded in Lamentations 3:21–23: *"This I recall to mind, therefore I have hope. The Lord's lovingkindnesses indeed never cease, for His compassions never fail. They are new every morning; great is Thy faithfulness."* Is there anything you need to "recall to mind" about God?

We saw in Day Four that God called Jeremiah to act in faith and acceptance of the future He had promised. He told Jeremiah to buy his cousin's farm. Jeremiah had to trust what God said about the future instead of trusting in the appearance of things. Is there an application in that for you?

Let's spend some time in prayer with the Lord right now.

Ah, Lord God, I thank You that before I was born You **knew** me, You **consecrated** me, and You **appointed** me for the tasks of my life. Sometimes I feel inadequate for those tasks. Thank You that where You guide, You provide. Help me to choose to speak Your truth even when I think there will be no response. Guard me from disobedience and circumstantial despair. Help me to act in faith on what You have promised in Your Word. Help me to look beyond the hopelessness of my circumstances and find my hope in You. Amen.

God is asking each of us to look at our "hopeless" situation and say with Jeremiah, "*. . . Nothing is too difficult for Thee*" (Jeremiah 32:17). Why not write out a prayer that fits your own circumstances, and express your trust in God.

Notes

Notes

Habakkuk

Following God in the Low Places of Life

The prophet Habakkuk wrote from a "low place" in the history of Israel. God had commissioned him to be the messenger of the coming judgment He was going to bring on Judah by the hands of the Chaldeans (Babylon). Because of the wickedness of His children, God was going to use a pagan nation even more wicked than Israel to discipline them. Judah's reigning king at this time was Jehoiakim, whom the prophet Jeremiah described this way: *"your eyes and your heart are intent only upon your own dishonest gain, and on shedding innocent blood and on practicing oppression and extortion"* (Jeremiah 22:17). The captivity Habakkuk prophesied about was the same captivity the prophet Daniel lived through. As Habakkuk heard what God was preparing to do, he struggled in his attempt to make sense of God's message. What we learn from his struggle is one of the most important lessons in following God. Following God is at the core of His message. This message includes following Him even when we fail to understand what He is doing, much less why He is doing it, and how to move from the "low place" of our circumstances to the "high place" of God's empowering grace as we live by faith.

HABAKKUK'S MINISTRY

Habakkuk prophesied during the first part of the reign of Jehoiakim (609–598 BC) at a time of great spiritual decline just after the righteous reign of Josiah and just before the Babylonians (Chaldeans) invaded in 605. His contemporaries included Zephaniah, Jeremiah, and young Daniel.

WHEN DID HE PROPHESY?

800	750	700	650	600
"A Prophet" (sent to Amaziah) **Amaziah 796–767** **Azariah (Uzziah) 790–739**	ISAIAH MICAH **Jotham 750–735** **Ahaz 735–715**	**Manasseh 697–642** **Hezekiah 715–686**	NAHUM ZEPHANIAH **Amon 642–640** **Josiah 640–609**	HABAKKUK HULDAH (a prophetess) JEREMIAH **Jehoahaz 609** **Jehoiachin (Jeconiah) 598–597** **Jehoiakim 609–598** **Zedekiah 597–586**
Jehoahaz 814–798 **Joash (Jehoash) 798–782** **Jeroboam II 793–753** JONAH	**Zechariah 753–752** **Menahem 752–742** **Hoshea 732–722** **Shallum 752** **Pekahiah 742–740** **Pekah 752–732** AMOS HOSEA ODED	There are no more kings or prophets in the Northern Kingdom. Foreign peoples are resettled into the land.		605—1st Captivity DANIEL Hananiah Mishael Azariah 597—2d Captivity EZEKIEL
	Tiglath-pileser I 745–727 Shalmaneser V 727–722	722—Assyria takes Israel into captivity Sennacherib 705–681		Nebuchadnezzar 605–562 612—Fall of Nineveh

Habakkuk's name, which means "embracer," speaks of his love for God. Habakkuk embraced the will and ways of God with His people. That was not an easy task for Habakkuk—in fact, it was one of the greatest struggles he had ever faced, and he did what we all should do—he took it to the Lord. Ultimately, he embraced the will of God as that which comes from loving, wise hands. As we study the story of Habakkuk through his journey of faith we too can learn to follow God, embracing Him and His will.

Habakkuk DAY ONE

THE SYMPTOMS OF BEING IN A LOW PLACE

The nation of Judah was sinking into spiritual depression. Doubtless, Habakkuk was in a spiritual valley himself. Not only was he surrounded by the sins of God's people, but he was also oppressed by the reality of what God was going to do about this rampant disobedience.

Not only was Habakkuk surrounded by the sins of God's people, but he was also oppressed by the reality of what God was going to do about this rampant disobedience.

What do we know about the times in which Habakkuk wrote? What was going on in the country? Habakkuk wrote from around 609 to 605 BC, just after the godly reign of King Josiah and just before the first wave of Babylonian armies in 605 BC. The order of events for those few years is as follows:

DATE	EVENTS
609BC	Josiah died in battle against Pharaoh Necco.
609	Josiah's son **Jehoahaz** became king and reigned three months.
609	The king of Egypt made Jehoahaz' brother, Eliakim, king of Judah and changed his name to **Jehoiakim**. He reigned for eleven years (**609–598 BC**).
609–605	The prophet **Habakkuk** ministered and wrote his prophecy most likely during the reign of Jehoiakim after the death of Josiah and before the Babylonians (Chaldeans) overran Judah in 605.
605	After Josiah's death, the nation *as a whole* had not continued to seek the Lord, though a remnant did seek Him. Within 4 years of Josiah's death, Judah encountered the first attack by **King Nebuchadnezzar** of Babylon. He besieged Jerusalem and took **Jehoiakim** captive to Babylon along with **Daniel** (around age 14) and several others.

📖 What do you discover in 2 Kings 23:31–32 about King Jehoahaz?

____

____

____

____

____

____

Jeremiah's early prophetic ministry included the reigns of Josiah, Jehoahaz, and Jehoiakim. Read 2 Kings 23:36–37, and record what you read about King Jehoiakim.

What do you discover about Jehoiakim in Jeremiah 22:18–19?

Jehoahaz reigned only three months, and in that short reign all that could be said of him was that he did evil in the sight of the Lord as many of his predecessors had done. His brother Eliakim, renamed Jehoiakim, followed the same trail. That path included idolatry and disobedience to the clear commands of God's Word. Jeremiah praised the life and reign of Josiah noting his just and righteousness ways, such as his care for the poor and needy. A stark contrast to his father, Jehoiakim was marked by greed and covetousness—even to the point of shedding innocent blood. He would be judged, however, as we read that he received the burial of a donkey. Many in Judah followed the lead of Jehoahaz and Jehoiakim into even lower depths of disobedience and defiance of their covenant with God (see 2 Kings 17:7–19; note verse 19). Judgment was inevitable upon the nation of Judah (Deuteronomy 28).

"Also Judah did not keep the commandments of the LORD their God, but walked in the customs which Israel had introduced."
2 Kings 17:19

Judah was at a low point spiritually, and Habakkuk found himself at a personal low point. Look at Habakkuk 1:1–4, and identify the symptoms you see of Habakkuk's depression.

In verse one Habakkuk identified his message as an "*oracle*." The word itself carries the idea of a burden, an awareness of impending peril. If we could sum up Habakkuk's disposition in these verses in one word, it would be **discouraged**. He was discouraged because he prayed, and God didn't seem to be listening. He was discouraged over the consequences of the sins of those around him and the seeming lack of concern on the part of God. He wondered what God was going to do about this situation.

In Habakkuk 1:5–11 we see the Lord's answer to Habakkuk's questions and the second indication of Habakkuk's low place. Read these verses, and write what stands out to you.

The word used to describe this second indication of Habakkuk's "low place" is **distressed**. God caused Habakkuk to recognize Judah's ominous future. He would judge them by allowing the *"fierce and impetuous"* Chaldeans (Babylonians) to overrun them. Habakkuk was distressed because as verse 5 relates, God had already said it would not be something he would understand.

Habakkuk 1:12–17 and 2:1 show Habakkuk's response to all that God had revealed. He had more questions for the Lord. Again, read these verses and write what stands out to you.

____

____

____

____

____

____

The word to describe this third symptom is **disgusted**. Habakkuk was disgusted with the idea that God would use the Chaldeans to *"swallow up those more righteous than they."* Habakkuk had placed God in a box and couldn't comprehend the fact that while God was going to use the Chaldeans, that **did not** mean that He approved of them or that they themselves wouldn't be judged for their sins. He chose to wait and see what God would do and say.

Have you ever been at a point where you were discouraged, distressed, even disgusted with certain events in your life? Or have you been frustrated that your prayers didn't seem to be making it past the ceiling? How did you handle it—or, how **are** you handling it right **now**? You may be like Habakkuk—a prime candidate for a new level of faith. Ask the Lord what your circumstances mean.

Habakkuk DAY TWO

THE SIN THAT A LOW PLACE REVEALS

A "low place" is not simply being in a difficult circumstance. As we will see later in our study of chapter three of Habakkuk, God made it clear that even though the difficulties would continue, Habakkuk could still have a positive attitude in the midst of turmoil. Being a Christian does not remove our difficulties or make us immune to the trials and tribulations unbelievers experience. In fact, being a Christian adds new dimensions of difficulty in the form of persecution. Yet, though the believer goes through the same hard times as an unbeliever, the believer can approach difficulties with a much brighter perspective. You see, our joy is not in our changing circumstances, it is in our relationship with God who never changes. However, we will not be able to hold the hand of God while still holding onto our pride. God opposes the proud, but He gives grace to the humble (James 4:6; 1 Peter 5:5). What can we learn from Habakkuk about pride?

📖 Look at Habakkuk 2:2–4, and noting verse 4, identify the sin which the low place reveals. (Remember that the text in verse 2 begins God's answer to Habakkuk.)

____

____

____

____

____

NEVER SATISFIED?

Habakkuk 2:5 mentions that **Sheol** and **death** are never satisfied. Proverbs 27:20 says the ***"eyes of man"*** are never satisfied. It is the nature of evil to always want more. How much is enough? For too many the answer is "more, more, more," the battle cry of greed. The peaceful state of the heart of God and those who follow Him by faith is contentment, gratitude, and an inner satisfaction given by His Spirit.

In verse 4, we see a contrast between two people: the proud one (whose soul is not right) and the righteous one (who lives by his faith). When a believer is angry and bitter because of what God has allowed into his life, he walks by pride, not by faith. If he walks by faith, he will trust a sovereign God's definition of what is good and beneficial. If he walks in pride and arrogance, he will look only at his limited definition of what is best.

A fallacy of Habakkuk's reasoning was that he believed that the proud walk of those in Judah had to be less offensive to God than the gross immorality of the Chaldeans. In chapter two, God laid out His indictment of the sins of the proud Chaldeans in a series of five "woes." While targeted at the Chaldeans, the judgment could also have been directed to His own people who were acting in pride and self-centeredness instead of in faith in the true God and His Word.

📖 Make note of each time the word "woe" appears in Habakkuk 3:6–20, and write your observations on what each reveals as symptoms of the pride of the Chaldeans (and by application, the pride of the people of God).

Woe #1 (2:6–8)

____

____

____

The first "woe" is found in verse six—to him who *"increases what is not his and makes himself rich with loans."* In other words, this person spends more than he earns. This display of pride in verse five is one of greed, which often manifests itself in piling up debt. That was true of the greedy Chaldeans. (We saw the same thing in the life of King Jehoiakim in Jeremiah 22:13–17.)

When a believer is angry and bitter because of what God has allowed into his life, he walks by pride, not by faith.

Woe #2 (2:9–11)

____

____

____

The second woe is found in verse 9—to him who *"gets evil gain for his house."* Why he does this is significant. The verse implies that his motive is to *"put his nest on high"* (be secure) and to be delivered from calamity (no difficulties). In essence his goal was to be self-sufficient, and because of his greed he was willing even to practice evil to get that security.

Woe #3 (2:12–14)

The third woe is in verse 12—to him who *"builds a city with bloodshed."* In other words, a characteristic of pride is violence, reflecting a belief that there is no accountability for one's actions, so one doesn't have to be just. Again, King Jehoiakim was guilty of this, too. Violent people don't realize that their labors are futile because God makes their violent efforts come to nothing.

Woe #4 (2:15–17)

Pride is reflected in our unwillingness to trust God with what we don't understand. It is always distinguished by a lack of faith—we have to try and fix things ourselves since we refuse to trust God.

The fourth woe is in verse 15—to him who takes advantage of others through drunkenness and immorality. The Chaldeans used others to gratify themselves, but in turn God would allow them to be used. He would bring their own actions back on them to judge them. Drunkenness and immorality are also characteristics of pride, for these sins are self-serving.

Woe #5 (2:18–20)

The fifth and final woe is found in verse 19—to him who worships the work of his own hands. While clearly, idolatry first comes to mind when interpreting this verse, the application is much broader than statue worship. Pride manifests itself by worshiping the efforts of self, whether it is in business, talents, or any other human venture. Over all things considered great in the eyes of the world, we read the verdict—*"there is no breath at all inside it"*—they are all lifeless, they can provide no true satisfaction, they can never build loving relationships, nor can they make life what God meant for it to be. In His judgment, God would expose the false and empty Chaldean gods. The foolish idolatrous ways of Judah would meet God's judgment as well.

Realizing that the sin often revealed in one's "low place" is pride, what is God's point in verse 20?

Pride is reflected in our unwillingness to trust God with what we don't understand. It is always distinguished by a lack of faith—we have to try and fix things ourselves since we refuse to trust God. Because of this, we often speak out against God when we don't really understand what is going on. Habakkuk had this problem, and God's response to him was pretty blunt. Verse twenty literally reads, "*Hush before Him*!" In light of His position as the Lord enthroned in His holy temple, and in light of His power at work that would eventually judge the Chaldeans, Habakkuk was ordered to hush and trust Him!

Coming Back to a Right View of God

Habakkuk chapter three verse one begins, *"A prayer of Habakkuk the prophet, according to Shigionoth."* I'm sure that the phrase, *"according to Shigionoth"* does not overwhelm you with spiritual insight, nor does it change your understanding of what it means to follow God. Understanding the word *"Shigionoth"* might help. It refers to a highly emotional form of Hebrew poetry that was probably set to music and intended to be sung (see also the end of Habakkuk 3:19). Most likely chapter three is this kind of song and reflects the fact that Habakkuk was deeply moved by what God had revealed. God had touched the depths of his heart.

📖 According to Habakkuk 3:2, what was Habakkuk's new perspective now that he had heard God's point of view?

____

____

____

____

____

With a right view of God, Habakkuk cried out for God in His mercy to revive His work among His chosen people.

Habakkuk said, "I heard what You had to say, and I fear." There was no more pride nor arrogance that made him think he knew better than God what ought to happen. The fear spoken of here is not fear of what God was going to do, rather it reflects respect and reverence for God Himself, and a recognition that His ways are greater than Habakkuk could see. In the midst of this view of God, Habakkuk cried out for God in His mercy to revive His work among His chosen people. Even in the midst of His judgment and wrath would He show mercy and revive His work? Would He bring His people back to life?

📖 Look at the adjectives in verses 3–5, and write down what Habakkuk saw with this new view of God.

____

____

____

____

____

____

Compare Deuteronomy 33:1–4. Note any similarities with what Habakkuk said.

As the Lord had revealed Himself and His plans through Moses, now God was revealing Himself and His revelation afresh to Habakkuk concerning His plans for Judah. Habakkuk was reminded of God's revealed glory when He brought Israel out of Egypt. Habakkuk spoke of God's splendor, which covered the heavens, and His praise, which filled the earth. When the Lord led Israel His radiance was "*like the sunlight*" (or like lightning as in Deuteronomy 33:2), but the implication is that the comparison is only with the rays flashing from His hand. In other words, the glory of the sun or of lightning bolts compares with only a minute fraction of His radiance, indicating that what is seen of God's power is only a small portion, the majority remains hidden from man's view. Not only that, but God also manifested His holy judgment in pestilence and fever both in Egypt and in the Wilderness. He was about to reveal His holy judgment on Judah

"The LORD is in His holy temple. Let all the earth be silent before Him." Habakkuk 2:20

📖 Read Habakkuk 3:6–12, absorbing all that God had done to reveal His judgments and His ruling power over any obstacle, whether of man or of nature. Over what does the Lord have power?

📖 Now look at 3:13, and identify why God did all these things.

God is Lord over all creation, the rivers, the seas, and all the earth. He rules over the nations; none can stop Him, His judgments, or His purposes. God's purpose for the perils His people were about to endure was not to punish them. His purpose was two-fold: **first**, He worked this coming oppression for the salvation of His people, Israel, and, **secondly**, He established this oppression for the preservation of His "*anointed*" (Christ), who would come out of His people and open salvation to all men. Everything God does in our lives has that two-fold purpose: to benefit us, and to benefit those He wants to bless through us, thus revealing Himself as Lord and Savior.

Habakkuk 3:14–15 invokes imagery of Pharaoh and his army storming in to scatter Israel, but the Lord routed them and destroyed them in the sea. Regardless of the oppression of Judah by other nations, the Lord wanted

Habakkuk to tell His people of the certainty that God would accomplish His will for His people. This revelation brought Habakkuk to an even greater depth of faith and trust in the Lord and His ways. God's revelation to him convinced him that He did indeed have everything under control, and that He would carry His plans for His people. God had some "high places" for Habakkuk to walk on, as He does for you and me. We will see those "high places" revealed in Day Four.

How to Walk on the High Places

God had a message to Habakkuk, and to us through his writings. None of us enjoy being led by God into hard times, yet even though the hard places deprive us of so many things that give our lives temporal happiness, it is still possible to walk with a positive outlook in the midst of the trial. The reason for this is simple: true joy is not the result of a circumstance, it is the result of a relationship with God. Sometimes it is only when we are robbed of everything that gives us material happiness that we are able to recognize the source of true joy. True joy is not found in things, but in a close walk with God.

Look at Habakkuk 3:16. Describe Habakkuk's emotional state at his realization of the frightful events God was going to bring upon Judah.

____

____

____

____

____

"I must wait quietly" (Habakkuk 3:16). Waiting on God is one of the foundation stones of learning to follow Him. In the Old Testament we are often told to "wait on the Lord." As we wait in faith, our waiting is not passive trust but active trust. Abraham, Joseph, Moses, Joshua, David, and Habakkuk all experienced times of waiting on the work of the Lord. Are you waiting patiently for the Lord to work in your life?

He shook on the inside (*"my inward parts trembled"*) and the outside (*"my lips quivered"*). He was in that difficult place of knowing the hard road ahead and having to simply wait for it to happen. Sometimes ignorance is bliss, for it is easier not knowing what the future holds. In the midst of knowing the days ahead would bring God's judgment on His people, Habakkuk would *"wait quietly for the day of distress,"* or *"rest in the day of trouble"* (NKJV), knowing that God would do what was right for His people and He would deal justly with the Chaldeans.

According to verse 17, exactly what circumstances did Habakkuk have to look forward to?

____

____

____

____

____

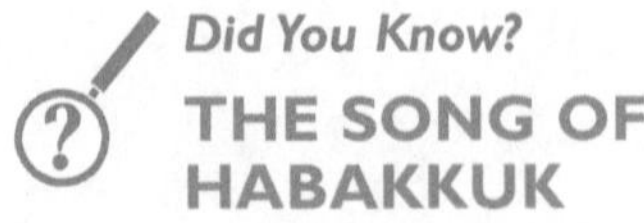

Did You Know?
THE SONG OF HABAKKUK

The Song of Habakkuk in Habakkuk 3:1–19 is one of many such "songs" in the Scriptures, including the Song of Moses and Miriam (Exodus 15:1–18, 21), of Moses (Deuteronomy 32:1–43), of Deborah (Judges 5:1–31), and of Hannah (1 Samuel 2:1–10). Other Old Testament "songs" include the songs of David (2 Samuel 22:1–51), Hezekiah (Isaiah 38:9–20), and Jonah (2:2–9). New Testament "songs" include the songs of Mary (Luke 1:46–55), Zacharias (Luke 1:68–79), and the New Song to the Lamb (Revelation 5:9–10).

Habakkuk listed five circumstances, all related to the livelihood of Israel: **a)** failure of the fig crop, **b)** failure of the grapevines, **c)** failure of the olive trees, **d)** failure of the field crops, **e)** failure of the livestock—the flock cut off (sheep) and no cattle in the stalls. All of the things associated with prosperity would be gone.

Against this black backdrop the truth of Habakkuk 3:18–19 shines. Where is Habakkuk's focus (3:18)?

____

____

____

____

____

____

Reflect on what Habakkuk is saying in verses 18 and 19. Write down your observations.

____

____

____

____

____

____

____

"Yet I will exult in the Lord, I will rejoice in the God of my salvation. The Lord God is my strength, and He has made my feet like hinds' feet, and makes me walk on my high places." Habakkuk 3:18, 19

While Habakkuk had a clear view of what lay ahead (the invasion of an enemy army, defeat, scarcity), his focus was on the Lord. He stated his faith—*"I will exult (or rejoice) in the LORD."* God was the God of his salvation and the salvation of Israel. The word *"Yet"* in verse 18 stands as a sharp contrast to the bleak circumstances awaiting the people of Judah. When Habakkuk said he would *"exult"* in the LORD, he used a word that suggests rejoicing in a victory already won.

Habakkuk's joy was based on four things God would do. First, God would give salvation (not so much eternally speaking, but here it means to *"rescue"*). Second, God would give him strength; in God Habakkuk would find the ability to handle the difficult road ahead. He knew that God would make his feet like a hind's feet. A hind is a deer, whose hooves are specially suited for rocky, uneven ground. God was preparing him to walk in difficulties. Finally, God would force Habakkuk into the places where, though difficult, he would be able to experience his full potential and accomplish more than he ever thought he could. His faith in the Lord (remember 2:4, *"the righteous will live by his faith")* would be met with the strength and skill only God could give.

For Me to Follow God

The Lord told Habakkuk *"the just shall live by his faith"* (2:4), and in the New Testament we find that same phrase repeated three times. Paul quoted Habakkuk in Romans 1:17 and Galatians 3:11, and we also find that phrase in Hebrews 10:38. The New Testament shows us that faith is rooted in being persuaded about the truth. As a matter of fact the Greek words *pistis* ("faith") and *pisteuo* ("to believe") are rooted in the Greek word *peitho* which means "to persuade." One believes when he has been persuaded about the truth of a matter. Throughout the Scriptures faith is based on truth—truth that persuades, truth about God, truth He has spoken (commanded or promised), and the truth about the choices He tells us to make. Habakkuk experienced that. God convinced him that what He was doing was right, and Habakkuk needed to trust Him as he eventually did. How can we apply this need for faith to our own lives?

APPLY Think about your own "low places." Where are your struggles? Check those places where you are wrestling with Habakkuk-like dilemmas.

☐ My finances	☐ My family	☐ My school
☐ My health	☐ My job	☐ My friends
☐ My church	☐ My future	☐ My nation
☐ My community	☐ Other ______________	

Where are you placing your faith?

Think for a moment. Where do you need to trust God? What is God taking you through that is stretching, challenging, or breaking you before Him? Consider this: God never allows or authors something in our lives unless it has passed through the gates of His **perfect love**, His **perfect knowledge and wisdom**, and His **perfect holiness and goodness**. Once it has cleared those gates then it goes through the gate of His **perfect choices**. This is the kind of God and Father we have, and the God in whom we can place our faith as Habakkuk did.

Let's review those characteristics of God and see what applications we can glean from the Scriptures.

First of all, God has **perfect knowledge and wisdom**. Read Romans 11:33–34, and record what you find.

____

____

____

____

Read Isaiah 40:12–14 and 25:1, and record what you discover about God.

____

____

____

____

God's wisdom and knowledge are like the outer reaches of the star-filled heavens or the immense depths of the oceans—unfathomable, unsearchable, beyond our limited comprehension. No one has ever had to counsel God or inform Him of anything. A friend once shared a very perceptive thought. He said, "Has it ever occurred to you that nothing ever occurred to God?" He already knows all that was, is, or ever will be. In Job 11:7 the question is asked, *"Can you discover the depths of God? Can you discover the limits of the Almighty?"* And verse eleven of that same chapter states, *"For He knows false men, and He sees iniquity without investigating."* He knows all that everyone has ever thought or done, good or bad, great or small. He doesn't need advice nor insight, and we can be assured that as in Isaiah's day, so even now He is working His perfect *"plans formed long ago, with perfect faithfulness"* (Is. 25:1).

APPLY In your "low place" do you doubt God's perfect knowledge of you and your situation? Trust Him!

"But God demonstrates His own love toward us, in that while we were yet sinners, Christ died for us."
Romans 5:8

God has **perfect love.** What do you discover about God's love in John 3:16–17?

____

____

____

Record what you find in Romans 5:6–11.

____

____

____

____

God's love is measured by the gift that He gave—He gave His only begotten Son to save us. He did not come condemning, He came giving and loving and seeking the lost. When the time came for Him to die for His "sheep," He gave His life willingly, purposefully, deliberately, and He did so as a covenant friend—first of all loyal to His Father, but also full of love for mankind (John 10:11, 18; 15:13). Think of the kind of "friends" He died for. We were in fact helpless, unable to do anything to save ourselves, but more than that, we were morally stained—ungodly in attitude and action. We were sinners, ever missing the mark and falling short of the holy character of God. We were even enemies of God and yet He showed His love for us by dying for us, and provided the way that we could be saved from His just wrath and could, instead, experience His eternal Life.

APPLY In your "low place" do you doubt God's perfect love for you or someone close to you?

Psalm 119:68 says *"Thou art good and doest good."* God is perfectly good. What do you discover about this **perfect holiness and goodness** of God in Psalm 86:5 and 25:8?

____

____

____

____

What do you glean from reading Deuteronomy 8:15–16 and Romans 8:28?

____

____

____

____

____

In His goodness and mercy God readily and willingly forgives those who call on Him. He is also ready to counsel, guide, teach, lead, and direct us in the way we should walk, knowing our weaknesses, our stubbornness, and our ignorance. His willingness to forgive and to lead is one of millions of reasons He is so worthy of praise and thanksgiving. He withholds what we so readily deserve and have earned (His wrath), and gives what we do not deserve but so desperately need (His lovingkindness and mercy). In Deuteronomy 8, we find that with His loving, guiding hands He may take us through some "wilderness" experiences, but it is always *"to do good for [us] in the end"* (Deuteronomy 8:16). It is all part of His causing *"all things to work together* **for good** *to those who love God, to those who are* **called according to His purpose**" (Romans 8:28). His goodness is perfect.

"Thou art good and doest good; Teach me Thy statutes."
Psalm 119:68

APPLY In your "low place" do you doubt God's perfect goodness in your situation? Are you struggling with some of the things that are seemingly not working together for your good? Remember that the Lord is weaving a tapestry that is not yet finished, and some of the strands He is using are the very dark colors you may be struggling with. When all is said and done He will show you a beautiful tapestry in which *"all things"* have worked together as only He, the Perfect Weaver, could weave them.

God makes **perfect choices** out of His perfect knowledge, His perfect love, and His perfect holiness and goodness. Never is there the least bit of uncertainty, never the slightest lack of genuine care and concern, never the trace of a stain on any choice He makes.

Think of this as you read Psalm 135:1–7. Note verse 6. What do you understand from this verse?

____

____

____

____

What do you see about God's perfect choices in the story of Joseph in Genesis. [If you are not familiar with the story it would be good to read it in Genesis 37, 39—50.] Note what you find in Genesis 45:1–15 and 50:15–21.

____

____

____

____

Psalm 135:6 says the Lord does whatever He pleases, whenever He pleases. Joseph certainly experienced that. When his brothers came to Egypt looking for grain, he eventually revealed himself to them and told them how Pharaoh had made him a ruler over all of Egypt. In telling them all that had happened, Joseph was very careful to point out two things over and over: **1)** it was not them that sent him to Egypt, it was God (Genesis 45:5, 7–9), and **2)** while they meant evil against him, God meant it all for good (Genesis 50:20). Joseph saw the perfect choices of God flowing out of His perfect knowledge of His plans for Jacob and his family which included provision in famine. With that choice Joseph also saw God's perfect goodness and love. We need to do the same in the events of our lives. We too have the same loving and wise heavenly Father making perfect choices for us. Let us trust and praise Him today!

APPLY In your "low place" do you struggle with God's perfect choices in your life?

"'For I know the plans that I have for you,' declares the LORD, 'plans for welfare and not for calamity to give you a future and a hope.'"
Jeremiah 29:11

Think about the greatest choice God ever made. Peter tells us in Acts 2:23 that Jesus was *"delivered up by the predetermined plan and foreknowledge of God"* to die on a Roman cross so that we might receive the forgiveness of our sins and the gift of the indwelling Holy Spirit giving us life forever (Acts 2:38–39). In the light of that kind of love, we can certainly trust the choices God makes in our lives.

Habakkuk had to learn to trust the Lord in the choices He made and of which He informed Habakkuk. The near future would not be easy for Judah, but it would be ultimately good for Judah and all Israel. Remember that one of the Lord's promises to Israel as they prepared for all that Habakkuk told them, is found in Jeremiah 29:11, *"'For I know the plans that I have for you,' declares the LORD, 'plans for welfare and not for calamity to give you a future and a hope.'"*

Take a moment to reflect on what you have learned through Habakkuk and the other Scripture verses in this lesson. Let what you have learned soak in. God is holy and good. God knows. God loves. God is at work even now. Talk to Him about **your life**.

Spend some time in prayer with the Lord right now.

Lord, I know You have plans for me as You did for Your people in Habakkuk's day. I know those plans come from Your perfect knowledge and wisdom, Your perfect goodness and holiness, and Your perfect love. Thank You that Your choices are always perfect choices, never tainted by lack of knowledge, purity, or love. May I learn to trust You with what You are doing in my life, even today. I thank You that You know where I am, the condition I'm in, and what the next step is for me. May I always surrender to You and Your ways even as Habakkuk did. Thank You for the "song" of faith You gave him. May I sing that song through the low places in life in which You lead me. I ask this in Jesus' Name, Amen.

Using what you have learned about the life and times of Habakkuk, record your prayer to the Lord, or make a journal entry expressing your trust in His plan.

Notes

Daniel

CONFIDENCE IN THE GOD OF HEAVEN

The prophet Daniel lived a remarkable life. Best known for his trip to the lion's den, Daniel was one of the many captives taken during the first Babylonian invasion of Judah in 605 BC. He was likely around 13 or 14, when taken on the four to five month journey to Babylon. Once in Babylon the king ordered Daniel and his three friends, Hananiah, Mishael, and Azariah (Shadrach, Meshach, and Abednego), to be trained in the Royal Academy for three years (around 604–601 BC, [Daniel 1:3–7]). They then entered into government service under the reign of Nebuchad-nezzar (1:19–20). Daniel served in that office almost seventy years, until *"the first year of Cyrus the king"* (ca. 536 BC, 1:21). Below is a brief chronology chart concerning the life of Daniel. A more exhaustive chart can be found at the end of this lesson.

With more than seventy years of government service in Babylon, Daniel served under at least six rulers and wrote the prophecies and accounts found in the book of Daniel.

Captured and taken to Babylon	In the Royal Academy	In the Service of the Kings	"Retirement"	Final Prophecies
605 BC	604–601 BC	601–536 BC	536 BC	534 BC
Age 14	Age 15–18	Age 18–83	Age 83/84	Age 85/86
Daniel 1:1–2	Daniel 1:3–7	Daniel 1:17–20	Daniel 1:21	Daniel 10:1

WHEN DID HE PROPHESY?

800	750	700	650	600
"A Prophet" (sent to Amaziah)	ISAIAH MICAH		NAHUM ZEPHANIAH	HABAKKUK HULDAH (a prophetess) JEREMIAH
Amaziah 796–767 **Azariah(Uzziah) 790–739**	**Jotham 750–735** **Ahaz 735–715**	**Manasseh 697–642** **Hezekiah 715–686**	**Amon 642–640** **Josiah 640–609**	**Jehoahaz 609** **Jehoiakim 609–598** **Jehoiachin (Jeconiah) 598–597** **Zedekiah 597–586**
Jehoahaz 814–798 **Joash (Jehoash) 798–782** **Jeroboam II 793–753** JONAH	**Zechariah 753–752** **Shallum 752** **Menahem 752–742** **Pekahiah 742–740** **Hoshea 732–722** **Pekah 752–732** AMOS HOSEA ODED	There are no more kings or prophets in the Northern Kingdom. Foreign peoples are resettled into the land.		605—1st Captivity DANIEL Hananiah Mishael Azariah 597—2d Captivity EZEKIEL Nebuchadnezzar 605–562
	Tiglath-pileser I 745–727 Shalmaneser V 727–722	722—Assyria takes Israel into captivity Sennacherib 705–681		612—Fall of Nineveh

During these many years Daniel followed God in a foreign land, in a pagan atmosphere, under the Babylonian government. How did he do it? In the midst of it all he knew that his life and circumstances did not depend on the rule of Jerusalem or the rule of Babylon because when all was said and done *"it is Heaven that rules,"* and Daniel was **confident in the God of Heaven** (Daniel 4:26). What he did and the way he did it can help us learn what it means to trust and follow God with confidence knowing He is Lord over all—whatever our circumstances may be.

Daniel DAY ONE

CONFIDENCE IN GOD'S RIGHTEOUSNESS

Daniel and his three friends Hananiah, Mishael, and Azariah were born around 619 BC in the land of Judah during the reign of the godly king, Josiah. Their parents and relatives would have known much about the joy of Josiah's leadership in the land.

📖 Read 2 Kings 23:24–25 and 2 Chronicles 34:33. What do you discover about Josiah's reign and the early years of Daniel's life?

___

___

___

"And Josiah removed all the abominations from all the lands belonging to the sons of Israel, and made all who were present in Israel to serve the LORD their God. Throughout his lifetime they did not turn from following the LORD God of their fathers."
2 Chronicles 34:33

In response to the revelation of the Word of God, Josiah removed the wicked elements of idolatry from the land. His reign was one of the greatest in the history of Israel, first of all because of his own whole-hearted seeking of the Lord and secondly, because of his desire to follow **all** the Law of Moses. He followed the Lord and led the people to follow Him throughout his lifetime. Daniel would have spent his childhood in that kind of atmosphere. In addition, the prophets Jeremiah and Habakkuk ministered during these days and doubtless had an impact on the families of Daniel and his friends.

The first chapter of Daniel gives us some of the introductory details about his captivity and early days in Babylon. Remember that Daniel and his fellow Israelites were approximately 14 years old when these events occurred.

📖 Read Daniel 1:1–7. What is the "atmosphere" of these verses? Pause and think about all that was going on at this time. Record your insights and thoughts.

___

___

___

___

___

Daniel chapter 1 starts off with a picture of trouble, gloom, and defeat—the city of Jerusalem was besieged and under full military alert, drawing nearer day-by-day to defeat, capture, and imprisonment. The king, the temple, the city, and the people were conquered. Many were marched to Babylon on a four to five month journey. Once there, Daniel and his friends found a different culture, different religion, a different education system, a different diet, and even different names for each of them. Everything had changed, except God. Their whole present situation was entirely different and their future would prove not only to be physically challenging, but also spiritually challenging as well.

Who is in charge in Daniel 1:1–2?

____

____

Who sent them to Babylon?

____

____

Why did the people have to go into exile? Read Leviticus 26:14–17, 30–35; 2 Chronicles 36:14–21; and Jeremiah 29:4, and record your insights.

____

____

____

____

Daniel 1:2 says, *"***The Lord** *gave Jehoiakim"* and some of the Temple vessels into the hand of Nebuchadnezzar. With king Jehoiakim's defeat came the defeat of the nation and ensuing deportations of the Jews to Babylon. Daniel and his friends were part of these deportations. The Lord sent them to Babylon just as He had warned the people through Jeremiah and others. Jeremiah 29:4 clearly states that **the Lord** sent the exiles to Babylon. He did so because of the sin of the people of God. They refused to heed the compassionate warnings of God's messengers which included Jeremiah, Habakkuk, and Zephaniah, contemporaries of Daniel (2 Chronicles 36:15–16). Instead, they continued in disobedience, and He brought to them what He had warned through Moses in Leviticus 26:14–15, 30–35.

As we look at the circumstances surrounding Daniel, it becomes clear that the nation in which he was born and spent his first 13 or 14 years did not hold to the truths king Josiah had emphasized in his reign. After Josiah died in 609 BC many in the land departed from the Lord and His Word. They ignored their covenant relationship with the Lord and did not pay heed to the Law of Moses and its warnings against the disobedience of idolatry and apostasy. What a powerful object lesson and application Daniel and the other exiles experienced at the hands of Nebuchadnezzar (as orchestrated by the Lord). Think of the four to five-month journey to Babylon and the different surroundings in which they found themselves. Think of what difficult circumstances Daniel may have encountered.

Read Daniel 1:8–16. Note what you learn about Daniel. Why did he respond the way he did?

____

____

____

"BABYLON THE GREAT"

Babylon, located in what is today Iraq, was an impressive city surrounded by double walls 21 feet high, and 11 feet thick, its outer wall containing eight gates and running for eleven miles around the city. The Euphrates River ran under the city walls and through the city providing an ample supply of water. Many temples stood in Babylon, the most elaborate being the Esagila temple of Marduk, and just north of that temple rested a 300-foot, seven-story ziggurat. Near the Ishtar Gate, Nebuchadnezzar constructed a 400-foot-high mound where he placed the famous "Hanging Gardens of Babylon," one of the seven wonders of the ancient world. This "garden," a series of terraces connected by marble stairways and containing a variety of trees, flowers and shrubs, was built for his wife to remind her of her mountainous home of Media. At the summit was a series of cisterns filled by slaves operating pumps connected to the Euphrates River. These cisterns fed the fountains and waterfalls that watered the gardens. Babylon was truly an impressive city.

ISRAEL AND THE MOSAIC COVENANT

Israel was under the conditional covenant of Moses. Obedience brought blessing and disobedience ultimately brought banishment from the land. *"But if you do not obey Me and do not observe all these commandments . . . I will bring a sword against you that will execute the vengeance of the covenant . . . I will scatter you among the nations. . . ."* (Leviticus 26:14, 25a, 33a—NKJV).

What is his attitude and response to authority?

What personal applications do you see?

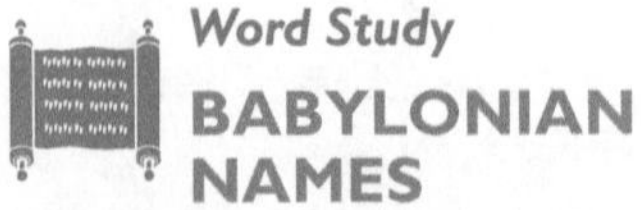

Word Study

BABYLONIAN NAMES

In an effort to re-orient and re-culturize them, the four Hebrew youths were given new names, those of Babylonian gods. Daniel whose name means "God (El) is my Judge," was changed to Belteshazzar, meaning, "Bel (Baal) protect the king." Hananiah ("Yahweh is gracious") became Shadrach ("command of Aku"), a Sumerian or possibly Elamite moon-god. Mishael ("who is what God (El) is?") was named Meshach ("who is what Aku is?"), and Azariah ("Yahweh is my Helper") was given the name Abed-nego, meaning, "servant of Nego," another Babylonian god.

Daniel was faced with tough choices. Either he could partake of the food and drink which was unclean according to Jewish Law (meats and strong drink most likely first offered to Babylonian gods), which would mean following the ways of the Babylonians or he could **follow God and His Word** and avoid defiling himself. He could have simply protested and rebelled against the king or even gone on a hunger strike, but he did not. First of all, Daniel *"made up his mind"* (literally, "set upon his heart") not to defile himself with the king's diet. Daniel responded with a respect for authority and a thoroughly tactful appeal with a reasonable option. The option he presented to the commander was that he could eat only vegetables (including grains) and water for ten days as a test diet. He concluded his appeal with the call for the commander to observe the results, *"and deal with your servants according to what you see"* (1:13b). God honored his heart attitude and his appeal (1:8) granting Daniel *"favor and compassion in the sight of the commander of the officials"* (1:9).

Think of the power of influence. Because king Josiah followed the Word of God so carefully, many in the land of Israel were strengthened to do the same. When captivity came, they remembered his example and sought to follow the Word in the land of their captivity. Daniel and his friends were witnesses of the fruit of the Word of God in the early years of their lives. The power of influence can be far-reaching.

FOOD LAWS

The Mosaic Law forbade certain foods for the covenant people of Israel. Those foods are listed in Leviticus 11:1-23 and include certain edible and non-edible animals, fish and seafood, birds, and insects. Included with the dietary concerns were concerns about pagan practices related to eating food offered to the various gods of Babylon. Exodus 34:14-16 specifically prohibited eating food sacrificed to false gods, lest it lead to the worship of those gods. Daniel desired to obey all the Law of Moses.

APPLY What is your heart attitude toward God and His Word? What about your influence on others? Is it toward the Word of God or away from the Word of God? What is your attitude toward authorities He has set over you? If necessary, how would you make a reasonable appeal?

Read Daniel 1:17–20. Note carefully **why** the four youths succeeded in school.

What is the point Daniel was trying to get across as he wrote this journal of his life?

____

____

____

THE POWER OF INFLUENCE

It was said of King Josiah, *"And before him there was no king like him who turned to the LORD with all his heart and with all his soul and with all his might, according to all the law of Moses; nor did any like him arise after him"* (2 Kings 23:25).

The youths were successful because *"God gave them knowledge and intelligence"* in their studies. Daniel carefully recorded the fact that God is above the kingdoms of this world and can guide and give success as it pleases Him for His purposes. He had not forgotten, does not forget, nor will He ever forget His people. Daniel was able to follow God even in the city of Babylon, the heart of the Babylonian Empire and the center of the established pagan religious system of that land.

CONFIDENCE IN GOD'S REVELATION

Daniel DAY TWO

When we turn to Daniel 2 we find Nebuchadnezzar very disturbed over some recurring dreams that he could not understand. Because none of his counselors could answer his concerns, he ordered that they all be executed which included Daniel and his three friends. This dilemma presented another opportunity for Daniel and his friends to follow God. How did Daniel respond?

Read Daniel 2:1–13. What do you see about Daniel's "co-workers" and the system in which he served?

____

____

____

Daniel served under a king who ruled by force and intimidation, one of the fiercest and strongest leaders in all of history. Daniel's co-workers were the Chaldean "wise men," men who continually searched the stars for their wisdom. Some of these were fellow schoolmates at the Royal Academy, young men trained in all the wisdom and literature of Babylon, including astronomy, science, and religion. In Daniel 2 the king's dream challenged them far beyond the limits of their education. No one could fulfill the king's wish; it seemed impossible. Only the *"gods, whose dwelling place is not with mortal flesh"* (2:11), could answer such a request as the king made. The king decreed their deaths, but Daniel knew the God of heaven, and his relationship with God would make all the difference in the world.

Did You Know?

THE KING'S DREAM

In order to reveal Himself and His will, God purposefully spoke through dreams to a number of people in the Scriptures. These included Jacob (Genesis 28, 31), Joseph (Genesis 37), the Baker and the Cupbearer (Genesis 40), Pharaoh (Genesis 41), Solomon (1 Kings 3), Joseph the husband of Mary (Matthew 1—2), and the wise men in Bethlehem (Matthew 2).

Read Daniel 2:14–18, and list the three things Daniel did in response to the king's decree.

____

____

____

____

Where was Daniel's focus?

First, Daniel did not panic but rather, *"replied with discretion and discernment"* to the officer who was to slay the wise men (2:14). He asked reasonable questions and did his homework, seeking to understand the whole situation. Secondly, he went to the king and made an appeal for extra time to bring an interpretation (2:16). Daniel responded with a servant's heart and with respect for the king and for the king's official, Arioch. Thirdly, Daniel made sure he had a foundation of prayer in place, so he went to his three friends and explained to them the whole situation—sparing no details—so they could pray with full understanding of the situation and the need. Daniel's focus was on *"the God of Heaven,"* who is above Israel and above Babylon, and who is the revealer of mysteries. Daniel and his friends knew that only by the Lord's compassionate answer would Daniel be able to give the king a sufficient understanding of his dream.

Word Study

PRAYING TO THE GOD OF HEAVEN

The name "God of Heaven" appears 22 times in the Old Testament with 16 of those occurring in Daniel, Ezra, and Nehemiah—books written when Israel was under the rule of a foreign nation. They each recognized that, in fact, it is heaven that rules (Daniel 4:26) and their God was the God of heaven, sovereign over all nations and fully able to care for His covenant people.

Daniel's focus was on the God of heaven. Read Daniel's prayer in Daniel 2:19–23. What did Daniel know about God?

God revealed the mystery to Daniel in a night vision (2:19), and Daniel discovered a new knowledge of the God who reveals mysteries (2:28). He honored God as the one whose name is to be blessed forever (2:20)! Wisdom and power belong to Him who changes times and directs the course of history and both establishes and removes kings (2:21). This God gives wisdom to wise men (2:21) and knowledge to men of understanding [literally, "knowers"—those with perception and insight]. He is the God who reveals profound and hidden things because He knows all—what is in darkness or light. Light always dwells with Him, and it is He who gives wisdom and power and can make known the matters we request of Him as He did with Daniel.

How did Daniel approach the king? What was the main truth he spoke to the king (2:24–28)?

Daniel first went to Arioch and appealed to him for an appointment with the king. He knew none of the king's wise men would be able to answer the king's questions concerning his dream, and Daniel was confident in what

God had revealed to him. He was sure the Lord would use this revelation in the life of the king, in his kingdom, and beyond.

What insights did Daniel give the king about his rule (2:37–38)?

____

____

____

____

As King over all, what would God do in the days ahead (2:44–45)?

____

____

____

____

____

What was the response of Nebuchadnezzar after the interpretation of his dream was revealed to him (2:47)?

____

____

____

____

"... let him who boasts boast of this, that he understands and knows Me, that I am the Lord who exercises lovingkindness, justice, and righteousness on earth. ..."
Jeremiah 9:24

God is the one who gives kingdoms to men. In Him are power, strength, and glory, and He causes men to rule. Since He is over all, He will set up an indestructible kingdom, a kingdom that will last forever. It was evident to Daniel that the God of heaven ruled unchallenged, and Babylon and its gods were no match. Nebuchadnezzar realized and acknowledged that there was indeed a God in heaven, who reigned as *"God of gods and a Lord of kings,"* the one who reveals mysteries. Daniel walked with confidence in that truth.

Daniel knew God as a God of revelation, one who could reveal mysteries, but more than that, he knew God wanted to reveal Himself so that man could walk in a personal relationship with Him. One of the prophets who ministered in Israel during Daniel's childhood and beyond was Jeremiah, who penned these words under the direction of the Spirit of God:

> *"Thus says the LORD, 'Let not a wise man boast of his wisdom, and let not the mighty man boast of his might, let not a rich man boast of his riches; but let him who boasts boast of this, that he understands and knows Me, that I am the LORD who exercises lovingkindness, justice, and righteousness on earth; for I delight in these things,' declares the LORD."* (Jeremiah 9:23–24)

Daniel was following this Lord as He revealed Himself and these mysteries, and, as we will see in the readings for Day Three and Day Four of this study, God was not finished revealing Himself or His mysteries to Daniel. As we see that, we can also learn some things God wants each of us to know about Him and about our relationship with Him.

CONFIDENCE IN GOD'S REIGN

The book of Daniel continually acknowledges the sovereign rule of God over the nations, over history, and over the individuals involved. Daniel was sure of God's authority and became even more convinced the longer he lived. He saw that truth worked out time after time, and his three friends had that same experience and same confidence. In Daniel 3 when Nebuchadnezzar ordered everyone to worship the golden image, they refused to do so. As a result, the king became very angry and decreed their execution in the flaming furnace, but the Lord went into the furnace with them so that the only thing that burned were the cords binding them. They were so well protected that not even the smell of smoke was on them. A higher decree by the God of heaven overruled the decrees of Nebuchadnezzar. The Most High God reigned.

Put Yourself In Their Shoes

THE FIERY FURNACE

Shadrach, Meshach, and Abed-nego were confident in God as they stood before Nebuchadnezzar and his fiery furnace. *"Our God whom we serve is able to deliver us from the furnace of blazing fire; and He will deliver us out of your hand, O king. But even if He does not, let it be known to you, O king, that we are not going to serve your gods or worship the golden idol that you have set up"* (Daniel 3:17-18).

When we turn to Daniel 4 we find the God of heaven, "the Most High God" (4:2), revealing Himself to Nebuchadnezzar in a very personal way. Let's see what we can learn from his experience with the Lord who reigns.

What stands out as the main point of Daniel 4:1–3?

____

____

____

____

In Daniel 4:1–3, Nebuchadnezzar focused attention on the Most High God and what He *"has done for me."* This chapter is a personal testimony that focuses on the greatness, the might, the rule, and the reign of the Most High God and how He got that point across to Nebuchadnezzar who, at this point in history, was the greatest ruler on earth, ruling the greatest kingdom in existence at that time.

📖 Read Nebuchadnezzar's testimony in Daniel 4:4–18. What was Daniel's reputation in Nebuchadnezzar's eyes?

____

____

____

"The Most High is ruler over the realm of mankind, and bestows it on whom He wishes, and sets over it the lowliest of men." Daniel 4:17b

Nebuchadnezzar had no confidence that the wise men of his kingdom would be able to interpret his dream. However, Daniel's reputation had spread and Nebuchadnezzar saw Daniel as one *"in whom is a spirit (or the Spirit) of the holy gods (or God)"* and therefore, was confident he could interpret his mysterious dream (4:8).

What advice did Daniel give Nebuchadnezzar (4:17–27)?

____

____

____

____

What was the basis of all the counsel Daniel gave (4:17, 25, 26)?

Daniel revealed the sovereign workings of God in what he revealed to Nebuchadnezzar, pointing to the decree of the Most High God. Daniel emphasized that *"the Most High is ruler over the realm of mankind"* and bestows power and authority *"on whomever He wishes"* (4:25). It was crucial that Nebuchadnezzar understood and acknowledged the Most High God and the fact that *"it is Heaven that rules"* not only over Babylon, but also over all the kingdoms of the world (4:26). The first thing Nebuchadnezzar had to do was acknowledge his sins, repent of them and turn to do that which was right in God's sight. It meant ruling with a compassionate heart, *"showing mercy to the poor,"* not judging with an iron fist (4:27). Daniel continually based his counsel on the sovereign Lordship of the Most High God, ruler over all men, who puts all rulers in place including the greatest and *"the lowliest of men"* (4:17).

DID NEBUCHADNEZZAR HAVE BOANTHROPY?

Some think Nebuchadnezzar had a disease known as boanthropy, a malady in which one imagines he is an ox and acts accordingly. Cases of this have been recorded in modern times. Whatever the malady of Nebuchadnezzar may have been, it was at the disciplinary hand of God that he was given a "beast's mind" (literally, "heart") for a period of seven years (Daniel 4:16).

What was Nebuchadnezzar's problem (4:28–33)?

Nebuchadnezzar was full of pride. He had an "I" problem focusing his attention on himself, using his "vanity mirror" three times as he walked on the rooftop over his palace in Babylon as recorded in verse 30. Notice the words, *"I myself," "my power,"* and *"my majesty."* Nebuchadnezzar still had not gotten the point. God knew the exact remedy for his pride and self-sufficiency; He humbled him by driving him into the pastureland to eat grass like a grazing ox. The king who boasted of almost superhuman building feats now moved about in the fields unable to do the simplest things. What a price to pay for rejecting the word of the Lord!

What was the result of God's work in Nebuchadnezzar's life (4:34–37)?

What a comfort for the child of God—Our Father is "the King of Heaven" and "It is Heaven that rules" (Daniel 4:26, 37).

After seven years, when Nebuchadnezzar raised his eyes toward heaven his understanding returned to him. He recognized God as the *"King of Heaven"* and that indeed *"it is Heaven that rules"* (4:26, 37). He humbled himself before this Most High God, praising Him as the eternal God who lives forever and who reigns forever. He saw himself and all mankind as nothing on the scale of significance and power compared to the Lord who does as He pleases, when He pleases. No one has power to restrain His hand or question His wisdom. When Nebuchadnezzar surrendered to the Lord of heaven and earth, the Lord returned him his kingdom, his authority, and his honor. His praise of the Lord knew no bounds, for he saw in Him not only absolute authority but also the perfection of purity in all He did as he exclaimed, *"all His works are true and His ways just"* (4:37). Then, surely as a personal testimony, Nebuchadnezzar concluded, *"and He is able to humble those who walk in pride."*

Three times we read that *"the Most High is ruler over the realm of mankind, and bestows it on whomever He wishes"* (4:17, 25, 32). What attributes of God are evident to you in your life? What about your attitude toward all you have and all you've done? How does it compare with the attitude of Nebuchadnezzar . . . that is, with what stage of Nebuchadnezzar's life does your life compare today?

____

____

____

____

Doctrine

CONFIDENCE ABOUT THE FUTURE

God gave Daniel a confidence about His plans for His people. Like three strands of a lifeline of hope, God revealed His plans for the kingdoms of the world, His purpose for the Messiah King in the world, and the place of Israel in the world. Daniel prophesied concerning the current and the coming world powers (Babylon, Medo-Persia, Greece, Rome, and revived Rome), the coming of the Messiah, and God's schedule for Israel.

Daniel continued to serve under Nebuchadnezzar throughout the remainder of his reign. Nebuchadnezzar died in 562 BC (a 43 year reign) and was followed by a series of short-term kings. His son, Evil-Merodach, reigned two years and was then murdered by his brother-in-law, General Neriglissar, who then ascended the throne, ruling four years before he died. His son, Labashi-Marduk, reigned after him, but was assassinated after nine months. Nabonidus, the son-in-law of Nebuchadnezzar, began to rule in 556, and in 554 made his eldest son Belshazzar co-regent with him while he left the city of Babylon to restore parts of the empire and conquer new territory. They reigned until 539 BC, when Darius the Mede conquered Babylon and the Medo-Persian Empire was established. Daniel served during all of this political turmoil, and through it all, he lived out the truth that *"it is Heaven that rules."* When we turn to Daniel chapter 5, Daniel is eighty years of age, and he has not stopped following God. (NOTE: The chronological order of the chapters of Daniel is as follows: 1, 2, 3, 4, 7, 8, 5, 9, 6, 10, 11, 12. For an overview of how the chapters of the book of Daniel fit together, see the Chronology at the end of this lesson.)

During the first three years of Belshazzar's reign God gave to Daniel two very unique visions of what would take place in world history and in the life of the people of God (see Daniel 7 and 8). In spite of the perplexing visions Daniel received, he was assured of at least two truths: **1)** The one who would arise to *"wear down the saints of the Highest One"* (7:25) would be judged, overthrown, and destroyed and **2)** *"the saints of the Highest One will receive the kingdom and possess the kingdom forever, for all ages to come"* (7:18; see also verse 27). Daniel 7 gives a quick view of the four beasts (kingdoms) as well as an assurance of the rule of the Ancient of Days and the everlasting dominion of the Son of Man (7:9–14). Daniel knew he was following the God who reigns!

Twelve years after the visions of Daniel 7 and 8, around 539 BC, we are introduced to Belshazzar at a *"great feast"* in the palace banquet hall, attended by a thousand nobles plus wives and concubines (Daniel 5). Belshazzar felt secure inside the well-fortified city of Babylon. Its massive double walls were 21 feet high and 11 feet thick with towers reaching up to ninety feet high. The outer wall stretched eleven miles around the city. While everyone inside enjoyed their sumptuous feast, outside the walls, the city was in the process of being besieged by the Persians, though the Babylonians saw little reason to be concerned. The city had enough supplies to take care of the people for twenty years, and Belshazzar, thinking he was safe, showed his contempt for the Persians. More dangerous than that, he showed contempt for the Lord of heaven in praising his gods while drinking from the Temple vessels taken from Jerusalem.

Read Daniel 5. Note especially 5:18–29. What do you see about how Daniel followed God?

____

____

____

____

____

____

What do you learn about the reign of the Lord? (NOTE: the lesson of Daniel 4:17, 25, 32 is repeated in 5:21.)

____

____

____

____

____

____

Belshazzar the king (co-regent) exalted himself, his position, and his gods in total disregard of the Most High God, the Lord of heaven about whom he had some knowledge. Because of the appearance of the handwriting on the wall, he feared greatly. When Daniel came into the banquet hall Belshazzar offered him gifts and a third share as ruler of Babylon alongside himself and his father Nabonidus. Daniel spoke with conviction, *"keep your gifts for yourself, or give your rewards to someone else"* (5:17). Then he clearly proclaimed the truth of Belshazzar's sin and his judgment. Belshazzar knew the story of his grandfather Nebuchadnezzar, but had ignored that truth as well as his own responsibility to honor and glorify the true God. Therefore, through the handwriting on the wall, the Lord miraculously revealed His message of judgment: Belshazzar's kingdom was at an end, and he was about to be slain. Daniel, who had no desire for the king's gifts or position, watched the king meet his demise. Daniel continued to follow God under the new king, Darius the Mede. (Darius is probably a title rather than a name, and most likely refers to Cyrus, who ruled as king of the Medo-Persian empire until 530 BC.)

We see in these events the Lord's continual reign in the midst of intense political rivalries, assassinations, and wars. The Lord's plans, purposes, and decrees stand unshaken regardless of the most wicked of men and kingdoms. He is always *"ruler over the realm of mankind, and He sets over it whomever He wishes"* (5:21b). Daniel followed this Lord who ever reigns over all, even when it meant that his co-workers became his enemies. We will see that in Day Four.

Did You Know?

THE GODS OF BABYLON

The people of Babylon worshiped several different gods. Daniel 5:4 mentions gods of gold, silver, bronze, iron, wood, and stone, referring to the materials used to craft their images. Those images represented such gods as Marduk, chief of the gods who was also called Bel (equivalent to Baal, meaning "lord"), Nebo (or Nabu) son of Marduk and god of writing, Sin the mood god, and Ishtar, goddess of the morning and evening star. She was also called the "Queen of Heaven" (Jeremiah 7:18; 44:17-19). God's message to the Babylonians was clear, *"you have praised the gods of gold . . . which do not see or hear or know; and the God who holds your breath in His hand and owns all your ways, you have not glorified"* (Daniel 5:23).

CONFIDENCE IN HIS RELATIONSHIP WITH GOD

Daniel 6 opens in 538 BC when Daniel was around 81 years of age and under the newly established reign of Darius the Mede. Daniel continued to prove himself an able leader, ruling as one of three commissioners overseeing 120 **satraps** (rulers over the provinces of the kingdom). God had prospered him in this pagan environment. He ruled with justice and proved such an able leader that *"the king planned to appoint him over the entire kingdom"* (6:3). Some of the leaders despised Daniel, knowing he was an exile from Judah and a potential threat to their positions. Therefore they resorted to political entrapment. Would Daniel follow God when others targeted their venomous rancor towards him?

📖 Read Daniel 6:4–9. What do you learn of Daniel's life in regard to his following God?

____

____

____

____

Daniel's confidence was not in prayer. His confidence rested in the God who answers prayer.

The leaders seemed jealous of Daniel because of the respect which Darius showed him, even though Darius' kindness was a result of Daniel's excellent leadership (6:3). As they sought to uncover something with which to accuse Daniel, they found absolutely no evidence of corruption or negligence. He was faithful in his job and that was evident, but there was one other matter that caught the attention of Daniel's rivals; Daniel followed God and His Word, and the men knew it. That's where they chose to direct their plot against him, specifically proposing to establish an irrevocable law against prayer (see Daniel 6:1–9).

📖 Read Daniel 6:10–15. What was Daniel's response to this new law (Daniel 6:7)?

____

____

____

____

____

What do you observe about Daniel's lifestyle?

____

____

____

____

Daniel knew about the law and *"continued kneeling on his knees three times a day, praying and giving thanks before his God"* (6:10). This was not something new for Daniel, but rather it was his lifestyle. He had a personal relationship with the God of heaven. He wasn't praying just to make a political statement. Verse 10 states, *"as he had been doing previously."* He did not try to hide himself or his praying. He could be seen through his roof chamber windows, and the jealous officials saw him, went to Darius, and accused him of disregarding the king and the law. They also revealed their prejudice against Daniel by calling him *"one of the exiles from Judah"* (6:13). Their accusation greatly distressed Darius who could see through their plot. Since he respected Daniel, he tried relentlessly to rescue Daniel—to no avail. As a result, Daniel was thrown into the lion's den.

Read Daniel 6:16–27. What further evidence do you see that Daniel followed God?

____

____

____

____

What do you see about Daniel's relationship to those in authority over him?

____

____

____

____

What impact did Daniel have on the king?

____

____

____

____

Doctrine

PICTURES OF THE MESSIAH IN DANIEL

Christ is seen in the Stone of Daniel 2:34-35, the "Fourth Person" whose appearance was *"like a son of the gods"* in the fiery furnace of Daniel 3, the Son of Man of Daniel 7:13-14, and the Anointed One (Mashiyach—Messiah) of Daniel 9:25-26.

The king himself testified that Daniel constantly followed God, and he knew Daniel's God would deliver him (*"your God whom you constantly serve will Himself deliver you"* [6:16b]). He called Daniel *"servant of the living God"* (6:20), and again pointed to the fact that he "*constantly*" served God. Daniel continually honored the king with a service marked by integrity (see 6:4). It is evident that the king cared deeply for Daniel since he neither ate nor slept that night (6:18). In the morning he rushed to the lion's den in great concern over Daniel (6:19–20). There, Daniel testified that *"my God sent his angels and shut the lion's mouths. . . . I was found innocent before Him; and toward you, O king, I have committed no crime"* (6:22). Verse 23 states, *"no injury whatever was found on him because he had trusted in his God."*

As a result of Daniel following God, the king issued a decree honoring the God who is to be feared, who is the living and enduring God, whose kingdom will never be destroyed, whose dominion is forever. He is the God who answers prayer, who rescues and performs signs and wonders in heaven and on earth. He revealed Himself, His power, and His dominion in delivering Daniel from the lions. However, Daniel's enemies experienced a much different outcome. Everyone saw the swiftness with which those same lions crushed the men and families who had plotted against Daniel. Daniel followed God, confident in prayer, even when he faced the enemies of God. You can do that when you know that the God of heaven rules.

In chapter 9 we find the account of Daniel (about age 80) reading the prophecy of Jeremiah concerning the seventy years of desolation decreed for Jerusalem (see Jeremiah 25:11, 12; 29:10). The year was 539 BC, 67 years since the Babylonian captivity began. Daniel set his heart and mind to seek the Lord concerning this. He knew God was about to end the captivity, he knew the captivity was deserved, and he knew he could trust God, His Word, and His promises. That's why he prayed.

📖 Read Daniel 9:1–14. What do you see in Daniel's confession?

____

____

____

____

____

____

What is the heart cry of Daniel according to 9:15–19?

____

____

____

____

____

____

"See how great a love the Father has bestowed upon us, that we should be called children of God; and such we are."

I John 3:1

Daniel honestly admitted the grave sin of his people Israel. Everything God had done in bringing them into captivity was righteous and necessary. Daniel was concerned with "the here and now" (9:15–16), and he called on the Lord to turn His anger away and *"let Thy face shine on Thy desolate sanctuary"* (9:17). He was quick to claim no merit; nothing deserved. He desired God to act out of His *"great compassion"* (9:18). He was concerned for God's people and God's name and honor. He earnestly prayed, *"For Thine own sake, O my God, do not delay, because Thy city and Thy people are called by Thy name"* (9:19b).

God sent Gabriel to answer Daniel and in his answer indicated something of the relationship Daniel had with the Lord. Gabriel told him in verse 23, *"you are highly esteemed"* or *"greatly beloved" (*NKJV*)*. Gabriel then gave him a vision of the Seventy Weeks set *"for your people and your holy city"* (9:24). God was far from finished with His people Israel. He promised to deal fully with transgression and make atonement for sin so that everlasting righteousness might arise. Jerusalem would be rebuilt and the promised Messiah would come, but Jerusalem would continually face much conflict and desolation. Still, God would ultimately triumph.

In 534 BC Daniel (about age 85), the *"man greatly beloved"* (10:11, 19), received yet another vision and message. The account of this vision is recorded in Daniel chapters 10, 11, and 12. The vision covered the period from Daniel's day all the way to the time when the Lord would set up His earthly kingdom and beyond when all His promises would be fulfilled. It was given to Daniel so that he could know and convey *"what will happen to your people in the lat-*

ter days" (10:14) and to assure him and the people of God of God's reign and God's rescue of His people. Then, the Lord had a personal message to Daniel. We will see that as we make applications to our own walk in Day Five.

For Me to Follow God

Daniel DAY FIVE

What an incredible life Daniel lived! What an incredible journey following God! We have looked at Daniel in some amazing circumstances. Right from the start he followed God and His Word wherever God placed him. He was confident in God's righteous ways. He knew the God of heaven, the Most High God, as the God who reveals mysteries, who could guide him regardless of the circumstances that threatened him. He found that the Lord of heaven reigned over all and was able to deal with his enemies in His way and in His timing. As a man who prayed with confidence because of his relationship with the God of heaven, Daniel found that the Lord never left him and never abandoned the plans he had for him or for His people. Although Daniel had reached the age of eighty-five, the Lord had something else to say to him, His beloved servant.

📖 Read Daniel 12:13, and record the heart of the promise of God to Daniel.

____

____

____

What does this say about following God?

____

____

____

____

God's command to Daniel was in essence, "Carry on all the way to the end. Keep on following Me like you have done for 85 years. Rest will come soon, and then a glorious resurrection and a gracious reward awaits you."

APPLY Are you being faithful following God in the "wherever" places He takes you? Are you confident in His righteous Word and His righteous ways?

____

____

____

____

"... For there is no authority except from God, and those which exist are established by God ... for it is a minister of God to you for good."
Romans 13:1b, 4a

Because Daniel had come to know and trust that God reigns supreme; because he had confidence that God raises up kings and puts down kings, he was able to trust the Lord even while working for the godless authorities in his life.

Do you trust the Ruler of heaven by respecting those who are your authorities? Take a moment to identify each of the authorities God has placed over you.

❒ Parents	❒ Policemen	❒ Governmental Leaders
❒ Husband	❒ Teachers	❒ Civic Leaders
❒ Employer	❒ Laws	❒ Church Leadership
❒ God	❒ Others ______________	

APPLY Are there any authorities toward whom you have been harboring a heart of rebellion?

____

____

____

____

"I also do my best to maintain always a blameless conscience both before God and before men."
Acts 24:16

Are there any "appeals" you need to make to keep a clear conscience toward God **and** your authorities?

____

____

____

____

One of the ways Daniel showed his trust in God and his submissive heart to those in authority over him was in the actions which led to his being thrown into the lion's den. Many have misinterpreted his willingness to disobey the law against prayer as justification for civil disobedience. But Daniel's actions were not a protest against an unjust law. He merely continued doing what he had always done. His submission to authority in this matter was expressed not in ceasing to pray, but in willingly accepting the consequences of his obedience to God. Daniel did not mount a protest rally or boycott Persia. He went to the lion's den without complaint. His submissive heart toward the king was reflected in the first words out of his mouth when the king came to check on him the next morning: *"O king, live forever!"* (Daniel 6:21).

When you have suffered injustice because of the stand of your faith, have you kept a submissive heart toward those God has allowed to be in authority, or has your heart been filled with bitterness and rebellion?

Is there any authority with whom you need to make things right?

____

____

____

We all have areas where **we** are the authority, a "kingdom" over which we are responsible—the home, the job, a little league team, a small group at church, and so forth. We are accountable to God for the way we "rule" in our "kingdom." He wants us to walk with a servant's heart, grateful to Him and depending on Him for wisdom and strength.

APPLY Nebuchadnezzar handled his kingdom with self-will, self-effort, and self-glory. How are you handling your kingdom? Do you see any of these in your life?

____

____

____

"There are six things which the LORD hates, yes, seven which are an abomination to Him." The first on the list is "haughty eyes" (Proverbs 6:16-18).

Think again of what Nebuchadnezzar faced in Daniel 4. He had to learn the hard way that the Lord *"is able to humble those who walk in pride"* (Daniel 4:37). Has this lesson exposed any areas of pride that need to be dealt with in your life? Have you been caught thinking too highly of yourself or your accomplishments? Sometimes what we defend the loudest and fight for the fiercest is an indicator of the infection of pride. It needs lancing and removing, and the infected area needs cleansing. Bring anything like this to the Lord, confessing it as sin. Submit whatever weaknesses you have to Him.

____

____

____

____

____

____

It is also important to thank Him for any blessings or successes He has given you. Hold those loosely as a gift from Him and use them as a gift to Him.

Another truth Daniel and his three friends teach us is how to handle the unexpected things in life. They certainly faced some surprises in their lives, and they faced them at a very tender age—first, an invading army and war, then capitulation and being moved to a foreign land. And not just any foreign land, it was Babylon! They faced a different school, a different career, and certainly a different future than they or their parents had planned for them. Of course, they didn't stop facing surprises once they were out of their teen years. Daniel faced them throughout his life, even after he passed the milestone of his eightieth birthday.

APPLY Have you faced any surprises recently? How have you responded to the unexpected (the big or little surprises)? (Check all that apply.)

❒ I have worried a lot.
❒ I am learning to go to the Lord in prayer.
❒ I have started seeking Him and His wisdom in the Bible.
❒ I stay on the phone a lot getting others' opinions.
❒ I have complained a lot.
❒ Sometimes I am tempted to blame God.

"The fear of the LORD is to hate evil; Pride and arrogance and the evil way, and the perverted mouth I hate."

Proverbs 8:13

Is your focus on the God of heaven?

____

____

____

"But to this one I will look, to him who is humble and contrite of spirit, and who trembles at My word." Isaiah 66:2b

Daniel faced some enemies **because He followed God.** Do you have some enemies because you are following God? Stay with what you know is true. Trust God with the results.

Think through what you have read and studied in this lesson. Are you surrendered to Following God "to the end?" Take some time to think through the life of Daniel.

Talk to the Lord about how you are "following" Him.

Lord, thank You for the life of Daniel, for his faithfulness to You, and for Your revelation to him passed down to me in Your Word. Thank you for Daniel's example of confidence **in You**—confidence in Your Word, in Your righteous ways, in Your ability to give just the right wisdom at just the right time, confidence in Your sovereign reign, and confidence in Your power to answer prayer. May I walk in that same confidence, surrendered to You and Your will. Lord, may my relationship with You grow in the way You desire, and I ask You to teach me to pray with the confidence Daniel had. That will make all the difference in how I walk and in how I pray in the places You take me. In Jesus' Name, Amen.

In light of all you have seen this week through the life of Daniel, write a prayer expressing the personal applications the Lord has shown you, or make a journal entry expressing what you have learned.

A General Chronology of the Life of Daniel

DATE	EVENTS	SCRIPTURE
619 BC— Birth	Daniel was born in Judah during the reign of the godly king, Josiah (640–609 BC).	2 Kings 23 2 Chronicles 35
609–605 BC Age 10 or 11 to 14	Daniel would have witnessed the corrupt reigns of Josiah's sons Jehoahaz and Eliakim (Jehoiakim).	2 Chronicles 36:1–5
605 BC Age 14	Jerusalem was conquered.	Daniel 1:1–2
605—Age 14	The first deportation of exiles, which included Daniel, Hananiah, Mishael, and Azariah.	Daniel 1:3–7, 8–16
605–602 BC Age 14 to 17	Daniel, Hananiah, Mishael, and Azariah went into training at the Royal Academy.	Daniel 1:4–5, 17–20
603/602 BC Age 16/17	Nebuchadnezzar's dream— "The Great Statue"	Daniel 2:1–49
602–562 (?)	Nebuchadnezzar's golden idol vision	Daniel 3:1–30
602–562 (?)	Nebuchadnezzar's dream—"The Great Tree"	Daniel 4:1–37
562— Age 57	Nebuchadnezzar died.	
562–556 Age 57–63	Short reigns of Evil-Merodach, Neriglissar, and Labashi-Marduk.	
556	Nabonidus, Nebuchadnezzar's son-in-law, began to rule.	
554–539	Nabonidus made his eldest son Belshazzar co-regent with himself.	
553—Age 66	Daniel's vision of the four beasts	Daniel 7:1–28
551—Age 68	Daniel's vision of the ram and the goat	Daniel 8:1–27
539—Age 80	Belshazzar's feast and defeat	Daniel 5:1–30
539—Age 80	Darius the Mede made king.	Daniel 5:31
539—Age 80	Daniel fasted and prayed, and the answer and vision of 70 weeks were given by the angel, Gabriel.	Daniel 9:1–27
538—Age 81	Daniel began serving as commissioner under Darius the Mede, also known as Cyrus. "Darius" was most likely a title of honor and not a proper name.	Daniel 1:21; 6:1–28;
534—Age 85	Daniel's 21 days of fasting and Vision of the Latter Days of Israel	Daniel 10:1–21; 11:1–45; 12:1–12
534—Age 85	Command to Daniel and comfort about His coming resurrection	Daniel 12:13

Haggai

A Call to Consider Your Ways

At a low point in the national and spiritual life of the people of God, Haggai appeared on the scene in Israel in 520 BC. He prophesied for only five months and was not heard from again, but his impact has endured for countless generations. In fact, through his book he will likely minister to you this week as you study, but before we begin, let's briefly review the time period in which Haggai lived. Israel had just come through a time of great turmoil and trial. The nation had experienced three waves of devastation and deportation under the Babylonians (605, 597, 586 BC). It was during this time that many citizens of Judah were taken into captivity for a period spanning seventy years (605–536 BC). The city of Jerusalem was destroyed, and worst of all, the glorious Temple Solomon had built was left in ruins (586 BC). All the treasures were gone, all the people were defeated; the nation was under the chastening hand of God Himself because of the people's idolatry and disobedience. But a fresh wind of change began to blow. In 538, King Cyrus of Persia issued a decree that the Jews should return to their land and rebuild the Temple (Ezra 1:1–3). Cyrus returned their sacred vessels and provided the necessary provisions and protection for the four-to-five month journey of over a thousand miles (1600 kilometers). In 537/536 BC, Zerubbabel led the first group back to

HAGGAI'S MINISTRY

Haggai began ministering in 520 BC, and ministered for only five months. His short prophecy of only two chapters impacted the nation of Israel in a significant way. Contemporaries of Haggai were Zechariah (who prophesied alongside him), Zerubbabel the Governor, and Joshua the High Priest.

WHEN DID HE PROPHESY?

550	500	450	400
HAGGAI ZECHARIAH		MALACHI	
Zerubbabel 536—First Return 536—Rebuilding the Temple 516—Temple completed		Ezra 458—Second Return Rebuilding the people	
586—Final Captivity Jerusalem and Temple destroyed		Nehemiah 445—Third Return Rebuilding the walls and the city of Jerusalem	The Jews are without a prophet, living under foreign rulers, and **AWAITING THE MESSIAH, THE GREATEST PROPHET OF ISRAEL.**
538–Decree of Cyrus to return	Queen Esther		
Amel-Marduk (Evil-Merodach) 562–560 Cyrus 539–530	Darius I 522–486 Xerxes 486–464	Artaxerxes 464–423 Socrates 470–399 Plato 428–348	Aristotle 384–322

miles (1600 kilometers). In 537/536 BC, Zerubbabel led the first group back to Israel and to the task at hand—rebuilding the Temple in Jerusalem (Ezra 1:4–11; 2:1–70). Suddenly there came renewed hope. [See *A Chronology of Ezra-Nehemiah-Haggai-Zechariah-Malachi* at the end of this lesson.]

When the people arrived they settled in and began the task. They finished the foundation but faced strong opposition from the Samaritans and other nations around them (Ezra 3:1–13; 4:1–5). After six years of opposition, the work stopped (530 BC), and for a decade (Ezra 4:24) this God-given task lay unfinished while the people went on with their new lives. In 520 BC the Lord brought up two prophets, Haggai and Zechariah, who began calling the people to their God-given responsibility (Ezra 5:1–2). Haggai led the people to consider their ways before the Lord. Would they follow God in what He had instructed them to do? Haggai's ministry can instruct us as we consider our ways and seek to walk in the joy of following God, obeying Him from a pure heart.

Haggai DAY ONE

FIRST THINGS FIRST—MAKING GOD'S PRIORITIES PREEMINENT

Haggai 1:1 opens in *"the second year of Darius the king."* This verse speaks of Darius I (Hystaspes) who became king over Persia in 521 BC, not Darius the Mede of Daniel 5:31 (539 BC). At that time Zerubbabel was Governor and Joshua was High Priest.

"Consider your ways."
Haggai 1:5

Who was Haggai? No background information is found anywhere in Scripture. We do know that his name means "festive" or "festal," which may indicate that he was born during one of the main Feasts of Israel (Unleavened Bread, Pentecost/Weeks, or Tabernacles). Haggai may have been an eyewitness of Solomon's Temple in its glory and in its destruction. If so, he would have been over seventy years of age at the time his book was written. However it is possible that he was born and lived in Babylon several years before coming to Israel during the First Return of 50,000 Jews. Either way, he would have known the shame of Israel's idolatry and disobedience that led to their captivity. He would have grieved over the idolatry of the land of Babylon with its many temples to various idols, and he would have longed to return to the covenant land of Abraham, Isaac, and Jacob. After sixteen years back in their homeland the Word of the Lord came to Haggai, and he began to proclaim God's message to a people in the midst of great hardship and need.

📖 Haggai 1:2 begins Haggai's first message. What is the main point of that verse?

____

____

____

____

📖 According to the Lord as recorded in Haggai 1:3–4, 9, what was the primary problem in Israel?

____

____

____

What was the focus of the people?

____

____

____

____

The people were saying it was not the right time to build the Temple (1:2). Haggai focused on the problem. Haggai did not place blame on the opposition that had caused the work to stop, for the problem was the people's focus—their concern only for their own houses—and their apathy and lethargy about the Temple. They were making sure they were well taken care of, often showing more concern for their own homes than for the Temple that was literally in shambles.

📖 What was the call of the LORD of Hosts in Haggai 1:5 and 1:7?

____

____

____

____

The Lord spoke very firmly, *"Consider your ways,"* or literally, *"Set your heart on your ways,"* on your lifestyles, on how you are living out your lives day after day. He wanted them to look at how they had made their houses and their personal concerns the priority of their lives. The Temple and the concerns of the Lord at that Temple were not preeminent to the people, nor were they secondary; they weren't even on the list, at least not for now. This was more than a concern over buildings and religious ceremonies. This had to do with their heart, their personal relationship with the LORD of Hosts, their covenant God.

"Set your heart on your ways" (Haggai 1:5), on your lifestyles, on how you are living out your lives day after day.

📖 What was a result of their lack of concern for the House of the Lord (1:6–11)?

____

____

____

____

____

Because of their refusal to rebuild the Temple as God had instructed them, the Lord withheld dew, and the land withheld its produce. A drought on all the land meant scarcity. The Lord touched the whole economy. There was a drought *"on men, on cattle, and on all the labor of your hands"* (v. 11). They sowed much, but harvested little. They ate and drank, but were not satisfied. They did not have adequate warmth and their wages disappeared like coins slipping through a bag with holes in it. The theme of considering your ways—which is alluded to five times in Haggai (1:5, 7; 2:15, 18)—was a clarion call for intense searching of **where** they were and **why** they were there. Haggai asked the people to look at their condition because of their disobedience.

Stop and think. Is there an area or item of disobedience that you have neglected to address? Are your ways pleasing to the Lord? Meditate on this paraphrase of Haggai's statement: "Set your heart on your ways . . . then 'go up' to the place of obedience."

Where are you now? Why are you there? Do you need to "go up" to the place of obedience?

It is important to remember that the people of Israel were in a conditional covenant. They should have made the connection with all that had been happening to them. Read what the Lord said about drought and scarcity in Deuteronomy 28:15, 23–24, and write your observations.

____

____

____

____

If the people obeyed they would experience the blessing of the Lord on their lands, their crops, and their families. Obedience results in blessings, but disobedience results in the opposite. If they disobeyed, He would make the heavens like brass and the ground like bronze—making it extremely difficult to grow crops in those conditions!

What was the solution (1:8)?

____

____

____

God called on them to *"Go up . . . bring wood and rebuild the temple."* This would please the Lord, and would glorify Him (1:8). Obedience to what the Lord had directed 16 years before was the main focus. Understanding that the Lord commanded them to rebuild the Temple, we are led to ask a very important question: What was so important about the Temple? We will see that in Day Two.

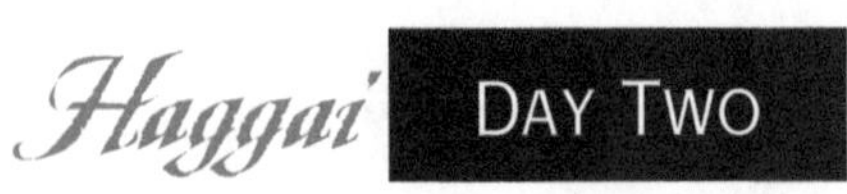

Rebuilding the Temple—Making God's Presence Preeminent

Why did God emphasize the rebuilding of the Temple in Haggai's day? What message was He seeking to get to His people? We find that answer in the original design of His "House" which He gave to Moses at Mount Sinai. The Tabernacle, a tent in the Wilderness, was the first "House" God commanded Israel to construct. This was God's idea, not something Moses conjured up in an effort to establish some sort of religious order. God had a very special design for His people and His "House" was a key component in that design.

📖 Read Exodus 25:1–8 (especially verse 8); 1 Kings 6:1, 12–13; and 8:12–13, 41–43. What is the main point of these verses? What is the main reason for this "House"?

____

____

____

____

____

____

📖 What do you see in 2 Corinthians 6:14–18 that coincides with Exodus 25 and 1 Kings 6 and 8?

____

____

____

____

____

"For we are the temple of the living God; just as God said, 'I WILL DWELL IN THEM AND WALK AMONG THEM; AND I WILL BE THEIR GOD, AND THEY SHALL BE MY PEOPLE.'"
2 Corinthians 6:16

The Lord wanted a "House" built among His people that He might permanently dwell with them. He wanted to walk with them as their God, and he wanted them to be His people. As in a family, He would be a Father to His people, and they would be sons and daughters walking with Him through all the events of life. This walk with God was the way life was always meant to be.

It is vital to understand the nature of this relationship. There is a difference between existing and living. Someone can exist in the finest house, with the most excellent food and drink, travel in the most luxurious form of transportation, and still not live the abundant life God desires for them. There are all kinds of ways to **exist**—poor ways, rich ways, and in-between ways. God knows we can exist in our "paneled houses" but we can't really **live** to our fullest potential apart from Him dwelling in our midst.

There is only one way to really live and that is in a right relationship with the Lord. That is the point of the Temple, the "House" of the Lord. In 1 Corinthians 6:19–20 we find that believers are the Temples of the Lord; the Lord Himself dwells in us by His Spirit. He who gives to all physical life and breath (Acts 17:25) **is our Life** (John 14:6; Philippians 1:21; Colossians 3:4). We will only experience the abundance of His life as we by faith obey Him, surrendering daily to His will, trusting Him to fill us with the abundance of His life—with the mark of the fruit of His Spirit (Ephesians 5:18–21; Galatians 5:22–25).

When the Lord sent Haggai and he began declaring the will and command of God, Zerubbabel the Governor of Judah and Joshua the High Priest took the lead in hearing and obeying God's Word through Haggai.

📖 Read Haggai 1:12, and describe their actions and attitudes.

Zerubbabel and Joshua and the remnant of the people (those who had returned from Babylon) obeyed the voice of the Lord. They honored Him as the Lord their God, and they honored Haggai as His prophet and spokesman. The people recognized that the Lord had sent Haggai and that what he spoke to them he had received from the Lord, not from his own self-initiated ministry. The heart of the people's response was their fear of the Lord. Verse 12 says *"the people showed reverence for the LORD,"* or literally, they "feared before the LORD," a picture of positioning themselves to seek His face and in that posture reverencing Him and seeking to please Him.

📖 As a result of the people's obedience, what **message** did the LORD send to them in Haggai's second sermon (1:13–15)?

"The fear of the LORD is the beginning of wisdom, and the knowledge of the Holy One is understanding."
Proverbs 9:10

The Lord wanted them to know He was glad to walk with them, for them to know the joy and the provision of His presence—*"I am with you."* They knew that meant the Lord was "*pleased*" (1:8). *"The LORD stirred up the spirit of Zerubbabel . . . and . . . of Joshua . . . and of the people."* They were energized because of their obedience.

📖 About one month later Haggai presented his third message. Read Haggai 2:1–3 (the first part of the sermon), and record the immediate concern of many of the people.

📖 Compare this with Ezra 3:12–13 (events from 15 or16 years earlier). What do you see?

There was a concern over how this Temple was going to look compared to Solomon's Temple. To those who had seen the first Temple this one seemed *"like nothing in comparison."* Haggai may have been referring to his own evaluation as an eyewitness as well (Haggai 2:3). The response in Ezra 3:12–13 after the foundation had been laid also focused on the comparison with Solomon's Temple. At that point there was loud weeping from the old men who had seen the first Temple. After fifteen or sixteen years and further construction, the grief was still felt. What was God's message in light of this concern of the people? We will see that in Day Three.

Experiencing the Presence and Provision of the Lord

In the midst of the people's comparisons of Zerubbabel's Temple with Solomon's Temple, the Lord had a very specific message for Haggai to deliver. The timing of this message is extremely significant, especially in light of the fuller revelation of Jesus Christ. It occurred on the twenty-first day of the seventh month (*Tishri*) or October 17, 520 BC. That would have been the last day of the Feast of Tabernacles, the feast that celebrated God's **presence** and **provision** throughout their wilderness journey (see Leviticus 23:39–44). It had been about 925 years since God had made His promises to Israel (1445–520 BC). For the people in Haggai's day this was a time when His **presence** and His **provision** would have been considered absolutely essential, just as they had been in the Wilderness in the past. The Lord wanted to remind them of the promise of His presence in their present need. And He wanted them to see beyond the present, beyond their limitations, to the bigger plans and promises of God for the future.

"'But now take courage' . . . declares the LORD . . .'and work; for I am with you,' declares the LORD of hosts."
Haggai 2:4

What specific truths and promises did the Lord give to Zerubbabel, Joshua, and the people (Haggai 2:4–5)?

____

____

____

____

____

What event did God call to mind?

____

____

____

____

"Be strong" or *"take courage and work; for I am with you."* For the task they faced, the Lord promised His presence once again, reminding them of the promise He made when they came out of Egypt—His presence would go with them and be in their midst. That meant His provision would be

available for all their needs and for whatever He called them to do (see Exodus 29:45–46; 33:12–16; 34:8–10). There was no need to fear because He would be with them personally through the presence of His Spirit.

"If any man is thirsty, let him come to Me and drink. He who believes in Me, as the Scripture said, 'From his innermost being shall flow rivers of living water.'" John 7:37–38

"We interrupt this study on the second chapter of Haggai to bring you a special revelation from the New Testament!"

What Jesus did and said on **this day** 550 years **later** is worthy of note. The events of John 7:37–39 occurred during the Feast of Tabernacles (or Booths). The people celebrated this feast the same as they did in Haggai's day—as a remembrance of the Wilderness experience of His presence and provision—that time when the Lord provided manna and fresh, flowing water as they needed. It was a reminder of the blessings of the coming Messiah, the Seed of Abraham, Isaac, and Jacob (Isaiah 44:3).

📖 Read John 7:37–39. What was [and is] Jesus' invitation and promise?

____

____

____

____

____

Jesus cried out to any who were thirsty, for He knew the deepest needs of each man and woman. They could have their thirst quenched by Him if they would come to Him. That meant believing in Him, and through that belief they would find rivers of Living Water by the power and presence of the Holy Spirit. This Living Water could be accessed after Jesus was glorified in His death, resurrection and ascension.

Doctrine

THE STONE THE BUILDERS REJECTED

Psalm 118:25 says, *"O Lord, do save, we beseech Thee; O Lord, we beseech Thee, do send prosperity."* That verse was spoken at the Feast of Tabernacles as the priests made their processions around the altar. The context of that verse (Psalm 118:22–29) mentions the stone the builders rejected and calls on the Lord to save now ("Hosanna"). As Jesus the Savior walked and taught among the Jews, many failed to recognize Him and eventually rejected Him as their Messiah. The Cornerstone they shouted and sung about in their festivities, they rejected when He stood before them. How easy it is to miss the very messenger or message that God has sent even though he stands right before us.

To better understand all that Jesus said it is important to see the historical context in which Jesus gave His invitation and promise. On each day of the Feast there would be several burnt offerings plus a sin offering. In addition, at the first of each day, the High Priest would walk to the Pool of Siloam south of the Temple area in Jerusalem, fill a golden pitcher with water and come with great procession back through the Watergate at the south side of the Temple area. His arrival was signaled by the sounding of trumpets (3 times) and the shout by the people (Isaiah 12:3). As the procession went around the altar, the Temple choirs sang Psalm 113—118 (the *Hallel*). Then at the time of the morning sacrifice, the water was poured out before the Lord.

The seventh day was *"the great day of the Feast"* (John 7:37) when there would be seven processions around the altar. With each procession the priests chanted Psalm 118:25, *"O Lord, do save, we beseech Thee; O Lord, we beseech Thee, do send prosperity."* In **this place** on **this same day** over 500 years before, Haggai had assured the people of the Spirit's presence and provision, and of His prosperity for the God-given task before them (Haggai 2:4–5). On **this day** of the Feast, Jesus cried out, *"If any man is thirsty, let him come to Me and drink."* Jesus' promise to those who believed in Him was Living Water—the Life and Fruit of the Spirit, the forever presence and provision of the Spirit of God Himself.

"Now back to Haggai Chapter Two . . ."

📖 Read Haggai 2:6–9. The Lord gave several promises. List those given in this passage.

____

____

____

____

____

> **"'The latter glory of this house will be greater than the former,' says the LORD of hosts, 'and in this place I shall give peace,' declares the LORD of hosts."**
> **Haggai 2:9**

The Lord promised to shake the heavens, the earth, the sea and land as well as the nations. The Lord promised that *"this House"* would be filled with glory greater than that of Solomon's day. The Lord who owns all the silver and gold could not only assure a greater splendor, but He also assured Haggai and those who listened to Haggai's prophecy that He would one day give peace *"in this place."*

📖 Read Haggai 2:7–9 with Zechariah 2:5, 10–11 (proclaimed 4 months later). What similarities do you see?

____

____

____

____

The words of the Lord imply that the silver and gold of the nations will come to the House of the Lord in Jerusalem and the glory of the House (the Temple) will be greater than ever. There will be a God-given peace—no nations threatening or warring against Jerusalem or Israel in any way.

In Zechariah the Lord Himself will be the wall of fire around Jerusalem and the glory in her midst. He will personally dwell in her midst, and many nations will come to the Lord and become His people. Both of these prophets were speaking the heart of God to the people and seeking to encourage, strengthen, and give them a confident hope in His plans for them.

All God ever wanted was to reveal Himself and His glory to a responsive creation who would in turn love Him with all their heart, mind, soul, and strength and reflect Him to others throughout the world. He still longs for us to know Him and honor Him as our Lord and God. He has revealed Himself for that purpose, and continues to reveal Himself through His Word and the work of His Spirit. In His revelation concerning the Tabernacle/Temple, He gave us an illustration of what is necessary for us to walk with Him and for Him to dwell with us. However, it is very easy for us to get distracted with our own plans and "houses" and things and forget Him and His will. God is very patient. He continually works at getting our attention, revealing Himself, and teaching us about Himself and about how He wants us to live. God especially wants us to learn how to **experience Him as our Life**. He wants to live in us and through us, showing us His character, His truth, His love, and His goodness. God wants us to continually experience His presence and provision, and He has not yet completed all He has planned. What else awaits us? We will see that in Day Four.

JESUS—THE GLORY OF GOD

"I will fill this house with glory" (Haggai 2:7). Was this fulfilled in Jesus' first coming? In Luke 2:32, Simeon referred to the infant Jesus as *"the glory of Thy people Israel"* in recognition of Him as the Messiah born in Israel. Jesus will certainly be the glory of God in the millennial Temple, but in Herod's Temple the glory of Jesus seemed to be veiled to all but the few who had eyes of faith like Simeon and Anna (Luke 2:25–38). Christ's appearance certainly was not the same manifestation of the glory of God as in the Tabernacle or in Solomon's Temple. Besides that, the prophesied events (the shaking of heaven, earth, the sea, dry land and all the nations) that must happen before this glory appears, has not yet occurred (Haggai 2:6–7).

Experiencing the Promises of God Then and Now

Haggai presented his fourth sermon on December 18, two months after his third sermon. The Lord wanted His people to know what it meant to live in His presence, walking in purity and holiness, not only ceremonially or externally, but more importantly with purity of heart. God planned to use the brief ministry of this prophet in some lasting ways. The Lord wanted Haggai's messages to help the people take inventory of their lives and priorities, and to help them repent of their disobedience.

"'For I,' declares the Lord, 'will be a wall of fire around her, and I will be the glory in her midst.'"
Zechariah 2:5

Read Haggai 2:10–19 (several times if needed), and note the two main questions concerning what is holy and what is unclean. What was his main point in these questions?

___

___

___

___

___

Haggai's main point in these questions was to show that someone cannot transfer holiness nor cleanliness from one thing or person to another, but someone or something unclean can defile anything it touches. The holiness of a sacrifice cannot be transferred any more than health can, but any sin can defile and contaminate just as disease can. The offerings the people had given while refusing to rebuild the Temple were considered unclean. Their sacrifices were out of place. They were not in line with God's revealed Word or His clear way. Because they were coming from a heart of partial obedience (which is really disobedience), the people could look back on God's judgment on their land and the meagerness that resulted (2:15–17, 19). Now that they were obedient to God, they could look forward to His promised blessings (2:19).

APPLY Is there any partial obedience or lingering disobedience that has contaminated your fellowship with the Lord Jesus? Is there anything out of place or not in line with His Word or His way? Deal with this situation quickly.

The Lord wanted the people to know His blessings and His rich and full promises for the future. He gave Haggai another message (the fifth message), on the same day as he delivered the fourth message (December 18, 520).

Read Haggai 2:20–23. Summarize the Lord's promise.

___

___

___

The Lord had a message for Zerubbabel. In relationship to the kingdoms of earth, He promised to shake the heavens and the earth, topple thrones, and destroy the power of the kingdoms of the Gentiles (the nations). In relationship to Zerubbabel, the Lord spoke of him as *"My servant,"* a title used of David from whom he was descended (2 Samuel 3:18) and of the Messiah who would one day come from this same family line (Isaiah 42:1–9). He was chosen of the Lord, who promised to make him *"like a signet ring."*

What is the significance of this last message to Zerubbabel? Before the exile to Babylon, God had judged Zerubbabel's great-grandfather Jehoiakim for his wicked rule as king of Judah (609–598 BC [see Jeremiah 22:18–23]). The Lord judged Jehoiakim's son Coniah (also called Jehoiachin or Jeconiah) for his iniquity as well. He said that if Coniah were His signet ring, He would take him off His hand and give him into the hand of the Babylonians. Coniah ruled only three months and 10 days before being taken into captivity (598–597 BC [Jeremiah 22:24–27]). Then the Lord declared that none of Coniah's descendants would rule on the throne of David or in Judah (Jeremiah 22:30; 36:30). From Coniah on, there were no more kings in Judah from the Davidic line (Jeconiah's line). What is the significance of the Lord calling Zerubbabel *"My servant"* (Haggai 2:23), a term used of David and of the Messiah (2 Samuel 3:18; Isaiah 42:1–9), and also *"signet ring"*?

The picture of the signet ring is important at this point. The signet ring was used to seal official documents, and also served as a symbol of authority, honor, and power. It was equivalent to an official signature—**a signed guarantee.** A signet ring could be used as a pledge of full payment to come. Even the words associated with it all convey this importance—*signet, signature, significance, sign, signed.* (For biblical examples see Genesis 38:18; 41:42; Esther 3:10; 8:8; Daniel 6:17.)

How could Zerubbabel find encouragement in being called "*My servant*" and the Lord's "*signet ring*" if he was in the line of descendants from Jehoiakim? The Lord chose to bypass His curse on Jeconiah and work through Zerubbabel, even raising him up as His signet ring—His guarantee of a future Son of David who would rule in peace. Zerubbabel would not be a king, but he would be in the legal Davidic line leading to the Messiah through Joseph (Matthew 1:12) and in the line of Mary (Luke 3:27).

God assured Zerubbabel and the people of the land that the Lord would be victorious. There would be a day of greater glory when the Messiah—the greater Son of David—would rule from Jerusalem. The nations would follow Him and bring honor and wealth to Israel. The Lord chose Zerubbabel as His guarantee of those promises. God chose him to be part of the Davidic line, the Messianic line.

Though Zerubbabel did not see the full picture, he and the people received enough of a glimpse to be strengthened and encouraged to faithfully finish the Temple, anticipating the glory to come. God continued to encourage Zerubbabel, Joshua, and the people as they worked on the Temple. They had to face the harassment of the Samaritans and others who had helped stop the work more than ten years earlier. They still faced the pressures of those who compared this Temple with Solomon's Temple, and they also had to deal with limited resources. However, God used Haggai to encourage them and to call them to obedience and the vision of the greater glory to come.

THE BEAUTY OF OBEDIENCE

The Lord delights to see obedience and desires to bestow His blessings. Samuel said, *"Has the LORD as much delight in burnt offerings and sacrifices as in obeying the voice of the LORD? Behold, to obey is better than sacrifice, and to heed than the fat of rams"* (1 Samuel 15:22).

"Do not fear, for I am with you; do not anxiously look about you, for I am your God. I will strengthen you, surely I will help you, surely I will uphold you with My righteous right hand."

Isaiah 41:10

After Haggai's messages ceased, the Lord continued to speak through Zechariah. One passage from Zechariah's prophecies will give us a good picture of the Lord's continued encouragement and call to trust Him.

Read Zechariah 4:1–10 (prophecy given on February 15, 519, two months after Haggai's last message). There are two very familiar verses in this passage, verses 6 and 10. Now that you are aware of the historical setting and what you know from Haggai's messages, what do you see in these two verses?

____

____

____

____

____

____

____

What message was [and is] God sending?

____

____

____

____

____

____

Doctrine

THE PROMISED PEACE

Haggai 2:9 promises the peace of the Lord of hosts *"in this place."* This prophecy has not yet been fulfilled to its fullest extent. Isaiah 9:6–7 promises that the Messiah's reign will be marked by endless peace (Isaiah 2:4; 11:6–9; Micah 4:1–4). Jesus promised His disciples the indwelling presence of His Spirit and His peace (John 14:25–27). The fruit of His Spirit is peace (Galatians 5:22), and Jesus is the *"Prince of Peace"* (Isaiah 9:6-7). The Hebrew words, *Sar Shalom* ("Prince of Peace") refer to the one who not only brings peace, but also maintains peace. That peace will one day be seen over all the earth when He reigns as Messiah.

In Zechariah 4:6 Zerubbabel was reminded again that it was the Lord who would strengthen and bless. They would complete the Temple by His Spirit, not by Zerubbabel's or Israel's might and power—they had no might nor power. They were under Persian domination and were coming out of a very depressed economy.

In Zechariah 4:10 we see that while the Temple may have appeared small in comparison to Solomon's Temple, and the nation may have seemed insignificant compared to the vast Persian Empire, the Lord was watching over the whole earth. He was pleased with what He saw taking place at the Temple sight, even though some considered it small or even insignificant. His all-seeing eyes would take care of and rejoice over Zerubbabel through the construction and completion of His Temple.

The Temple was completed in 516 BC, seventy years after its destruction. Ezra 6:13–18 describes the completion of the Temple and the celebration that followed. The Lord has always wanted to walk with His people. He wants us to experience His presence. One day we will enter into the new heaven and new earth where His nature and character are fully revealed, His presence is most clearly manifested, every need is met, and every righteous desire is satisfied to the fullest (Revelation 21—22).

For Me to Follow God

Haggai **Day Five**

What would Haggai say to us today about **following God**? The first statement he would make might be, *"Consider your ways"*—honestly evaluating your priorities first. Are your priorities and God's priorities one and the same? If not, why not?

Are you following God's priorities, or do you have some misplaced priorities? What are the most important things in your life? *"Consider your ways."* Check those that apply.

☐ Making sure my house is "paneled" (furnishings, location, size).
☐ Making sure I spend time in the Word of God every day.
☐ Taking care of my finances. I want to catch up, then I want to get ahead.
☐ Making sure I spend time with my family seeking to help each member be all God wants him or her to be.
☐ Taking time to pray—thanking the Lord for all He has done, interceding for my family, my church, and its leaders, my leaders in government, people at work or in the neighborhood.
☐ I like sports a lot, especially________________________________.
☐ Spending time with other believers to encourage them and to be encouraged.
☐ There are some things I want to do, places to see, experiences to have.
☐ Investing time and money in the advancing of the gospel worldwide.
☐ There are some things I really want to buy.
☐ Being open and available to sharing the gospel where I live and work.
☐ I want to be more involved (have more prominence) in certain community activities.

Could it be that there is an area (or areas) of disobedience in your life? Perhaps the Lord has spoken to you through a verse of Scripture, a message, or a song, and you have ignored that message—you may have even tried to cover it over with something louder, or have run in the opposite direction from it (like Jonah). Now is the time to deal with this disobedience. As someone has wisely said, **"If not here, where? If not now, when? If not you, who?"** *"Consider your ways."*

Another area Haggai might emphasize is the promise of the presence of God. God wants to dwell with us. He wants us to walk—not **ahead** of Him, trying to control our own lives; not **behind** Him, rebelling against Him and His ways—but **with** Him, cooperating and enjoying the fellowship of the journey. Think about the many promises God has made and fulfilled to His people over the years.

We have seen how the Lord chose the Tabernacle, a tent, to picture His dwelling with His people. He always communicates in the language we understand. Moses and the people of Israel were living in tents at Mount Sinai—thus a tent was the exact picture to convey that God wanted to dwell with them. In Jewish history, the pillar of cloud by day and fire by night was often considered as a picture of a Shepherd leading His flock through the

"For thus says the LORD of hosts, 'Once more in a little while, I am going to shake the heavens and the earth, the sea also and the dry land.'"
Haggai 2:6

"...Who has despised the day of small things?"
Zechariah 4:10

land to places of food and water. Again, the Lord communicated in a way they understood—the language of shepherds. In the case of the pillar of cloud and fire, He would not only dwell with them as in a tent, He would be their Leader dwelling with them—He would be their Shepherd God.

The smallest act of obedience is never small to God. From it He can bring great things.

In the New Testament we see this picture again. In John 1:14, John chose to use a word often translated "dwelt" that literally means "tabernacled." What significance do you see in that word picture based on what you have learned about the Tabernacle/Temple of the Old Testament?

____

____

____

____

John testified that Jesus, the Word, became flesh and *"dwelt* (or tabernacled) *among us"* so that they beheld His glory in a way similar to the way the Israelites beheld the cloud of glory in the tent in the Wilderness. However, this glory was *"as of the only begotten from the Father, full of grace and truth."* In the tent of the Old Testament only Moses could talk face to face with God as friend to friend. In Jesus many could talk face to face with God as friend to friend. Then, as Christ prepared to go to the cross, knowing His days on earth were limited, He promised to send another Comforter, the Holy Spirit, one just like Himself, who would be with them forever and in them forever (John 14:16–18).

Think about your walk with the Lord and the presence of the Spirit in your life. Do you walk in recognition of His presence? Do you take Him places that grieve or quench Him or places that please and delight Him? *"Consider your ways."*

When I was in school hundreds of miles from home, I received one of those "I-needed-that" kind of letters from a friend with the words of Isaiah 41:10 written in it. That was a great encouragement to me in a time of particular pressure and discouragement. Are you at a pressure point?

Are you walking in recognition of His presence? Do you take Him to places that grieve or quench Him or to places that please and delight Him? "Consider your ways" (Haggai 1:5).

📖 Read Isaiah 41:10, and note what encouragement you find.

____

____

____

Is there a task God has given to you that seems too big, too uncertain from your point of view? Or has He given you a task that seems too small—one of those of which the Lord would say, "Don't despise *the day of small things*" (Zechariah 4:10)? Is it time to act instead of argue? Obey instead of whine? *"Consider your ways."* Follow the Lord. He never gives us something unless it fits into His plans. Trust Him.

Spend some time with the Lord in prayer.

Father, You have many wonderful plans for Your children, things You've had in mind since before Creation. Thank You for making me part of those plans. Thank You for calling me to Yourself and making me Your child. Thank You for Your presence in my life. I ask You to show me how to practice Your presence more consistently. Also there's much I need to learn about misplaced priorities and neglected obedience. Teach me about prompt obedience. Thank You for Your patience and mercy. May I walk more in the light of Your priorities and eternal promises and less in the dim and fading, faltering hopes this world gives. Thank You that Your Word is ever true and that Your Spirit is my guarantee of all Your promises, not only for now but for eternity. I love You. Teach me to love You more fully and more consistently till I see You face to face. In Jesus' Name, Amen.

WALKING WITH GOD

God wants to dwell with us. He wants us to walk with Him—not ahead of Him trying to control our own lives; not behind Him rebelling against Him and His ways—but with Him cooperating and enjoying the fellowship of the journey.

In light of all you have seen in Haggai and related passages of Scripture write a prayer to the Lord expressing your heart.

A Chronology of Ezra-Nehemiah-Haggai-Zechariah-Malachi

SCRIPTURE	DATE	EVENT
Isaiah 44:28	688 BC 538 BC	Prophecy about Cyrus being used by God to return His people to His land Fulfillment
Jeremiah 25:12	605 BC 539 BC	Prophecy of Babylon's judgment for the destruction of Jerusalem and captivity of God's people Fulfillment
Jeremiah 29:10	594 BC 536 BC	The people of God would be ruled by Babylon for 70 years and then return to Israel. The people return after 70 years (605–536 BC).
Some date the 70 year period from 586, when the Temple was destroyed, to 516, when the people finished and dedicated the Temple. The Temple in Jerusalem was the focal point of the nation of Israel.		
Daniel 5:17–30	539 BC	Daniel prophesied the fall of the Babylonian Empire and the victory of the Medes and Persians. The prophecy was immediately fulfilled.
2 Chronicles 36:22, 23; Ezra 1:1–3	538 BC	Cyrus' Decree
Ezra 1:4–11; 2:1–70	536 BC	FIRST RETURN led by Zerubbabel—4 month journey
Ezra 3:1–7	536 BC	Altar consecrated and Feast of Booths
Ezra 3:8–11	536 BC	Temple reconstruction begins. The foundation is completed, and there is a celebration by many.
Ezra 3:12–13	536 BC	Many grieve over comparison with First Temple (Solomon's Temple).
Ezra 4:1–5	536–530 BC	Opposition to Temple reconstruction
Ezra 4:24 Haggai 1:4	530–520 BC	No work on the Temple—People work on their own houses.
Ezra 5:1	520 BC	HAGGAI and ZECHARIAH begin prophesying.
Haggai 1:1–11	August 29, 520 BC	Haggai's FIRST Message (6th month, 1st day, 2nd year)
Ezra 5:2 Haggai 1:12–15	September 21, 520 BC	Temple construction begins (6th month, 24th day, 2nd year) Haggai's SECOND Message
Haggai 2:1–9	October 17, 520 BC	Haggai's THIRD Message (7th month, 21st day, 2nd year)
Zechariah 1:1–6	October-November, 520 BC	Zechariah begins prophesying.
Haggai 2:10–19	December 18, 520 BC	Haggai's FOURTH Message (9th month, 24th day, 2nd year)
Haggai 2:20–23	December 18, 520 BC	Haggai's FIFTH Message (9th month, 24th day, 2nd year)
Ezra 5:3–17; 6:1–14	519–518 BC	Temple work continues.
Zechariah 1:7—6:8	February 15, 519 BC	Zechariah's eight visions
Zechariah 6:9–15	February 16(?), 519 BC	Joshua's crowning as high priest
Zechariah 7–8	December 7, 518 BC	The call to hear, the promise of good
Ezra 6:15–18	March 12, 516 BC	Dedication of the Temple
Ezra 4:6	486 BC	Accusation is sent to Ahasuerus (Xerxes) against the inhabitants of Judah and Jerusalem.
Book of ESTHER	483–473 BC	
Zechariah 9—14	489 or later 480(?) BC	
Ezra 4:7–23	ca. 464–460 BC	Letter is written to Artaxerxes I, who then stops the rebuilding of the wall and city of Jerusalem.
Ezra 4:23; Nehemiah 1:2, 3	ca. 464–460 BC	The walls of Jerusalem are torn down again and the gates burned.
Ezra 7:1–10	458/457 BC	A summary of the SECOND RETURN under Ezra
Ezra 7:11–28	458 BC	The letter and decrees are given to Ezra in preparation for the journey to Israel.
Ezra 7:9; 8:1–20	Nisan 1–12, 458 BC (March/April)	Many join Ezra in preparing for the journey. Ezra calls for some Levites to join them in the journey.
Ezra 8:21–23	Nisan, 458 BC	Ezra calls for a time of fasting and seeking the Lord for His protection.

SCRIPTURE	DATE	EVENT
Ezra 8:24–30		Ezra distributes the silver, gold, and various vessels to be carried to the temple in Jerusalem.
Ezra 7:8, 9; 8:31, 32	Nisan 12–Ab 1, 458 BC	Ezra and the exiles depart for Jerusalem on the twelfth day of the first month, and arrive there on the first day of the fifth month.
Ezra 8:33–36	Ab, 458 BC	They deliver the gifts to the temple, then offer sacrifices and worship the Lord. Then they deliver the orders from King Artaxerxes to the various officials.
Ezra 9:1–15; 10:9	Chislev, 458 BC	Four months later, some of the leaders report that some in Israel have married foreign wives. Ezra begins to grieve and prays to the Lord.
Ezra 10:1–6	Chislev, 458 BC	The people gather together and Shecaniah calls for a covenant agreement to put away the foreign wives. Ezra agrees.
Ezra 10:7, 8	Chislev 17–19, 458 BC	They issue a proclamation calling for an assembly in Jerusalem in three days to deal with the problem of intermarriage with foreign wives.
Ezra 10:9–15	Chislev 20, 458 BC	The men of Judah and Benjamin gather in Jerusalem, and Ezra calls them to separate from the peoples of the land and from their foreign wives. The people agree and call for an orderly investigation into the matter.
Ezra 10:16–44	Tebeth 1, 458 BC through Nisan 1, 457 BC	Over a period of three months, Ezra and the leaders of the assembly in Jerusalem lead the investigation of each man in the presence of the elders and judges from each man's town—after which the men are called to put away their foreign wives and children.
Nehemiah 1—12	445 BC	THIRD RETURN, rebuilding of the walls, and restoration of the city under Nehemiah. He serves his first term as governor from 445 to 433 BC
Nehemiah 1:1	Month Chislev (November-December) 446 BC (20th year)	Nehemiah serving as Cupbearer to King Artaxerxes. It is in the twentieth year of the king's reign.
Nehemiah 1:2, 3		He receives a report on the distressful condition of Jerusalem from his brother Hanani.
Nehemiah 1:4–11; 2:1	Chislev, 446 BC to the month Nisan (March-April), 445 BC	Nehemiah continues to pray to the God of heaven about the situation in Jerusalem. He prays for four months.
Nehemiah 2:1–8	Nisan, 445 BC	By serving the king and queen, Nehemiah is given the opportunity to present his burden for the needs in Jerusalem.
Nehemiah 2:6–8; Daniel 9:25	Nisan, 445 BC	Some believe the decree of Artaxerxes giving Nehemiah permission and provisions to go to Jerusalem is a fulfillment of the prophecy in Daniel.
Nehemiah 2:9	Nisan-Ab, (April-July) 445 BC	Nehemiah travels with officers of the army and horsemen on a three to four month journey.
Nehemiah 2:11	Ab 1–3, 445 BC (ca. July 16–18)	Three-day wait upon arrival in Jerusalem
Nehemiah 2:12–15	Ab 3, 445 BC	Nehemiah leads a night inspection of the condition of the walls of Jerusalem.
Nehemiah 2:16–18	Ab 4, 445 BC (ca. July 19)	Nehemiah meets with the leaders and people of Jerusalem concerning the needs of the city and the rebuilding of the walls.
Nehemiah 2:19, 20		Opposition and distraction begins. Nehemiah faces them and begins the process of rebuilding.
Nehemiah 3:1–32	Ab 4, 445 BC	Nehemiah and the people begin work on the wall.
Nehemiah 4:1–6	Around the 29th day of Ab, 445 BC	In the midst of the threats and opposition of others, the wall was built to half its height only 26 days after construction began (half the time it took to complete the wall).
Nehemiah 4:7–23		The work continues in the face of threats and distractions from the enemies of the Jews.
Nehemiah 5:1–19		Nehemiah deals with problems in the Jewish community.
Nehemiah 6:1–14		Opposition continues, as does the building of the wall.
Nehemiah 6:15–19	Elul 25, 445 BC (September 10)	The wall is completed in 52 days to the praise and honor of the Lord God of Israel. (based on 30-day months)
Nehemiah 7:1–4		Nehemiah puts Hanani and Hananiah in charge of the city of Jerusalem.
Nehemiah 7:5–73		Nehemiah gathers the people and conducts a census.

SCRIPTURE	DATE	EVENT
Nehemiah 7:53; 8:1–12	Tishri 1, 445 BC (September 16)	Ezra and Nehemiah gather the people for instruction from the Law and the celebration of the Feast of Trumpets (seventh month, first day).
Nehemiah 8:13	Tishri 2, 445 BC (September 17)	Ezra leads a continuing study of the Law and finds the instructions for the upcoming Feast of Booths. The Day of Atonement (seventh month, tenth day) is probably celebrated as well.
Nehemiah 8:14–18	Tishri 15–21, 445 BC (Sept. 30-Oct. 6)	The people celebrate the Feast of Booths/Tabernacles from the fifteenth to the twenty-first of the month (seven days).
Nehemiah 8:18	Tishri 22, 445 BC (October 7)	A solemn assembly is held on the eighth day of the Feast.
Nehemiah 9:1–38; 10:1–39	Tishri 24, 445 BC (October 9)	The leaders (Ezra, Nehemiah, and others) and the people read the Law, confess their sins, worship the Lord, and establish and sign a renewal of their covenant with the Lord to walk in His law.
Nehemiah 11:1–36		The people settle in their respective towns, and several volunteer to live in Jerusalem to continue the rebuilding process.
Nehemiah 12:1–26		Nehemiah records the names of those who came with Zerubbabel in the first resettling and those who have worked alongside Nehemiah and Ezra.
Nehemiah 12:27–47; 13:1	Tishri, 445 BC (mid October)	Soon after the Feasts and the assemblies of the seventh month, the people celebrate the dedication of the wall with praise, singing, and the reading of the Word of God.
Nehemiah 13:1–3		All foreigners are excluded from Israel.
Nehemiah 13:6	433 BC	Nehemiah returns to King Artaxerxes in Babylon.
Nehemiah 13:4	433–430 BC (?)	Eliashib the high priest prepares a room for Tobiah in the Temple.
Book of MALACHI	ca. 433 BC–420 BC	Malachi prophesies.
Nehemiah 13:4–9	ca. sometime between 430 BC and 425 BC	Nehemiah returns to Jerusalem for a second term as governor. He evicts Tobiah from the Temple building and gives orders to cleanse those rooms.
Nehemiah 13:10–31	ca. 430 BC–415 BC	Nehemiah restores order in the Temple service, as well as in the day-to-day order of business, the Sabbath, marriage among the people of God, and the duties of priests and Levites.
With the completion of Malachi *and the last part of* Nehemiah*, the Old Testament writings were complete, awaiting the promised coming of the Messiah, the Lord Jesus Christ, in the fullness of time (Galatians 4:4; see also Genesis 49:10; Matthew 1; Mark 1; Luke 1–2; John 1).*		

Notes

Notes

Christ the Prophet

WORSHIPING IN SPIRIT AND TRUTH

When we think of the prophets of the Old and New Testaments, certainly none rival the majesty and power of the Lord Jesus Christ. He opened the Scriptures as no man ever could and spoke as no man ever spoke (see John 7:46). He prayed as no man ever prayed and walked as no man ever walked. He walked in truth and spoke truth in all He did. Jesus Christ fulfilled the prophecies of the Old Testament that spoke of **The Prophet to come**.

The call of any prophet was to listen faithfully to God and speak His word, nothing more, nothing less, and nothing else. Any added opinion was disobedience to the Lord and a distortion of His message. That message was always to bring people to a right relationship with the living Lord, to genuine

"And this is eternal life, that they may know Thee, the only true God, and Jesus Christ whom Thou hast sent."

John 17:3

WHO IS "THE PROPHET"?

The Lord Promised Moses in Deuteronomy 18:18–19 . . .	Jesus Christ Is . . .	The Scriptures Speak . . .
"I will raise up a prophet	"THE PROPHET"	*"This certainly is the Prophet." John 7:40; 4:19; 6:14; Acts 3:20–26*
from among their countrymen like you,	"THE SON OF ABRAHAM" "THE SON OF DAVID"	*"The son of Abraham . . ." Matthew 1:1; 27:37; John 4:9*
and I will put My words in his mouth,	"THE SON OF THE FATHER" "THE SON OF MAN" "A DISCIPLE"	*"I speak these things as the Father taught Me." John 8:26, 28; Isaiah 50:4*
and he shall speak to them all that I command him.	"THE MESSIAH" "THE ANOINTED ONE"	*"He anointed Me to preach the gospel . . ." Luke 4:18; John 12:49–50*
And it shall come about that whoever will not listen to My words which he shall speak in my name, I myself will require it of him."	"MY BELOVED SON" "MY CHOSEN ONE" "JUDGE	*"The Father . . . gave to the Son . . . authority to execute judgment. . . . As I hear I judge." John 5:26–30, 43; Matthew 12:18–81; 17:5; Luke 9:35; Acts 17:30–31*

worship in spirit and truth. Just before the eventful Passover week when Jesus prepared to give His life as the Passover Lamb, He gave this testimony of His life and ministry: *"For I did not speak on My own initiative, but the Father Himself who sent Me has given Me commandment, what to say, and what to speak. And I know that His commandment is eternal life; therefore the things I speak, I speak just as the Father told Me"* (John 12:49–50). That was true of the Lord Jesus in His life and ministry. Though we live 2,000 years later, through His Word we too can hear Him speak the Father's will, and through that we can come to worship Him in spirit and truth.

A PROPHET LIKE UNTO MOSES

The Lord has always wanted His people to walk in truth. That is His nature. He is the Truth and walking in truth is as natural to Him as breathing is to us. He speaks truth, lives truth, and delights in truth. Lies and deception have no part in His ways, His character, or His Kingdom. It is not just that He does not lie, Scripture teaches us that He **cannot** lie (Titus 1:2). When He chose Israel as His own people, He wanted them to walk in truth. All the laws He gave Moses were to help them walk in the truth and experience the freedom truth always brings. As He walked them out of Egypt and through the Wilderness, He sought to show them how they could encounter the blessed experience of following Him. When people did not walk in line with the truth, He dealt with them and showed Moses and the elders how to do the same. In the midst of those journeys, He made a promise to Moses. Today, we will look at that promise and see how that can help us walk more fully in the truth.

Put Yourself In Their Shoes

WHAT IS A PROPHET?

A prophet:

- is raised up by God
- is able to hear God
- speaks what He has heard from God
- is always true in what he says

📖 Read Deuteronomy 18, and answer the following discussion questions.

What is the main point of verses 9–14?

____

____

____

____

What is the main point of verses 20–22?

____

____

____

In general terms, how do verses 15–19 relate to verses 9–14 and verses 20–22? Is there a connection?

____

____

____

____

The Lord warned the people about the abominations of the nations then inhabiting the land of Canaan, practices so detestable and unlawful they required the immediate removal of those nations from the land. The Canaanites were guilty of child sacrifice, witchcraft, consulting mediums (psychics), sorcerers, and spiritists and things associated with all these. The Lord wanted His people to walk following Him in truth, not in the lies and deceptions of the occult. The Lord wanted His people to listen to **Him**, not to false teachers and spiritists. The Lord promised to raise up a Prophet who would lead the people in truth, in all He said. They must ever be cautious of one who would speak presumptuously out of his own thinking or out of the lies and superstitions connected with the gods of Canaan and the surrounding nations.

In looking at Deuteronomy 18:15–19, what was God's promise to Moses about **The Prophet** (18:15)?

___

___

___

Where would He come from (18:15)?

___

___

The Lord promised to raise up a Prophet from among their brethren, the chosen people of Israel. He would be a man like Moses raised up by God for them, to lead and guide them as Moses had done.

What was God's reasoning in providing for this **Prophet to come**? How were the people connected to this promise (18:16–17)?

___

___

___

___

When the Lord spoke at Horeb (Mount Sinai) the people were intensely afraid in the presence of the awesome majesty and holiness of God. The fire and smoke on the mountain, the flashes of lightning, and the thundering voice of God from the cloud caused them to fear for their very lives (Exodus 19:16–20; 20:18–19). In this intense encounter with the holiness and power of God, they asked Moses to be their mediator between God and them (Deuteronomy 5:23–33). This is the role every prophet of God fills.

"I will put My words in His mouth, and He shall speak to them all that I command Him."
Deuteronomy 18:18b

What would be the chief characteristic of this Prophet that God would raise up (18:18)?

___

___

___

What authority would this Prophet have (18:19)?

___

___

The Lord promised to put His words in the mouth of this Prophet so He would speak all that God commanded Him. He would speak in the name of the Lord, with the authority of the Lord. This would not be a self-promoting prophet; He would be God-centered and faithful to deliver only the messages God the Father gave Him to speak.

What would happen to the one who would not listen to this Prophet (18:19)?

____

____

____

The man or woman who heard this Prophet would be held accountable to answer to the Lord for how he responded to Him. Would people respond to Him with obedience or apathy or willful ignorance? All who listened to Him would have to answer for the way they responded to all they heard, implying accountability for how they obeyed. This not only refers to hearing the sound of this Prophet's voice, but to obeying from the heart the Lord's intent in the messages, the commands, and the statutes given.

What contrast does the Lord present in verses 20–22?

____

____

____

____

"'Let him who has My word speak My word in truth. What does straw have in common with grain?' declares the LORD. 'Is not My word like fire?' declares the LORD, 'and like a hammer which shatters a rock?'"
Jeremiah 23:28-29

📖 Read Jeremiah 23:9–32. Compare the message God gave through Jeremiah to God's message in Deuteronomy 18:20–22.

____

____

____

____

____

Some would presume to speak for the Lord, while others would boldly declare that their messages were from other gods. Such prophets should surely die. By checking their accuracy, one could be sure whether the prophets were speaking presumptuously or from their own imagination. One hundred percent accuracy was the requirement. Therefore, if a prophet's prophecy did not come true as it had been stated, this prophet was a false prophet, an imposter whose message should be ignored. Jeremiah describes the messages of false prophets as straw that offers no benefit whatsoever, while he describes the Lord's words as grain that feeds, nourishes, and strengthens.

The Lord told Moses that He would raise up a Prophet and would give Him the words to say. That Prophet is Jesus Christ (Acts 3:22), and God His Father gave Him the words He spoke on earth. How did that work out in the life of Jesus? We will see that in Day Two.

"I Will Put My Words in His Mouth"

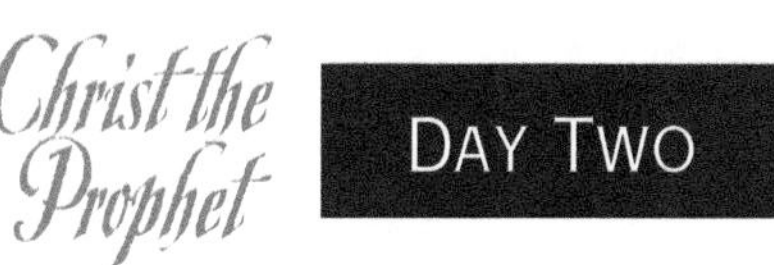

A prophet speaks for God. This is what every true prophet has done through the ages. But all of the Old Testament prophets were precursors to the One that God promised to raise up. How would **this Prophet** know what to say and when to say it? The Lord told Moses that He would be faithful to give this Prophet the message He was to speak, *"I will put My words in His mouth, and He shall speak to them all that I command Him"* (Deuteronomy 18:18). To speak for God, a Prophet had to hear from God. We will see that process at work in today's lesson.

PROPHET, PRIEST, AND KING

Jesus Christ came as the promised Prophet, Priest, and King, the one worthy and able to live and speak the truth in every situation, able to be the mediator between God and man, and able to reign in righteousness and peace.

There are over three hundred prophecies concerning the coming of the Messiah, and they speak of His various roles. Some speak of Him being the King, others of Him being our High Priest, and still others speak of Him being the Prophet.

Read the messianic prophecies in Isaiah 50:4–9. What do you see in verse 4 concerning what this Messiah will speak?

____

____

____

How was the Messiah to receive His instructions (50:4–5a)?

____

____

____

The Messiah would be one who spoke as a disciple, or a learner. He would learn from His Teacher and speak those words to the weary and downtrodden so that they would be sustained. The Hebrew word (*'uwth)* translated "*sustain*" refers to running to the aid of others, to support them and help them. Though He was God in the flesh, in His humanness the Messiah would learn by personal experience how to teach others, how to encourage others, how to run to the aid of others. He would learn this as He was awakened morning by morning to *"listen as a disciple"* (or learner). The ear of the Messiah, the God-Man, would be opened to hear and obey all the commands God the Father would give.

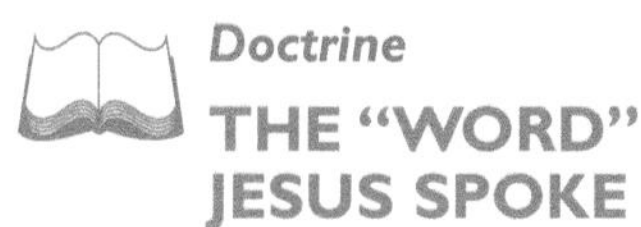

Doctrine

THE "WORD" JESUS SPOKE

The Hebrew word, *dabar,* translated "a word" in Isaiah 50:4, is used 225 times in the Old Testament to speak of the *"word of the LORD,"* the word of prophetic revelation. The Messiah in Isaiah 50 would also be the prophesied Prophet raised up by the Lord.

What is revealed about the heart of this Messiah (50:5–6)?

____

____

____

Where was His confidence (50:7–9)?

____

____

____

The Messiah in Isaiah 50 is revealed to have a heart of obedience and submission even to the point of humiliation, a humiliation the New Testament graphically pictures in crucifixion. He would be surrendered to the Father, confident in His help. He would walk into death knowing He would come out of His tomb in glorious resurrection.

📖 Read Mark 1:35–38, and answer the questions below.

What do you discover about Jesus in Mark 1:35? (Note this was after a very long day of ministry in Capernaum.)

____

____

____

____

How does Mark 1:35 relate to Isaiah 50:4? What was Jesus' reply to their suggestion concerning the day's schedule (Mark 1:36–38)?

____

____

____

____

"For I did not speak on My own initiative, but the Father Himself who sent Me has given Me commandment, what to say, and what to speak. And I know that His commandment is eternal life; therefore the things I speak, I speak just as the Father has told Me."

John 12:49-50

Jesus arose while it was still dark, and went out to a lonely place outside the city of Capernaum, perhaps somewhere along the shore of the Sea of Galilee or in the hills surrounding that lake. There He spent time with His Father listening with a learner's heart as described in Isaiah 50:4. When the disciples found Him, they informed Him that there were many yet in Capernaum who expected Him to minister there again that day. Jesus was quick to respond that He and they must go to other villages and proclaim the message the Father had given Him. This declaration of the truth was the purpose of His coming. Jesus followed the designs of His Father, listening to Him and obeying all He commanded.

📖 Read Luke 5:16. What is significant about this verse?

____

____

____

📖 Read John 7:14–18 and 8:28–30, and record what you discover about Jesus.

____

____

____

____

Jesus often slipped away to uninhabited areas away from the crowds and village businesses in order to spend time with His Father. Christ's relationship with the Father was His delight and the source of His ministry. The people (including some of the leaders) were amazed at what Jesus taught, wondering where He acquired such insight and how He taught with such power. Jesus made it plain that all He taught did not originate with Him but, in fact, came from God the Father. All that Christ said was true and righteous. In everything, He had the goal of pleasing His Father and bringing glory to Him. He wanted people to see and to know Him for who He was and surrender their lives to Him in worship and obedience.

John 8:30 tells us many came to believe in Him because of what He taught. What was at the heart of all Jesus spoke and taught? Read the next two verses (John 8:31–32), and write your findings.

Jesus heard from the Father what to speak, and He faithfully proclaimed the message His Father gave Him. He spoke the truth and promised that those who chose to abide in His word (those who would receive and live by His word) would know the truth and walk in freedom. Lies only divide and bring bondage. Truth sets a person free and leads to oneness. Jesus wanted His disciples walking in that freedom and oneness, so He came as a Prophet declaring the truth. As a result, those who followed Him and His word could be free—open, transparent, and unhindered in their relationship to the Father and others.

"It was for freedom that Christ set us free. . . . who hindered you from obeying the truth? . . . For you were called to freedom. . . ." Galatians 5:1a, 7b, 13a

Are you walking in the freedom Jesus desires for you? Are you open, transparent, and unhindered in your relationship with Him? What about your relationship with others—your spouse, your parents, your friends, fellow Christians? Is there an area of division, bondage, lack of oneness? Ask the Lord to reveal the truth that is missing in that relationship or that area of your life. He wants you walking in truth and freedom.

What else can we learn of this Prophet? As we look at His words to a woman wrapped up in many lies, we begin to see some added details in our portrait of this Prophet who spoke the words of God. We will discover those details in the Day Three discussion.

"I Perceive That You Are a Prophet"

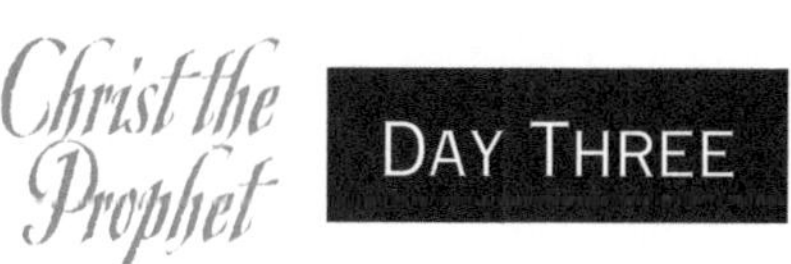

Would you know a prophet if you saw (or heard) one? What would he be like? The Lord said that the Prophet He would raise up out of Israel would *"speak to them all that I command Him."* (Deuteronomy 18:18). As we look through the photo album of the New Testament, we see several settings in which **this Prophet** did just that. Jesus Christ came as **The Prophesied Prophet**, able to live and speak the truth in every situation, faithfully speaking what the Father gave Him to say. We see one of the clearest examples of His ministry as **The Prophet** in an incident near the Samaritan village of Sychar, an occurrence that would forever change that village and its people.

Read John 4:1–42, and answer the questions throughout this Day Three discussion.

BRIDGING BARRIERS

There were several barriers that Jesus bridged to reach out to the Samaritan woman: **Racial and Religious**—Jew and Samaritan, **Gender**—Man and Woman, and **Character**—Prophet and Adulteress.

Let's establish the background of this incident. What did the woman from Sychar notice about Jesus in her first encounter (John 4:7–9)?

____

____

____

____

This incident came in the fall of AD 27 during the first year of Jesus' ministry. With His ministry growing in popularity and with the potential for controversy with the Pharisees in Judea, He chose to leave Judea and travel to Galilee. Christ chose the shorter route through Samaria, and approached the village of Sychar around noon. While the disciples went to gather some food, Jesus stayed at Jacob's well outside town, and there at the noon hour a woman from Sychar came to draw water. Jesus asked her for a drink. She recognized that He was a Jew and responded with surprise, perhaps even offense—a Jewish man asking a Samaritan woman for a drink was not the norm, *"for Jews have no dealings with Samaritans."*

Jesus was not offended by her response. Where did He direct her attention (4:10)?

____

____

____

SAMARITANS AND JEWS

The Samaritans were the race that originated from the intermarriage of the Assyrians with the Israelites after the Assyrian conquest of Israel in 722 BC. The Samaritans were despised by the Jews because of their continual idolatry and adaptation of foreign culture. With the intermarriage came many compromises of the Mosaic Law in family and society.

What was the woman's response (4:11–12)?

____

____

____

____

Jesus directed the woman's attention to God, specifically on what He wanted to give her—*"the gift of God"*—and on Himself as the one who could give her this gift. He spoke to her of *"living water."* She wanted to know where this living water was found and how He could give it to her since He had nothing with which to draw from the well. Was He greater than Jacob himself who gave the well, a well that was able to provide so abundantly for Jacob's family as well as for many generations since that day?

How did Jesus answer her question? Where was His focus (4:13–14)?

____

____

____

What was the woman's concern in John 4:15? Where was her focus?

____

____

____

____

Jesus spoke of water that would forever quench thirst, versus the water of Jacob's well that satisfied temporarily. Jesus promised a source of Living Water that would be like a perennial fountain satisfying forever, picturing everlasting life. Jeremiah 2:13 spoke of the Lord as a fountain of Living Water that Israel rejected. Here Jesus was offering a fountain of Living Water in Himself, but that point had not yet become clear to the woman. She was still thinking of literal water (H_2O). She was very interested in this kind of water that eternally quenched thirst since she was evidently thirsty and tired of coming to the well everyday.

"For My people have committed two evils: They have forsaken Me, the fountain of living waters, to hew for themselves cisterns, broken cisterns, that can hold no water."
Jeremiah 2:13

Upon what idea did Jesus focus in John 4:16, and how did the woman answer Him (4:17)?

____

____

____

____

____

What was the woman's response to Jesus' piercing statement (4:17–20)?

____

____

____

____

____

Note the woman's new focus in John 4:20. What did she bring up?

____

____

____

____

Jesus began dealing with the barriers to this Living Water. He pointed to a spiritual boulder stopping up the well. The woman admitted she did not have a husband and left it at that, but Jesus did not leave it there—she had to deal with her past and present sin, the five husbands and the current live-in boyfriend. Because of her sinful life, Jesus' pointed analysis of this Samaritan woman was a sore subject to her. Jesus dealt with her sin, but she decided she wanted to change the subject and talk about theology. She correctly perceived He was a prophet, for no ordinary man could analyze her life like Jesus had just done. Since He was a prophet they could talk about "prophet things" like which was the best place to worship, Jerusalem or Mount Gerizim.

With pinpoint accuracy, the Lord Jesus had a message for this woman (and for us). What did Jesus say about her worship (and Samaritan worship [4:21–22])?

____

____

____

____

📖 What was the heart of the message from **this Prophet**, Jesus (4:23–24)?

____

____

____

____

Did You Know?

MOUNT GERIZIM

Located in the Judea mountain range in central Israel, Mount Gerizim and Mount Ebal stand opposite one another with the site of Shechem resting in the valley between them. When Abraham first came into the land of Canaan, he built an altar at Shechem (Genesis 12:6–7). Mount Gerizim (with Mount Ebal) was the place of the reading of the Blessings and Curses of the Law when Israel entered the land under Joshua (Deuteronomy 11:29–20; 27:11–12; Joshua 8:30–35). The Samaritans placed a temple there since they considered this the best place for worship, not accepting Jerusalem as God's chosen place for the Temple (2 Chronicles 3:1–2; 6:4–11).

Jesus took the woman's focus off the **place** of worship, or the externals associated with any place, whether Mount Gerizim or Jerusalem, and focused her on the **Person** of worship, God the Father. Jesus confronted her doubts about what the Scriptures taught, and about the fact that the Jews truly did have God's revelation concerning salvation. The Samaritans, who only accepted the Pentateuch (Genesis—Deuteronomy), had corrupted their worship and refused what God had spoken through the many prophets and writers of the Old Testament. They did not know the truth. They worshiped a lie.

Jesus directed her attention on true worship of the Father and the fact that *"the hour"* was present for *"true worshipers"* to *"worship the Father in spirit and truth."* That *"hour"* was His death on the cross that would provide redemption and open the way to the Father for this woman and for any who would come and accept this redemptive gift of salvation. At the heart of Jesus' words was the truth that God is Spirit, and a relationship with Him must be on a spirit to Spirit level—from the heart and based on truth. The Father is seeking those who will worship Him based on the revelation of Scripture and the revelation of Jesus Christ, who is the Word and the Truth (John 1:1–5, 14; 14:6). The depth of our relationships is always based on the truth of revelation. The greater the understanding between two people and the stronger the commitment to truth in their relationship, the deeper the relationship can grow.

What do you find in the woman's statement in John 4:25? Compare this with what she told her fellow villagers in John 4:28–29.

____

____

____

____

What is significant about Jesus' response and revelation in John 4:26?

____

____

____

She quickly understood that He knew all about her, and the words He spoke about true worship being *"in spirit and truth"* pierced her heart. She believed (as did many other Samaritans) that a Messiah was coming. This Messiah would know and explain all that was necessary. **This Prophet** in her midst certainly told her all the things about her that would convince her of her need for Him. Then Jesus clearly stated who He was, literally, *"**I** who speak to you **am** He"* (emphasis added), pointing to Himself as the Messiah and using the language emphasizing the "I AM" as He did on several other occasions. He revealed who He was, and He revealed who she was. As a matter of fact, the way He exposed the condition of her heart as it truly was became the heart of her testimony to the townspeople—*"Come, see a Man who told me all things that I ever did"* (4:29).

THE SEVEN "I AM" STATEMENTS OF JESUS

I AM . . . the Bread of Life (John 6:35), . . . the Light of the World (8:12), . . . the Door of the Sheep (10:7, 9), . . . the Good Shepherd (10:11, 14), . . . the Resurrection and the Life (11:25–26), . . . the Way, the Truth, and the Life (14:6), . . . the True Vine (15:1, 5).

📖 What did the townspeople come to believe (4:30, 39–42)?

____

____

____

____

____

This Christ, the Messiah, the Prophet who speaks truth and leads people to know the truth, is the Savior of the world. He brings people to a true understanding of who God is in His nature and character. He reveals the meaning of all the Lord has said through the many prophets He has sent and through whom He has spoken in the Old Testament. He also reveals to men and women the truth about their own hearts, their true condition before God and what He requires of them, and He leads them to true worship of the one true God. Unlike the Old Testament Prophets however, Jesus doesn't only speak truth, He **is** truth—*"the way, the truth, and the life"* (John. 14:6).

"He Who Receives a Prophet"

What do you do with a prophet? Throughout the ages, prophets were controversial figures. Their messages required change, and not everyone wanted to change. No one was more controversial than Jesus, **The Prophet**. Quoting the Old Testament, Peter called Him a Stone to stumble over (1 Peter 2:8). The issue God addressed with Moses in Deuteronomy 18 (and in many other passages) was the issue of refusing and receiving—refusing what is a lie (that which takes a person further and further away from the true God), and receiving the truth (that which brings one into a right relationship with God). Truth builds relationships and brings one into closer fellowship and friendship, while lies divide and destroy—sometimes eating away at the relationship like cancer, and at other times slicing the relationship in two as with an enemy sword. When Jesus came proclaiming what the Father taught Him, He knew the life and death nature of what He said, and how important it was that it be received. Today we will look at the importance of receiving **this Prophet** and His word.

Near the end of His second year of ministry (fall of AD 28), Jesus sent out the Twelve instructing them about ministry and its rewards (Matthew 10:1–42). Read Matthew 10:40–41. What did Jesus say about a prophet in these two verses?

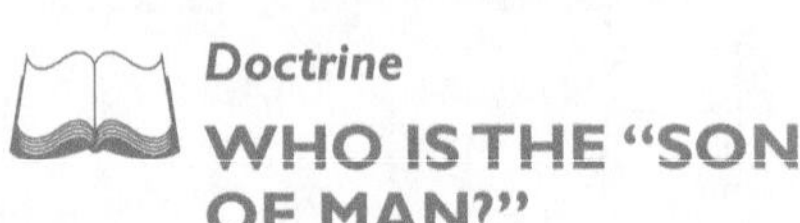

Doctrine

WHO IS THE "SON OF MAN?"

Jesus asked *"Who do people say that the Son of Man is?"* The disciples replied, *"Some say John the Baptist; and others Elijah; but still others, Jeremiah, or one of the prophets."* Then Jesus asked, *"But who do you say that I am?"* Peter answered, *"Thou art the Christ the Son of the Living God"* (Matthew 16:13–16).

Jesus promised that those who received the Twelve as His messengers (as they would receive a prophet) would receive a prophet's reward. In Matthew 10:40–41 Jesus used the word *dechomai,* which is translated *"receives."* This word refers to one who receives wholeheartedly, readily, and deliberately. It is literally, *"he who is receiving,"* with the idea of an ongoing reception and welcoming of the prophet and his message, not just a "tip of the hat" nod.

In light of the full meaning of *dechomai* (*"receives"*) in Matthew 10:40–41, how would Jesus want to be received as **The Prophet**?

How does this compare with Deuteronomy 18:19?

Extra Mile

A PROPHET WITHOUT HONOR

How did the people of Nazareth (Jesus' hometown) receive Him the first time He returned there after His ministry had begun? Read Luke 4:16–30 to discover their reception of, or reaction to Jesus.

If someone would be given a prophet's reward for receiving **one sent by Jesus,** then how much more would one be rewarded who **received Jesus** readily and deliberately with a whole heart. To receive Him as **The Prophet** sent from the Father was to receive the Father and His message of truth. At the same time, to reject Jesus and His message was to reject the Father as well. He stated in Deuteronomy 18:19, if anyone does not *"listen to My words which He shall speak in My name, I Myself will require it of him."*

What about Jesus' own family? How did His brothers and sisters receive Him? Jesus came to Nazareth for the first time in the early part of AD 28, near the beginning of His second year of ministry. He came once again in the fall of AD 28.

Read the account in Mark 6:1–4. Who is present?

What happened? What did Jesus do?

What was the response of the crowd?

Jesus came to Nazareth, and on the Sabbath went into the synagogue, as was His custom. The townspeople were there, including Mary, His four brothers, and at least two sisters. (There is no mention of Joseph at this time.) Jesus taught and obviously performed some miracles since miracles are mentioned in verse 2. Regardless of the wisdom of His teaching and the power of His miracles, the crowd took offense at Him.

"Jesus said to them, 'A prophet is not without honor except in his home town and among his own relatives and in his own household.'" Mark 6:4

What did Jesus say concerning the whole incident?

What does this tell you about the family situation, at least among His brothers and sisters?

Jesus spoke forthrightly. A prophet has no honor in his home town, among his own relatives, and in his own household. This statement sums up the whole crowd **including** Christ's own family. They did not believe in Him as the Messiah, and they were offended at what He taught. Only the power of God could change their hearts. The next time we hear of Jesus' brothers it was about a year later in the fall of AD 29 as they mockingly told Jesus to go up to the Feast of the Tabernacles and show Himself to His followers. Jesus told them His time had not yet fully come (John 7:1–9). In light of their rejection of Him, Jesus would trust His Father to draw them to Himself.

📖 How did the religious leaders receive Jesus as the Prophet? Read Matthew 23:29–39, and summarize what you find.

____

____

____

____

____

____

What was the heart of Jesus toward the people of Jerusalem (Matthew 23:37–39)?

____

____

____

____

____

____

Anyone can know forgiveness of sins and new life within by the presence and power of the Holy Spirit, if he or she will receive Jesus and the truth He has proclaimed.

Some of the multitudes who heard Jesus and saw His miracles considered Him to be a prophet, some even considered Him to be **The Prophet** who was to come (Matthew 21:11, 46; John 6:14; 7:40). Philip, a disciple of Jesus, saw Him as **The Prophet** (John 1:45). Even Herod Antipas the tetrarch over Galilee saw Jesus as a prophet of some sort (Matthew 14:1–2). However, the Pharisees and chief priests did not share these opinions or convictions; they saw Him as a threat to their political and religious power. Jesus rebuked their unbelieving hearts. He also wept over Jerusalem because she would not receive those sent to her by the Lord, nor would she receive **The Prophet**, the Lord Jesus. As a result judgment would soon come, but judgment would not have come to the people of Jerusalem if only they had believed the message of the prophets and the message of Jesus Christ.

So it is with us today. The Lord has spoken His Word, which we have recorded in the Old Testament, in the Gospels and Acts, in the Letters written by the Apostles, and in the prophetic Revelation to John. Will we receive and heed His Word? In the early days of the Church, the apostle Peter told the leaders and people of Jerusalem, *"TO HIM YOU SHALL GIVE HEED in everything He says to you,"* for He was sent by God *"to bless you by turning every one of you from your wicked ways"* (Acts 3:22b, 26b). In turning from sin to Jesus Christ, they could know forgiveness of sins and new life by the power and presence of His Holy Spirit, the Spirit He had promised and prophesied just months before. That same promise holds true for us today, if we will receive Him and what He has said.

If you do not know Jesus Christ as your personal Lord and Savior, now is the time to settle that issue in your life. It is as simple as **receiving Him** into your life **readily, deliberately,** and **wholeheartedly**. You can turn to the end of this workbook to the section entitled **"How to Follow God"** and find step-by-step instructions on how to begin the journey of knowing and following Jesus Christ.

For Me to Follow God

Day Five

Jesus always spoke truth. Truth was behind every word He said, as it is in any word of inspired prophecy, whether it **directs** someone regarding what they should do in the present or whether it **reveals** what is to come in the future. The issue of receptivity coincides with the issue of truth. Will I, will you, receive **The Prophet's** words of command, or exhortation, or instruction? What about the words of things yet to happen? Will we live in the light of what He has revealed? Will we prepare? God will hold us accountable for the way we receive the message of **The Prophet**. Deuteronomy 18:19 states, *"And it shall come about that whoever will not listen to My words which He shall speak in My name, I Myself will require it of him."* We must answer to the Father and to Christ as both Prophet and Judge.

Doctrine

TRUTHFULNESS IN THE INNER MAN

God has always wanted truthfulness from the innermost part of a man or woman. The first question posed to Adam after he sinned was *"where are you?"* implying more than location. The Lord wanted Adam to admit where he was in his relationship with the Lord. He wanted Adam to admit why he was hiding and covering himself with fig leaves. God essentially asked Adam, "Where are you? What is true of you, Adam, in the inner man?" David declared, *"Behold, Thou dost desire truth in the innermost being"* (Psalm 51:6a). John 4 reminds us that the Father seeks those who will worship Him in spirit and truth—from the heart with a cleansed conscience. Ephesians 6 tells us the first piece of necessary armor is the belt of truth, which implies truthfulness, or an open, honest heart. God wants truthfulness to exude from our innermost being.

APPLY Are you hearing Him? Are You heeding Him? When do you spend time in His Word?

- ☐ In the morning
- ☐ At night
- ☐ On my lunch break
- ☐ Sometimes during the week
- ☐ Usually on Sunday morning
- ☐ Rarely
- ☐ I need to start spending more time in His Word.

Has God spoken to you about some things through this lesson? Have you heard Him clearly? Are you heeding what He has said?

____

____

____

Is your relationship with the Lord clear? Do you need to make restitution to someone, for something you have done or promised to do and have not yet done? Do you need to ask forgiveness for something you have said?

____

____

____

____

____

Is there an area of disobedience in your life that He has pinpointed?

____

____

Hear and heed what He has said to you. You will discover that as you apply truth to your life; you will experience the joyous freedom that He wants for you. *"You shall know the truth, and the truth shall make you free"* (John 8:32).

We get a glimpse of the wonders of the salvation the prophets proclaimed when we turn to Revelation 19:1–2, *"Hallelujah! Salvation and glory and power belong to our God; BECAUSE HIS JUDGMENTS ARE TRUE AND RIGHTEOUS. . . ."* As John saw and heard the proclamation of the Lord's salvation

Extra Mile

PROPHET AND JUDGE

As Moses and Samuel were both Prophet and Judge, so we see the same in Jesus—We read in Exodus 18:13–26 how Moses served as a judge for Israel in the Wilderness. Speaking of the way the Lord knew Moses face to face, and the way he performed so many mighty works, Deuteronomy 34:10 says: *"No prophet has risen in Israel like Moses."* In I Samuel 3:20 we read, *"Samuel was confirmed as a prophet of the LORD,"* and I Samuel 7:15 declares that *"Samuel judged Israel all the days of his life."* The Lord Jesus is also Prophet and Judge (Matthew 13:57; Luke 13:33; John 5:24–30; Acts 17:31; Revelation 19:11). Read John 5:19–47 and see how Jesus spoke of Himself as the Son of God, Son of Man, Judge, and the one about whom Moses wrote.

he was tempted to worship the angel who brought him the message, but the angel focused his attention on the heart of the message the Old Testament prophets gave—**"worship God"** (19:10). Then the angel pointed him to the heart of all prophecy, *"For the testimony of Jesus is the spirit of prophecy."* Jesus is both **The Prophet** and **The Message.**

We know the Lord Jesus prophesied of many things to come—His Return for His Church, His judgment of the nations, etc. How are we to live in the light of all He has prophesied?

📖 Read Revelation 22:6–9. What do you find about the words of God?

___

___

___

What does the Lord Jesus promise in verse 7?

___

___

___

What command did the angel give John in verse 9?

___

___

___

With the prophecy given in the Revelation to John, the Lord concluded His prophetic tapestry, and is now working to carry it through to fulfillment in history. All these words given by God are *"faithful and true,"* never failing, never deceiving, never bringing someone into bondage. His words guide us in paths of righteousness and peace. He is continually bringing us into a walk of freedom. The theme of salvation was behind all the prophets He sent and all the messages they proclaimed. Jesus Himself promised *"I am coming quickly,"* and those who heed His words will be *blessed* (fully satisfied within [22:7]). This is the picture He painted of the day of His return when the Jews will say, *"BLESSED IS HE WHO COMES IN THE NAME OF THE LORD"* (Matthew 23:39). Second Thessalonians 1:7–10, on the other hand, paints a picture of both judgment and worship:

> *. . . when the Lord Jesus shall be revealed from heaven with His mighty angels in flaming fire, dealing out retribution to those who do not know God and to those who do not obey the gospel of our Lord Jesus. And these will pay the penalty of eternal destruction away from the presence of the Lord and from the glory of His power, when He comes to be glorified in His saints on that day, and to be marveled at among all who have believed—for our testimony to you was believed.*

The goal of Christ the Prophet, the One sent by the Father, is to bring us to worship and obey Him in spirit and truth.

The goal of all truth, all prophecy, all that God has spoken is to bring people to worship and obey Him. The goal of **Christ The Prophet**, the one sent by the Father, is to bring us to worship and obey Him in spirit and truth.

Spend some time with the Lord in prayer right now.

Lord, I honor You as **The Prophet**, the One who ever speaks the truth. Thank You for the freedom that comes as I apply Your Word throughout the landscape of my life—dealing with myself, in my family, in my relationships, in my finances, in my workplace, with other brothers and sisters in Christ, and with those who do not know You nor Your truth. May I always surrender to Truth, knowing You cannot lie. Open my eyes to see what Your Spirit reveals, and teach me to clearly hear and fully heed all You reveal. Teach me to walk in the light of Your true Word for today as well as in the light of what You have prophesied concerning the future. May I worship You in spirit and truth openly and transparently, surrendering to You every detail of life and experiencing the joyous freedom You came to give. In Jesus' Name, Amen.

Prayer of Application

In light of all you have learned this week write your own prayer to our Lord and Savior Jesus Christ, **The Prophet** who ever speaks Truth.

____

____

____

____

____

____

____

____

____

____

____

Notes

How to Follow God

Starting the Journey

Did you know that you have been on God's heart and mind for a long, long time? Even before time existed you were on His mind. He has always wanted you to know Him in a personal, purposeful relationship. He has a purpose for your life and it is founded upon His great love for you. You can be assured it is a good purpose and it lasts forever. Our time on this earth is only the beginning. God has a grand design that goes back into eternity past and reaches into eternity future. What is that design?

The Scriptures are clear about God's design for man—God created man to live and walk in oneness with Himself. Oneness with God means being in a relationship that is totally unselfish, totally satisfying, totally secure, righteous and pure in every way. That's what we were created for. If we walked in that kind of relationship with God we would glorify Him and bring pleasure to Him. Life would be right! Man was meant to live that way—pleasing to God and glorifying Him (giving a true estimate of who God is). Adam sinned and shattered his oneness with God. Ever since, man has come short of the glory of God: man does not and cannot please God or give a true estimate of God. Life is not right until a person is right with God. That is very clear as we look at the many people who walked across the pages of Scripture, both Old and New Testaments.

Jesus Christ came as the solution for this dilemma. Jesus Christ is the glory of God—the true estimate of who God is in every way. He pleased His Father in everything He did and said, and He came to restore oneness with God. He came to give man His power and grace to walk in oneness with God, to follow Him day by day enjoying the relationship for which he was created. In the process, man could begin to present a true picture of Who God is and experience knowing Him personally. You may be asking, "How do these facts impact my life today? How does this become real to me now? How can I begin the journey of following God in this way?" To come to know God personally means you must choose to receive Jesus Christ as your personal Savior and Lord.

- First of all, you must admit that you have sinned, that you are not walking in oneness with God, not pleasing Him or glorifying Him in your life (Romans 3:23; 6:23; 8:5–8).
- It means repenting of that sin—changing your mind, turning to God and turning away from sin—and by faith receiving His forgiveness based on His death on the Cross for you (Romans 3:21–26; 1 Peter 3:18).
- It means opening your life to receive Him as your living, resurrected Lord and Savior (John 1:12). He has promised to come and indwell you by His Spirit and live in you as the Savior and Master of your life (John 14:16-21; Romans 14:7–9).
- He wants to live His life through you—conforming you to His image, bearing His fruit through you and giving you power to reign in life (John 15:1,4–8; Romans 5:17; 7:4; 8:29, 37).

You can come to Him now. In your own words, simply tell Him you want to know Him personally and you willingly repent of your sin and receive His forgiveness and His life. Tell Him you want to follow Him forever (Romans 10:9–10, 13). Welcome to the Family of God and to the greatest journey of all!!!

Walking on the Journey

How do we follow Him day by day? Remember, Christ has given those who believe in Him everything pertaining to life and godliness, so that we no longer have to be slaves to our "flesh" and its corruption (2 Peter 1:3-4). Day by day He wants to empower us to live a life of love and joy, pleasing to Him and rewarding to us. That's why Ephesians 5:18 tells us to *"be filled with the Spirit"*—keep on being controlled by the Spirit who lives in you. He knows exactly what we need each day and we can trust Him to lead us (Proverbs 3:5–6). So how can we cooperate with Him in this journey together?

To walk with Him *day by day* means ...

- reading and listening to His Word day by day (Luke 10:39, 42; Colossians 3:16; Psalm 19:7-14; 119:9).
- spending time talking to Him in prayer (Philippians 4:6-7).
- realizing that God is God and you are not, and the role that means He has in your life.

This allows Him to work through your life as you fellowship, worship, pray and learn with other believers (Acts 2:42), and serve in the good works He has prepared for us to do—telling others who Jesus is and what His Word says, teaching and encouraging others, giving to help meet needs, helping others, etc. (Ephesians 2:10).

God's goal for each of us is that we be conformed to the image of His Son, Jesus Christ (Romans 8:29). But none of us will reach that goal of perfection until we are with Him in Heaven, for then *"we shall be like Him, because we shall see Him just as He is"* (1 John 3:2). For now, He wants us to follow Him faithfully, learning more each day. Every turn in the road, every trial and every blessing, is designed to bring us to a new depth of surrender to the Lord and His ways. He not only wants us to do His will, He desires that we surrender to His will His way. That takes trust—trust in His character, His plan and His goals (Proverbs 3:5–6).

As you continue this journey, and perhaps you've been following Him for a while, you must continue to listen carefully and follow closely. We never graduate from that. That sensitivity to God takes moment-by-moment surrender, dying to the impulses of our flesh to go our own way, saying no to the temptations of Satan to doubt God and His Word, and refusing the lures of the world to be unfaithful to the Lord who gave His life for us.

God desires that each of us come to maturity as sons and daughters: to that point where we are fully satisfied in Him and His ways, fully secure in His sovereign love, and walking in the full measure of His purity and holiness. If we are to clearly present the image of Christ for all to see, it will take daily surrender and daily seeking to follow Him wherever He leads, however He gets there (Luke 9:23–25). It's a faithful walk of trust through time into eternity. And it is worth everything. Trust Him. Listen carefully. Follow closely.

THE LEADER'S GUIDEBOOK

LIFE PRINCIPLES FROM THE PROPHETS OF THE OLD TESTAMENT

Preface

A Leader's Guide is for leaders. What does it mean to be a leader? The apostle Paul stands as one of the most noteworthy leaders in all of human history. In 1 Corinthians 3:10, Paul states, *"According to the grace of God which was given to me, as a wise master builder I laid a foundation, and another is building upon it. But let each man be careful how he builds upon it."* Upon close examination, that verse speaks volumes about leadership. As a small group leader you are building on a foundation laid by someone before you. What is the counsel of the Holy Spirit to us through the apostle Paul? What was he saying to the Corinthians that applies to us today?

First, Paul speaks of being a wise master builder. The Greek word he uses for master builder, *architekton*, is where we get our word, "architect." But *architekton* pictures more than simply the act of designing a building. It comes from two root words: *arche,* meaning "beginning," "origin," or "the person that begins something" and *tekton,* which means "bringing forth," "begetting," or "giving birth." *Architekton* carries the idea of one who leads forth, who goes first, who is the first to bring something to light. As a small group leader, you have the opportunity to guide people in the discovery of what it means to follow God. As you discuss each of the lessons and the people and concepts you will meet in those lessons, you and your group will learn some eternal truths about what it means to follow Jesus day by day.

Paul speaks of another aspect of being a Spirit-filled leader, and it is the essential work of *"the grace of God."* All Paul did, all he taught, every spiritual truth he helped others to see, was by the grace of God. It should be the same for you. You must depend on the Lord to be the Teacher for these lessons. By His Spirit, He will guide you in understanding His Word and His ways with His children. He will open the pages of Scripture. He alone knows the heart of each group member, and He alone has the wisdom you and your group need to walk through these lessons and to make the applications to daily life.

In 1 Corinthians 3:10, the Greek word for "*building*" refers to continuous, ongoing building, and pictures placing brick upon brick, stone upon stone. We are building day by day as we spend time with the Lord in His Word and obey what He is teaching us. As you walk through each lesson week after week, another stone can be added to the life of each group member, another truth can be built into each life, and another set of truths can be added to what God is doing in you as a group. Each group will be unique. Each week will be unique. The creativity and work of the Spirit of God will ebb and flow in different ways in each heart and in the group as a whole. You as a leader have the opportunity to encourage your group to be watching for the building work of the Spirit of God. Some insights will come when each is alone with the Lord. Other insights will not be seen until you come together as a group. The Spirit of God uses both means. It is a continuous adventure of discovering more about Him, His ways, and what it means to follow Him.

With this Leader's Guide, we want to come alongside and help you lead your small group in **following God** more closely and more consistently. Be a focused, attentive leader/builder. Paul said *"let* **each** *man be careful how he builds."* That means each of us. No one is exempt. As a small group facilitator, you will have the opportunity to lead others and experience one of the greatest times of building lives. Let us lead as "*careful*" builders, depending on the grace and the wisdom of God.

Following His leadership,

Wayne A. Barber — Eddie Rasnake — Richard L. Shepherd

Table of Contents

Causes of a Poor Study Group

The best way to become a better discussion leader is to regularly evaluate your group discussion sessions. The most effective leaders are those who consistently look for ways to improve.

But before you start preparing for your first group session, you need to know the problem areas that will most likely weaken the effectiveness of your study group. Commit now to have the best Bible study group that you can possibly have. Ask the Lord to motivate you as a group leader and to steer you away from bad habits.

How to Guarantee a Poor Discussion Group:

1. Prepare inadequately.
2. Show improper attitude toward people in the group (lack of acceptance).
3. Fail to create an atmosphere of freedom and ease.
4. Allow the discussion to wander aimlessly.
5. Dominate the discussion yourself.
6. Let a small minority dominate the discussion.
7. Leave the discussion "in the air," so to speak, without presenting any concluding statements or some type of closure.
8. Ask too many "telling" or "trying" questions. (Don't ask individuals in your group pointed or threatening questions that might bring embarrassment to them or make them feel uncomfortable.)
9. End the discussion without adequate application points.
10. Do the same thing every time.
11. Become resentful and angry when people disagree with you. After all, you did prepare. You are the leader!
12. End the discussion with an argument.
13. Never spend any time with the members of your group other than the designated discussion meeting time.

Helpful Hints

One of the best ways to learn to be an effective Bible discussion leader is to sit under a good model. If you have had the chance to be in a group with an effective facilitator, think about the things that made him or her effective. Though you can learn much and shape many convictions from those good models, you can also glean some valuable lessons on what not to do from those who didn't do such a good job. Bill Donahue has done a good job of categorizing the leader's role in facilitating dynamic discussion into four key actions. They are easy to remember as he links them to the acrostic ACTS:

*A leader ACTS to facilitate discussions by:

Acknowledging everyone who speaks during a discussion.

Clarifying what is being said and felt.

Taking it to the group as a means of generating discussion.

Summarizing what has been said.

*Taken from *Leading Life-Changing Small Groups* ©1996 by the Willow Creek Association. Used by permission of Zondervan Publishing House.

Make a point to give each group member ample opportunity to speak. Pay close attention to any nonverbal communication (i.e. facial expressions, body language, etc.) that group members may use, showing their desire to speak. The four actions in Bill Donahue's acrostic will guarantee to increase your effectiveness, which will translate into your group getting more out of the Bible study. After all, isn't that your biggest goal?

Dealing with Talkative Timothy

Throughout your experiences of leading small Bible study groups, you will learn that there will be several stereotypes who will follow you wherever you go. One of them is **"Talkative Timothy."** He will show up in virtually every small group you will ever lead. (Sometimes this stereotype group member shows up as "Talkative Tammy.") "Talkative Timothy" talks too much, dominates the discussion time, and gives less opportunity for others to share. What do you do with a group member who talks too much? Below you will find some helpful ideas on managing the "Talkative Timothy's" in your group.

The best defense is a good offense. To deal with "Talkative Timothy" before he becomes a problem, one thing you can do is establish as a ground rule that no one can talk twice until everyone who wants to talk has spoken at least once. Another important ground rule is "no interrupting." Still another solution is to go systematically around the group, directing questions to people by name. When all else fails, you can resort to a very practical approach of sitting beside "Talkative Timothy." When you make it harder for him (or her) to make eye contact with you, you will create less chances for him to talk.

After taking one or more of these combative measures, you may find that "Timothy" is still a problem. You may need to meet with him (or her) privately. Assure him that you value his input, but remind him that you want to hear the comments of others as well. One way to diplomatically approach "Timothy" is to privately ask him to help you draw the less talkative members into the discussion. Approaching "Timothy" in this fashion may turn your dilemma into an asset. Most importantly, remember to love "Talkative Timothy."

Silent Sally

Another person who inevitably shows up is **"Silent Sally."** She doesn't readily speak up. Sometimes her silence is because she doesn't yet feel comfortable enough with the group to share her thoughts. Sometimes it is simply because she fears being rejected. Often her silence is because she is too polite to interrupt and thus is headed off at the pass each time she wants to speak by more aggressive (and less sensitive) members of the group. It is not uncommon in a mixed group to find that "Silent Sally" is married to "Talkative Timothy." (Seriously!) Don't mistakenly interpret her silence as meaning that she has nothing to contribute. Often those who are slowest to speak will offer the most meaningful contributions to the group. You can help "Silent Sally" make those significant contributions. Below are some ideas.

Make sure, first of all, that you are creating an environment that makes people comfortable. In a tactful way, direct specific questions to the less talkative in the group. Be careful though, not to put them on the spot with the more difficult or controversial questions. Become their biggest fan—make sure you cheer them on when they do share. Give them a healthy dose of affirmation. Compliment them afterward for any insightful contributions they make. You may want to sit across from them in the group so that it is easier to notice any nonverbal cues they give you when they want to speak. You should also come to their defense if another group member responds to them in a negative, stifling way. As you pray for each group member, ask that the Lord would help the quiet ones in your group to feel more at ease during the discussion time. Most of all, love "Silent Sally," and accept her as she is—even when she is silent!

Tangent Tom

We have already looked at "Talkative Timothy" and "Silent Sally." Now let's look at another of those stereotypes who always show up. Let's call this person, **"Tangent Tom."** He is the kind of guy who loves to talk even when he has nothing to say. "Tangent Tom" loves to chase rabbits regardless of where they go. When he gets the floor, you never know where the discussion will lead. You need to understand that not all tangents are bad, for sometimes much can be gained from discussion that is a little "off the beaten path." But diversions must be balanced against the purpose of the group. What is fruitful for one member may be fruitless for everyone else. Below are some ideas to help you deal with "Tangent Tom."

Evaluating Tangents

Ask yourself, "How will this tangent affect my group's chances of finishing the lesson?" Another way to measure the value of a tangent is by asking, "Is this something that will benefit all or most of the group?" You also need to determine whether there is a practical, spiritual benefit to this tangent. Paul advised Timothy to refuse foolish and ignorant speculations, knowing that they produce quarrels. (See 2 Timothy 2:23.)

Addressing Tangents:

1) Keep pace of your time, and use the time factor as your ally when addressing "Tangent Tom." Tactfully respond, "That is an interesting subject, but since our lesson is on ________________, we'd better get back to our lesson if we are going to finish."
2) If the tangent is beneficial to one but fruitless to the rest of the group, offer to address that subject after class.
3) If the tangent is something that will benefit the group, you may want to say, "I'd like to talk about that more. Let's come back to that topic at the end of today's discussion, if we have time."
4) Be sure you understand what "Tangent Tom" is trying to say. It may be that he has a good and valid point, but has trouble expressing it or needs help in being more direct. Be careful not to quench someone whose heart is right, even if his methods aren't perfect. (See Proverbs 18:23.)

5) One suggestion for diffusing a strife-producing tangent is to point an imaginary shotgun at a spot outside the group and act like you are firing a shot. Then say, "That rabbit is dead. Now, where were we?"

6) If it is a continual problem, you may need to address it with this person privately.

7) Most of all, be patient with "Tangent Tom."God will use him in the group in ways that will surprise you!

Know–It-All Ned

The Scriptures are full of characters who struggled with the problem of pride. Unfortunately, pride isn't a problem reserved for the history books. It shows up today just as it did in the days the Scriptures were written. Pride is sometimes the root-problem of a know-it-all group member. **"Know-It-All Ned"** may have shown up in your group by this point. He may be an intellectual giant, or only a legend in his own mind. He can be very prideful and argumentative. "Ned" often wants his point chosen as the choice point, and he may be intolerant of any opposing views—sometimes to the point of making his displeasure known in very inappropriate ways. A discussion point tainted with the stench of pride is uninviting—no matter how well spoken! No one else in the group will want anything to do with this kind of attitude. How do you manage the "Know-It-All Ned's" who show up from time to time?

Evaluation

To deal with "Know-It-All Ned," you need to understand him. Sometimes the same type of action can be rooted in very different causes. You must ask yourself, "Why does 'Ned' come across as a know-it-all?" It may be that "Ned" has a vast reservoir of knowledge but hasn't matured in how he communicates it. Or perhaps "Ned" really doesn't know it all, but he tries to come across that way to hide his insecurities and feelings of inadequacy. Quite possibly, "Ned" is prideful and arrogant, and knows little of the Lord's ways in spite of the information and facts he has accumulated. Still another possibility is that Ned is a good man with a good heart who has a blind spot in the area of pride.

Application

"Know-It-All Ned" may be the most difficult person to deal with in your group, but God will use him in ways that will surprise you. Often it is the "Ned's" of the church that teach each of us what it means to love the unlovely in Gods strength, not our own. In 1 Thessalonians 5:14, the apostle Paul states, *"And we urge you, brethren, admonish the unruly, encourage the fainthearted, help the weak, be patient with all men."* In dealing with the "Ned's" you come across, start by assuming they are weak and need help until they give you reason to believe otherwise. Don't embarrass them by confronting them in public. Go to them in private if need be. Speak the truth in love. You may need to remind them of 1 Corinthians 13, that if we have all knowledge, but have not love, we are just making noise. First Corinthians is also where we are told, *"knowledge makes arrogant, but love edifies"* (8:1). Obviously there were some "Ned's" in the church at Corinth. If you sense that "Ned" is not weak or faint-hearted, but in fact is unruly, you will need to admonish him. Make sure you do so in private, but make sure you do it all the same. Proverbs 27:56 tells us, *"Better is open rebuke than love that is concealed. Faithful are the wounds of a friend, but deceitful are the kisses of an enemy."* Remember the last statement in 1 Thessalonians 5:14, *"be patient with all men."*

Agenda Alice

The last person we would like to introduce to you who will probably show up sooner or later is one we like to call **"Agenda Alice."** All of us from time to time can be sidetracked by our own agenda. Often the very thing we are most passionate about can be the thing that distracts us from our highest passion: Christ. Agendas often are not unbiblical, but imbalanced. At their root is usually tunnel-vision mixed with a desire for control. The small group, since it allows everyone to contribute to the discussion, affords "Agenda Alice" a platform to promote what she thinks is most important. This doesn't mean that she is wrong to avoid driving at night because opossums are being killed, but she is wrong to expect everyone to have the exact same conviction and calling that she does in the gray areas of Scripture. If not managed properly, she will either sidetrack the group from its main study objective or create a hostile environment in the group if she fails to bring people to her way of thinking. "Agenda Alice" can often be recognized by introductory catch phrases such as "Yes, but . . ." and "Well, I think. . . ." She is often critical of the group process and may become vocally critical of you. Here are some ideas on dealing with this type of person:

1) **Reaffirm** the group covenant.
At the formation of your group you should have taken time to define some ground rules for the group. Once is not enough to discuss these matters of group etiquette. Periodically remind everyone of their mutual commitment to one another.

2) **Remember** that the best defense is a good offense.
Don't wait until it is a problem to address a mutual vision for how the group will function.

3) **Refocus** on the task at hand.
The clearer you explain the objective of each session, the easier it is to stick to that objective and the harder you make it for people to redirect attention toward their own agenda. Enlist the whole group in bringing the discussion back to the topic at hand. Ask questions like, "What do the rest of you think about this passage?"

4) **Remind** the group, "Remember, this week's lesson is about ______________."

5) **Reprove** those who are disruptive.
Confront the person in private to see if you can reach an understanding. Suggest another arena for the issue to be addressed such as an optional meeting for those in the group who would like to discuss the issue.

Remember the words of St. Augustine: "In essentials unity, in non-essentials liberty, in all things charity."

Adding Spice and Creativity

One of the issues you will eventually have to combat in any group Bible study is the enemy of boredom. This enemy raises its ugly head from time to time, but it shouldn't. It is wrong to bore people with the Word of God! Often boredom results when leaders allow their processes to become too predictable. As small group leaders, we tend to do the same thing in the same way every single time. Yet God the Creator, who spoke everything into existence is infinitely creative! Think about it. He is the one who not only created animals in different shapes and sizes, but different colors as well. When He created food, He didn't make it all taste or feel the same. This God of creativity lives in us. We can trust Him to give us creative ideas that will keep our group times from becoming tired and mundane. Here are some ideas:

When you think of what you can change in your Bible study, think of the five senses: (sight, sound, smell, taste, and feel).

SIGHT:
One idea would be to have a theme night with decorations. Perhaps you know someone with dramatic instincts who could dress up in costume and deliver a message from the person you are studying that week. Draw some cartoons on a marker board or handout.

SOUND:
Play some background music before your group begins. Sing a hymn together that relates to the lesson. If you know of a song that really hits the main point of the lesson, play it at the beginning or end.

SMELL:

This may be the hardest sense to involve in your Bible study, but if you think of a creative way to incorporate this sense into the lesson, you can rest assured it will be memorable for your group.

TASTE:

Some lessons will have issues that can be related to taste (e.g. unleavened bread for the Passover, etc.). What about making things less formal by having snacks while you study? Have refreshments around a theme such as "Chili Night" or "Favorite Fruits."

FEEL:

Any way you can incorporate the sense of feel into a lesson will certainly make the content more invigorating. If weather permits, add variety by moving your group outside. Whatever you do, be sure that you don't allow your Bible study to become boring!

Handling an Obviously Wrong Comment

From time to time, each of us can say stupid things. Some of us, however, are better at it than others. The apostle Peter had his share of embarrassing moments. One minute, he was on the pinnacle of success, saying, *"Thou art the Christ, the Son of the Living God"* (Matthew 16:16), and the next minute, he was putting his foot in his mouth, trying to talk Jesus out of going to the cross. Proverbs 10:19 states, *"When there are many words, transgression is unavoidable. . . ."* What do you do when someone in the group says something that is obviously wrong? First of all, remember that how you deal with a situation like this not only affects the present, but the future. Here are some ideas:

1) Let the whole group tackle it and play referee/peacemaker. Say something like, "That is an interesting thought, what do the rest of you think?"
2) Empathize. ("I've thought that before too, but the Bible says. . . .")
3) Clarify to see if what they said is what they meant. ("What I think you are saying is. . . .")
4) Ask the question again, focusing on what the Bible passage actually says.
5) Give credit for the part of the answer that is right and affirm that before dealing with what is wrong.
6) If it is a non-essential, disagree agreeably. ("I respect your opinion, but I see it differently.") Let it go —some things aren't important enough to make a big deal about them.
7) Love and affirm the person, even if you reject the answer.

Transitioning to the Next Study

For those of you who have completed leading a **Following God** Group Bible Study, congratulations! You have successfully navigated the waters of small group discussion. You have utilized one of the most effective tools of ministry—one that was so much a priority with Jesus, He spent most of His time there with His small group of twelve. Hopefully yours has been a very positive and rewarding experience. At this stage you may be looking forward to a break. It is not too early however, to be thinking and planning for what you will do next. Hopefully you have seen God use this study and this process for growth in the lives of those who have participated with you. As God has worked in the group, members should be motivated to ask the question, "What next?" As they do, you need to be prepared to give an answer. Realize that you have built a certain amount of momentum with your present study that will make it easier to do another. You want to take advantage of that momentum. The following suggestions may be helpful as you transition your people toward further study of God's Word.

- ❑ Challenge your group members to share with others what they have learned, and to encourage them to participate next time.
- ❑ If what to study is a group choice rather than a church-wide or ministry-wide decision made by others, you will want to allow some time for input from the group members in deciding what to do next. The more they have ownership of the study, the more they will commit to it.
- ❑ It is important to have some kind of a break so that everyone doesn't become study weary. At our church, we always look for natural times to start and end a study. We take the summer off as well as Christmas, and we have found that having a break brings people back with renewed vigor. Even if you don't take a break from meeting, you might take a breather from homework—or even get together just for fellowship.
- ❑ If you are able to end this study knowing what you will study next, some of your group members may want to get a head start on the next study. Be prepared to put books in their hands early.
- ❑ Make sure you end your study with a vision for more. Take some time to remind your group of the importance of the Word of God. As D. L. Moody used to say, "The only way to keep a broken vessel full is to keep the faucet running."

Evaluation

Becoming a Better Discussion Leader

The questions listed below are tools to assist you in assessing your discussion group. From time to time in the Leader's Guide, you will be advised to read through this list of evaluation questions in order to help you decide what areas need improvement in your role as group leader. Each time you read through this list, something different may catch your attention, giving you tips on how to become the best group leader that you can possibly be.

Read through these questions with an open mind, asking the Lord to prick your heart with anything specific He would want you to apply.

1. Are the group discussion sessions beginning and ending on time?
2. Am I allowing the freedom of the Holy Spirit as I lead the group in the discussion?
3. Do I hold the group accountable for doing their homework?
4. Do we always begin our sessions with prayer?
5. Is the room arranged properly (seating in a circle or semicircle, proper ventilation, adequate teaching aids)?
6. Is each individual allowed equal opportunity in the discussion?
7. Do I successfully bridle the talkative ones?
8. Am I successfully encouraging the hesitant ones to participate in the discussion?
9. Do I redirect comments and questions to involve more people in the interaction, or do I always dominate the discussion?
10. Are the discussions flowing naturally, or do they take too many "side roads" (diversions)?
11. Do I show acceptance to those who convey ideas with which I do not agree?
12. Are my questions specific, brief and clear?
13. Do my questions provoke thought, or do they only require pat answers?
14. Does each group member feel free to contribute or question, or is there a threatening or unnecessarily tense atmosphere?
15. Am I allowing time for silence and thought without making everyone feel uneasy?
16. Am I allowing the group to correct any obviously wrong conclusions that are made by others, or by myself (either intentionally to capture the group's attention or unintentionally)?
17. Do I stifle thought and discussion by assigning a question to someone before the subject of that question has even been discussed? (It will often be productive to assign a question to a specific person, but if you call on one person before you throw out a question, everyone else takes a mental vacation!)
18. Do I summarize when brevity is of the essence?
19. Can I refrain from expressing an opinion or comment that someone else in the group could just as adequately express?

20. Do I occasionally vary in my methods of conducting the discussion?
21. Am I keeping the group properly motivated?
22. Am I occasionally rotating the leadership to help others develop leadership?
23. Am I leading the group to specifically apply the truths that are learned?
24. Do I follow through by asking the group how they have applied the truths that they have learned from previous lessons?
25. Am I praying for each group member?
26. Is there a growing openness and honesty among my group members?
27. Are the group study sessions enriching the lives of my group members?
28. Have I been adequately prepared?
29. How may I be better prepared for the next lesson's group discussion?
30. Do I reach the objective set for each discussion? If not, why not? What can I do to improve?
31. Am I allowing the discussion to bog down on one point at the expense of the rest of the lesson?
32. Are the members of the group individually reaching the conclusions that I want them to reach without my having to give them the conclusions?
33. Do I encourage the group members to share what they have learned?
34. Do I encourage them to share the applications they have discovered?
35. Do I whet their appetites for next week's lesson discussion?

Getting Started

The First Meeting of Your Bible Study Group

Main Objectives of the first meeting: The first meeting is devoted to establishing your group and setting the course that you will follow through the study. Your primary goals for this session should be to . . .

- ❑ Establish a sense of group identity by starting to get to know one another.
- ❑ Define some ground rules to help make the group time as effective as possible.
- ❑ Get the study materials into the hands of your group members.
- ❑ Create a sense of excitement and motivation for the study.
- ❑ Give assignments for next week.

Before the Session

You will be most comfortable in leading this introductory session if you are prepared as much as possible for what to expect. This means becoming familiar with the place you will meet, and the content you will cover, as well as understanding any time constraints you will have.

Location—Be sure that you not only know how to find the place where you will be meeting, but also have time to examine the setup and make any adjustments to the physical arrangements. You never get a second chance to make a first impression.

Curriculum—You will want to get a copy of the study in advance of the introductory session, and it will be helpful if you do the homework for Lesson One ahead of time. This will make it easier for you to be able to explain the layout of the homework. It will also give you a contagious enthusiasm for what your group will be studying in the coming week. You will want to have enough books on hand for the number of people you expect so that they can get started right away with the study. You may be able to make arrangements with your church or simply order books online. We would encourage you not to buy books for your members. Years of small group experience have taught that people take a study far more seriously when they make an investment in it.

Time—The type of group you are leading will determine the time format for your study. If you are doing this study for a Sunday morning time or other regular meeting time, the time constraints may already be prescribed for you. In any case, ideally you will want to allow forty-five minutes to an hour for discussion.

What to Expect

When you embark on the journey of leading a small group Bible study, you are stepping into the stream of the work of God. You are joining in the process of helping others move toward spiritual maturity. As a small group leader, you are positioned to be a real catalyst in the lives of your group members, helping them to grow in their relationships with God. But you must remember, first and foremost, that whenever you step up to leadership in the kingdom of God, you are stepping down to serve. Jesus made it clear that leadership in the kingdom is not like leadership in the world. In Matthew 20:25, Jesus said, *"You know that the rulers of the Gentiles lord it over them, and their great men exercise authority over them."* That is the world's way to lead. But in Matthew 20:26–27, He continues, *"It is not so among you, but whoever wishes to become great among you shall be your servant, and whoever wishes to be first among you shall be your slave."* Your job as a small group leader is not to teach the group everything you have learned, but rather, to help them learn for themselves and from each other. It is a servant's role.

If you truly are to minister to the members of your group, you must start with understanding where they are, and join that with a vision of where you want to take them. In this introductory session, your group members will be experiencing several different emotions. They will be wondering, "Who is in my group?" and deciding "Do I like my group?" They will have a sense of excitement and anticipation, but also a sense of awkwardness as they try to find their place in this group. You will want to make sure that from the very beginning your group is founded with a sense of caring and acceptance. This is crucial if your group members are to open up and share what they are learning.

During the Session

OPENING: 5–10 MINUTES GETTING TO KNOW ONE ANOTHER

Opening Prayer—Remember that if it took the inspiration of God for people to write Scripture, it will also take His illumination for us to understand it. Have one of your group members open your time together in prayer.

Introductions—Take time to allow the group members to introduce themselves. Along with having the group members share their names, one way to add some interest is to have them add some descriptive information such as where they live or work. Just for fun, you could have them name their favorite breakfast cereal, most (or least) favorite vegetable, favorite cartoon character, their favorite city or country other than their own, etc.

Icebreaker—Take five or ten minutes to get the people comfortable in talking with each other. Since in many cases your small group will just now be getting to know one another, it will be helpful if you take some time to break the ice with some fun, non-threatening discussion. Below you will find a list of ideas for good icebreaker questions to get people talking.

____ What is the biggest risk you have ever taken?

____ If money were no object, where would you most like to take a vacation and why?

____ What is your favorite way to waste time?

____ If you weren't in the career you now have, what would have been your second choice for a career?

____ If you could have lived in any other time, in what era or century would you have chosen to live (besides the expected spiritual answer of the time of Jesus)?

____ If you became blind right now, what would you miss seeing the most?

____ Who is the most famous person you've known or met?

____ What do you miss most about being a kid?

____ What teacher had the biggest impact on you in school (good or bad)?

____ Of the things money can buy, what would you most like to have?

____ What is your biggest fear?

____ If you could give one miracle to someone else, what would it be (and to whom)?

____ Tell about your first job.

____ Who is the best or worst boss you ever had?

____ Who was your hero growing up and why?

DEFINING THE GROUP: 5–10 MINUTES SETTING SOME GROUND RULES

There are several ways you can lay the tracks on which your group can run. One is simply to hand out a list of suggested commitments the members should make to the group. Another would be to hand out 3x5 cards and have the members themselves write down two or three commitments they would like to see everyone live out. You could then compile these into the five top ones to share at the following meeting. A third option is to list three (or more) commitments you are making to the group and then ask that they make three commitments back to you in return.

Here are some ideas for the types of ground rules that make for a good small group:

Leader:

____ To always arrive prepared

____ To keep the group on track so you make the most of the group's time

____ To not dominate the discussion by simply teaching the lesson

____ To pray for the group members

____ To not belittle or embarrass anyone's answers

____ To bring each session to closure and end on time

Member:

____ To do my homework

____ To arrive on time

____ To participate in the discussion

____ To not cut others off as they share

____ To respect the different views of other members

____ To not dominate the discussion

It is possible that your group may not need to formalize a group covenant, but you should not be afraid to expect a commitment from your group members. They will all benefit from defining the group up front.

INTRODUCTION TO THE STUDY: 15–20 MINUTES

As you introduce the study to the group members, your goal is to begin to create a sense of excitement about the Bible characters and applications that will be discussed. The most important question for you to answer in this session is "Why should I study ________?" You need to be prepared to guide them to finding that answer. Take time to give a brief overview of each leson.

CLOSING: 5–10 MINUTES

❑ Give homework for next week. In addition to simply reminding the group members to do their homework, if time allows, you might give them 5–10 minutes to get started on their homework for the first lesson.

❑ Key components for closing out your time are **a)** to review anything of which you feel they should be reminded, and **b)** to close in prayer. If time allows, you may want to encourage several to pray.

Samuel

"Only fear the L*ORD and serve Him in truth with all your heart; for consider what great things He has done for you."*

Before the Session

- ❒ Be sure to familiarize yourself with the chart on the life and ministry of Samuel at the end of Lesson 1.
- ❒ Spread your homework out rather than trying to cram everything into one afternoon or night. Perhaps use this as your daily quiet time.
- ❒ Always look for some personal applications which the Lord may have you share with the group. The more impact the Word makes in your heart the more enthusiasm you will communicate.
- ❒ As you study, write down any good discussion questions as they come to mind.
- ❒ **For additional study,** you can grasp the times in which Samuel lived and better prepare yourself towards leading the discussion by reading the book of Judges and/or Ruth. You may also want to look at some of the other **Following God** lessons centered around this period—**Gideon** and **Samson** in *Following God: Life Principles from the Old Testament*, **Ruth** and **Hannah** in *Following God: Life Principles from the Women of the Bible*, and **Saul** and **David** in *Following God: Life Principles from the Kings of the Old Testament*. The lessons in these **Following God**™ titles will help you see the times and the ways of the people in Samuel's day.
- ❒ A good Bible dictionary article on "Samuel" will give you more background information. Dictionaries often help you see the historical setting in which the man or woman lived.
- ❒ Be transparent before the Lord and before your group. We are all learners—that's the meaning of the word "disciple."

What to Expect

Samuel was born because of the surrender of his mother, Hannah, to the Lord's will. This attitude of surrender became an indelible characteristic of Samuel's life. Samuel's attitude was not genetically inherited, but it became evident as he learned to walk with the Lord, hearing Him and obeying His Word. Samuel's life, as is the case in all our lives, was a process of growth, of knowing the Lord at deeper and deeper levels, of hearing and obeying by faith. Studying the life of Samuel can help us know the Lord at greater depths of faith when we listen to His Word. If we will listen with a teachable heart we will learn much more readily.

It is quite possible that many in your group will experience new insights or rich applications from their study this week. Some will realize how far they have strayed from the Word of God. Others will be affirmed in the steps of obedience they have taken. Expect the Lord to do a fresh work in you as well as in the members of your group. He waits to show Himself strong toward *"those whose heart is fully His"* (see 1 Chronicles 16:9a). Some may have questions about the study or even about the validity of some portions of the Word of God. You can help them see the Bible as God's Word written in love. They can discover that this Book is eternal wisdom and is ever able to teach, reprove, correct, and train in righteousness (2 Timothy 3:16–17).

THE MAIN POINT

It is necessary to pay close attention to God's Word and obey Him promptly and fully.

During the Session

OPENING: 5–10 MINUTES

Opening Prayer—You or one of your group members should open your time together in prayer.

Opening Illustration—A very dear missionary to China, Miss Bertha Smith, was part of the great Shantung Revival there in the 1930's. During her time in China, she faced the attack of the Japanese and was one of those expelled by the Communists in 1949. For years (until she died at the age of 100), she used countless opportunities to testify of the redemption found in Christ, the power of the Holy Spirit, and the sufficiency of the Word of God. Often when she gave her testimony, she would sing "How Firm a Foundation," a hymn she sang during the shelling of Yenchow by the Communists and also a hymn that she declared had seen her through three or four wars. The first verse declares:

"How firm a foundation, ye saints of the Lord,
Is laid for your faith in His excellent Word!
What more can He say than to you He hath said,
To you who for refuge to Jesus have fled?"

The members of your group can find that to be true for their lives as well. Ask God to solidify the faith of each one as you study the life of Samuel.

DISCUSSION: 30–40 MINUTES

__Main Objective in Day One__: The days in which Samuel was born were a time of spiritual decline when *"everyone did what was right in his own eyes"* (Judges 21:25). We want to see the heart and life of Hannah, Samuel's mother, and the life of Samuel (even as a young boy) against this backdrop. Below are some possible discussion questions for the Day One discussion. Check which questions you will use.

____ What do you sense Samuel's home was like?

____ How would you describe Hannah, Samuel's mother?

____ What stands out about the spiritual atmosphere around the Tabernacle at Shiloh?

____ How was Samuel different from Eli's sons?

__Main Objective in Day Two__: Just as the Word of God was the final word in Samuel's life, it is vital for us to make the Word central to all we think, say, and do. Check which discussion questions you will use for Day Two.

____ Someone has well said, "You can choose your sin, but you cannot choose your consequences." How do you see that being worked out in the lives of Eli's sons?

____ What does Samuel show us regarding how we are to respond to the Word of God?

____ How would a fresh, clear understanding of the Word of God change the way things are in your home? At your job? In your community?

__Main Objective in Day Three__: The people of Israel had to learn that **knowing** the Word of God meant they were accountable to follow the will of the Lord as a nation and as individuals. Day Three focuses on surrender to the will of the Lord. Check which discussion questions for Day Three you might use.

____ Israel did not have an in-depth knowledge of the Word of God. They treated the Ark of the Covenant in a somewhat superstitious way, almost like a "good-luck" charm. In what ways do we act like that in our Christian lives?

____ Why do you think 1 Samuel 3:1 indicates that the *"word from the Lord was rare in those days"*?

____ What are some "idols" that we must deal with? How do they distract us from hearing and seeing God and His will for our daily lives?

Main Objective in Day Four: Just as important as finding God's will is **doing** His will **in His way.** In Day Four, we see that Samuel learned this lesson when God made His choice for king of Israel. We must learn this lesson too. Some good discussion questions from Day Four might be . . .

____ What have you learned from Samuel's life about dealing with sin (from both good or bad examples)?

____ As Samuel grew older, he still had some things to learn about the Lord's ways. How does that relate to us?

____ Like Samuel, we live in an era of spiritual decline. What does Samuel's life and ministry say to us today?

Day Five—Key Points in Application: The most significant application point from the life of Samuel is the importance of following the Word of the Lord with a humble, teachable heart. Choose one or two discussion questions from the list below.

____ Samuel was **available** to the plan of God. Being available means being surrendered to do His will His way—when He says, how He says. Do you ever struggle with "I'm not available for that" attitudes? As leaders, you may want to share some struggles you have had.

____ Samuel was also **teachable.** What do you think gets in the way of us being teachable?

____ What are some ways you are honoring the Word of God as your source of wisdom and direction?

____ What do you think of people who treat the Scriptures as just another book of good opinions, another option on the shelf of options?

CLOSING: 5–10 MINUTES

❒ **Summarize**—Restate the key points highlighted in the class. Take a few moments to preview next week's lesson, **"Elijah: Following God When Those Around You Do Not."**

❒ **Encourage** the group to do their homework.

❒ **Pray**—Close in prayer.

Tools for Good Discussion

Some who are reading this have led small-group Bible studies many times. Here is an important word of warning: experience alone does not make you a more effective discussion leader. In fact, experience can make you **less effective**. You see, the more experience you have the more comfortable you will be at the task. Unfortunately, for some that means becoming increasingly comfortable in doing a bad job. Taking satisfaction with mediocrity translates into taking the task less seriously. It is easy to wrongly assert that just because one is experienced, he or she can successfully "shoot from the hip," so to speak. If you really want your members to get the most out of this study, you need to be dissatisfied with simply doing an adequate job and make it your aim to do an excellent job. A key to excellence is to regularly evaluate yourself to see that you are still doing all that you want to be doing. We have prepared a list of over thirty evaluation questions for you to review from time to time. The list of questions can be found on page 218 in this Leader's Guide. The examination questions will help to jog your memory and, hopefully, will become an effective aid in improving the quality of your group discussion. Review the evaluation questions list, and jot down below two or three action points for you to begin implementing next week.

ACTION POINTS:

1. ____

____

2. ____

____

3. ____

____

Elijah

MEMORY **Colossians 4:17** VERSE

"Take heed to the ministry which you have received in the Lord, that you may fulfill it

Before the Session

- ❑ An important historical note is that Elijah ministered after the division of Israel into two kingdoms—the conservative Southern Kingdom (Judah), ruled over by the descendents of David, and the liberal Northern Kingdom (still called Israel), ruled by whoever could seize power. Elijah was a prophet to that Northern Kingdom.
- ❑ Remember that your goal is not to teach the lesson, but to facilitate discussion. Think of open-ended questions that will generate dialogue.
- ❑ For an enhanced understanding of the times in which Elijah ministered, see *Following God: Life Principles from the Kings of the Old Testament*, Lesson 6, on **"King Ahab: The Sins of Serving Self."** This wicked king reigned in Israel during the ministry of the prophet Elijah.
- ❑ Make sure your own heart is right with God. Be willing to be transparent with the group about your own life experiences and mistakes. This will make it easier for them to open up.
- ❑ Don't be afraid of chasing tangents for a while if they capture the interest of the group as a whole, but don't sacrifice the rest of the group to belabor the questions of one member. Trust God to lead you.

What to Expect

The danger of dealing with a character as familiar as Elijah is that, although most everyone will have some knowledge of certain events in his life, few will have seriously studied him. What they know of Elijah is woven from the snippets they have heard of him in sermons and the like. Make sure that, if nothing else, everyone goes away with some kind of grasp on the "received vs. achieved" principle. Many will find this principle to be an unfamiliar concept, but hopefully the concept will be a liberating one to them. God will be prompting many in your group to follow Elijah's example. They will need to be reminded that the keys are **a) walking** with God, and **b) waiting** on God. To experience "received" ministry and a "God-initiated" life, we have to be willing to be patient and let God have His way with us.

THE MAIN POINT

True ministry is "received, not achieved." Elijah models for us what it means to live a God-initiated life instead of a self-initiated, self-directed life.

During the Session

OPENING: 5–10 MINUTES

Opening Prayer—Ask someone to open your time in prayer.

Opening Illustration—The great hymn, "Have Thine Own Way" was written in 1902 by Adelaide Pollard during a time she referred to as suffering "a great distress of soul." Shortly before, she had tried unsuccessfully to raise funds for a missionary trip to Africa. God met with her in a prayer meeting, and the result was these words to this powerful hymn:

"Have Thine own way, Lord! Have Thine own way!
Thou art the Potter; I am the clay.
Mould me and make me after Thy will,
While I am waiting, yielded and still."

She had learned that true ministry is **received**, not achieved.

DISCUSSION: 30–40 MINUTES

Once your group gets talking, you will find that all you need to do is keep the group directed and flowing with a question or two or a pointed observation. You are the gatekeeper of discussion. Don't be afraid to ask someone to elaborate further or to ask a quiet member of the group what they think of someone else's comments. Time will not allow you to discuss every single question in the lesson one at a time. Instead, make it your goal to cover the main ideas of each day and help the group to share what they learned personally. You don't have to use all the discussion questions. They are there for you to pick and choose from.

Main Objective in Day One: The main objective here is to see the central role in Elijah's life of *"the Word of the Lord."* This refers not just to the Scriptures, but specifically to his hearing from God and being directed by God as he walked in fellowship with Him. While we will not experience God audibly speaking to us on a day-to-day basis, we are going to experience His leading as we walk with Him. Check which discussion questions you will use.

____ What do you think the text means by the phrase, *"the word of the Lord"*?

____ How was Elijah's hearing from God different than what we experience today?

____ How was it the same?

____ A companion idea here is that "where God guides, He provides." How do we see that in Elijah's experience?

____ What things get in the way of us hearing from God?

Main Objective in Day Two: Here we see that the miracle on Mt. Carmel was not a matter of Elijah coming up with a good idea and asking God to bless it, but rather doing all, Elijah says, *"at thy word"* (1 Kings 18:36).

____ From where does the idea come for Elijah's challenge?

____ What do you think God is trying to show Israel through His dealings here at Mt. Carmel? Why?

____ James says Elijah's prayer is an example of "effective prayer." What do you learn about prayer from his example?

____ Does prayer have to be long to be effective?

____ What keeps our prayers from being effective?

Main Objective in Day Three: Day Three introduces us to some of Elijah's humanness. There is always the danger of placing the people God uses on such a pedestal that we lose our ability to relate with them. Not only does Elijah show us that the Christian life is going to have its share of "highs" and "lows," but through him we also see that the highs are often followed by lows. Examine the discussion questions below, and determine which questions you might want to use in your discussion for Day Three.

____ How is this experience of Elijah different than what we saw on Mt. Carmel?

____ Why do you think Elijah struggled with trusting God with the threat on his life?

____ What is the good news in how God dealt with Elijah's suicidal prayer?

____ What conclusions can we draw from Elijah's experience concerning how we manage our own spiritual highs and lows?

Main Objective in Day Four: In Day Four we see the potential pitfall into which each of us can stumble: that is, thinking we are the only one standing for God. Like Elijah, we can convince ourselves that God needs us and wrongly assume that without us His purposes cannot be realized. Check which discussion questions you will use from Day Four.

____ What is wrong with Elijah's perspective here?

____ Have you ever felt that you were the only one standing for God?

____ What does Elijah's experience say to you about loneliness?

____ Did anything else stand out to you from Day Four?

<u>**Day Five—Key Points in Application:**</u> The most important application point from Elijah's life is that he followed God's initiation and direction most of the time. When he followed God, he was able to see God do more for him than anything he could do for God. Check which discussion questions you will use for Day Five.

____ Can you see any examples in your own life or those around you of ministry that is **achieved** (man-initiated) instead of **received** (initiated by God)?

____ Did God show you anything through this lesson you need to do differently?

CLOSING: 5–10 MINUTES

- ❑ **Summarize**—restate the key points that were highlighted in the class.
- ❑ **Remind** your group that the Christian life is not about trying hard to be like Jesus, but it is about totally surrendering our lives to God and letting Him work through us.
- ❑ **Preview**—Take a few moments to preview next week's lesson on **"Elisha: Putting Down the Idols in our Lives."** Encourage the group to be sure to do their homework.
- ❑ **Pray**—Close in prayer.

Tools for Good Discussion

Bill Donahue, in his book, *Leading Life-Changing Small Groups* (Grand Rapids: Zondervan Publishing House, 1996), lists four facilitator actions that will produce dynamic discussion. These four actions are easy to remember because they are linked through the acrostic method to the word, **ACTS.** You will profit from taking time to review this information in the "Helpful Hints" section of **How to Lead a Small Group Bible Study,** which is on page 212 of this Leader's Guide.

Elisha

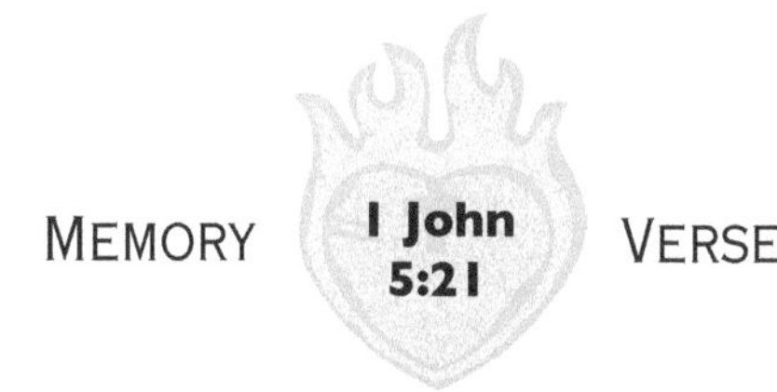

"Little children, guard yourselves from idols."

Before the Session

- ❑ Pray each day for the members of your group—that they spend time in the Word, grasp the message God wants to bring to their lives, and that they surrender to what God is saying.
- ❑ Do your homework—don't procrastinate!
- ❑ Remember, Elijah (last week's lesson) was mentor to Elisha. Keep that connection in view.
- ❑ Mark those ideas and questions you want to discuss as you go through the study. Those, along with the questions listed below, can personalize the discussion to fit your group. Think of the needs of your group and be looking for applicable questions and discussion starters.
- ❑ To better understand the times and the depths of Israel's idolatry, see *Following God: Life Principles from the Kings of the Old Testament,* Lesson 6, entitled **"Ahab: The Sins of Serving Self"** as well as Lesson 7 on **"Jehoshaphat: Unequally Yoked."**
- ❑ Ever remain teachable. Look first for what God is saying to you.
- ❑ Prepare yourself to be transparent and open about what God is teaching you. Nothing is quite as contagious as the joy of discovering new treasures in the Word.

What to Expect

For some in your group the dangers of idolatry are something reserved for some tribe on an island in the middle of the Pacific, not for modern society. However, we see in the life of Elisha just how close idols can be—as close as the breath we breathe. This can be an eye-opening and heart-revealing truth. Take this opportunity to sharpen your group's awareness of the idols of today, and then help them see the subtlety of idolatry. Elisha can be a true friend to help lead them out of the pit of idolatry and onto the solid ground of a surrendered walk with the true and living God.

THE MAIN POINT

We are to faithfully follow the true and living God and ever guard ourselves against idolatry in any form.

During the Session

OPENING: 5 MINUTES

Opening Prayer—Remember that the Lord is the Teacher, and He wants us to depend on Him as we open the Scriptures.

Opening Illustration—In one of His acts of judgment on faithless Israel in the wilderness, God sent poisonous serpents among the people. In Numbers 21, we read the story of God directing Moses to make a bronze serpent and lift it on a pole. All who had been bitten by these snakes need only look at the pole and be healed. The bronze serpent pole is an Old Testament picture of Christ (John 3:14). Yet in King Hezekiah's day, we learn that it had to be destroyed. It had become an idol to the people (2 Kings 18:4). They named it *"Nehushtan"* and burned incense to it. The human heart is able to take things that should point us to God and turn them into objects of worship. Whether it is creation or our blessings or even the past working of God, there is ever the danger of placing something ahead of God in our hearts. That is the danger we see Elisha confronting.

DISCUSSION: 30–40 MINUTES

Keep the group directed along the main highway of Elisha. You may have a pointed observation that helps sharpen the focus of the group. Encourage some to elaborate further on a key point, or ask a quiet member of the group what he or she thinks of someone's comments. Watch the time, knowing that you cannot cover every single question in the lesson. Seek to cover the main ideas of each day and help the group to share what they learned personally.

Main Objective in Day One: You should desire that you and your group see the necessity of following the true God in the midst of any tests or challenges that you may face. Elisha faced certain tests concerning his willingness to follow Elijah. He learned to trust in God's ways and experienced God's power as Elijah had done. He also had to trust God that the people would listen to him as God's spokesman. Check which discussion questions you will use from Day One.

____ What was Israel like in the days of Elijah and Elisha? What parallels do you see today?

____ Elijah faced some struggles. How did the Lord deal with him and with his struggles? How did the Lord encourage Elijah?

____ What do you think it meant for Elisha to leave behind his parents and the family business? Are you facing a similar challenge or call on your life?

____ How did Elisha respond to the various tests he faced? What can we learn from Elisha's responses for the tests we face?

Main Objective in Day Two: Here we learn that the Lord is the **living** God, the true provider, who longs for His people to look to Him and to follow Him—not some **dead** idol. You want to make sure your group catches that one point. Check which discussion questions you will use for your discussion of Day Two.

____ Why do you think many in Israel superstitiously followed Baal and Baal worship like the nations around them? How did Elisha show them the truth about the true God?

____ What are some modern "gods/idols" today? How do we follow the "popular" gods of those around us? How can we show them the truth about the true God?

____ Think of the many ways God used Elisha to reveal Himself as the **Living God** in today's Scriptures. Name or list those ways or write them on a marker board.

____ How has God revealed Himself as the **Living God** today? Some in your group may want to share ways they have seen God alive in their lives and circumstances this week or in recent weeks.

Main Objective in Day Three: Day Three introduces us to the ways of God among "the nations." He is Lord of all the earth, not just Israel. Check a discussion question or two below that you find to be useful for your discussion about Day Three.

____ How does God deal with those from other nations? What does God's dealings with Naaman tell you about the ways of God?

____ How did Elisha deal with someone from another nation? What was his focus? In the New Testament, Peter declared *"I most certainly understand now that God is not one to show partiality"* or is *"no respecter of persons"* (Acts 10:34). Neither was Elisha partial. What does that say to you?

____ What do you see about God's protective care for His people in the incident of the army surrounding Elisha? Ask different members of your group to give one of the purposes of the angels according to Hebrews 1:14.

____ What is God's desire for the nations? You may want to read some additional Scriptures not found in this lesson, such as Joshua 4:19–24 (especially verse 24), 1 Kings 8:41–43, and Matthew 28:18–20.

Main Objective in Day Four: For Day Four, we want to emphasize the faithfulness of God. He is faithful to His people in every detail of their lives and is committed to seeing them walk with Him, following Him as their God. Therefore, He is committed to child-training and discipline. Check which discussion questions you will use from Day Four .

____ What kind of discipline did God bring upon Israel through Hazael of Syria? What does this show us about God's faithfulness to His people?

____ What role did Jehu play in God's dealings with Israel? What do you discover about the faithfulness and the ways of God in all Jehu did?

____ What does 2 Kings 13:22–23 mean to you personally?

____ Read Hebrews 12:1–13. How does that passage speak to you about the faithfulness of God in training and dealing with His children?

Day Five—Key Points in Application: The most important application point is found in the delight of walking with the true and living God, while always being aware of the ever-present danger of idolatry. Below, check the questions that you might consider using in your discussion.

____ We need to be nourished on "sound" or "healthy" doctrine—the Word of God. How can you be sure to guard yourself from unhealthy teaching?

____ Has this lesson brought to mind any worldly opinions that have gotten mixed in with what you know in Scripture? Share some of these.

____ What about idolatry in **your** life? Remember when the apostle John was writing 1 John, he was talking to Christians (*"little children"*) who knew the Scriptures. The dangers of idolatry are always near. That's why we must "guard" ourselves. Review some of the idols we may face in today's world.

____ What can you do to increase your intake of the Word of God and intensify your watchfulness against idolatry?

CLOSING: 5–10 MINUTES

- ❑ **Summarize**—Restate the key points the group shared (Review the objectives for each of the days found at the beginning of these leader notes).
- ❑ **Remind**—Using the memory verse (1 John 5:21), remind the group that idols are still around today. We must stay on guard.
- ❑ **Preview**—Take time to preview next week's lesson, **"Jonah: Following God When You Don't Want To."**
- ❑ **Pray**—Close in prayer.

Tools for Good Discussion

One of the people who shows up in every group is a person we call **"Talkative Timothy."** Talkative Timothy tends to talk too much and dominates the discussion time by giving less opportunity for others to share. What do you do with a group member who talks too much? In the "Helpful Hints" section of **How to Lead a Small Group Bible Study** (p. 212), you'll find some practical ideas on managing the "Talkative Timothy's" in your group.

MEMORY **I Samuel I 15:22** VERSE

"Has the Lord as much delight in burnt offerings and sacrifices as in obeying the voice of the Lord? Behold, to obey is better than sacrifice, and to heed than the fat of rams."

Before the Session

- ❑ Be sure to do your own study far enough in advance so as not to be rushed. You want to allow God time to speak to you personally.
- ❑ Don't feel that you have to use all of the discussion questions listed below. You may have come up with others on your own, or you may find that time will not allow you to use them all. These questions are to serve you, not for you to serve.
- ❑ You are the gatekeeper of the discussion. Do not be afraid to "reel the group back in" if they get too far away from the lesson.
- ❑ Remember to keep a highlight pen ready as you study to mark any points you want to be sure to discuss.

What to Expect

The story of Jonah is the most human portrait of any of the prophets. It accurately records his rebellion against God's plan for him and shows how God dealt with him to bring him to a place of obedience. The account of Jonah and the great fish is so familiar that we run the risk of resembling that old adage, "familiarity breeds contempt." Yet, as you can see, there are some very practical lessons to be learned from his life—the main one being that we cannot succeed in running from God. Because God is who He is, He is able to keep turning up the heat through the circumstances of our lives, until we yield to His will and way. An important point to acknowledge, however, is that even submitting to God's will can be done with a wrong heart. To do the right actions alone is not enough. God desires that our hearts become yielded to Him, not simply that we acquiesce to His will because we have to.

THE MAIN POINT

The main point to be seen here is God's grace in the midst of Jonah's very reluctant obedience.

During the Session

OPENING: 5–10 MINUTES

Opening Prayer—Remember that if it took the inspiration of God for people to write Scripture, it will also take His illumination for us to understand it. Have one of the more serious minded members of your group open your time together in prayer.

Opening Illustration—A good hook for introducing this lesson might be the story of the little school boy who was made to sit in the corner during class as punishment for repeatedly standing when he should not. When the teacher came by and said, "Now, that is more like it," he replied in rebellion, "I may be sitting down on the outside, but I am standing up on the inside!" Such reluctant submission is not what the Lord desires. Yet that is what we see in Jonah.

DISCUSSION: 30–40 MINUTES

Here is a little tip to enhance the quality of your group's discussion. Don't be afraid to ask someone to elaborate further on their comments ("Explain what you mean, Barbara.") or to ask a quiet member of the group what he or she thinks of someone else's comments ("What do you think, Dave?"). Time will not allow you to discuss every single question in the lesson one at a time. Instead, make it your goal to cover the main ideas of each day, and help the group to share what they learned personally.

Main Objective in Day One: In Day One, the main objective is to reveal the downward spiral Jonah experiences when he runs from God's plan and purpose. Jonah was called to a purpose that he didn't like, so instead of obeying, he rebelled and ran from God. Every Christian has done the same thing at some point, so you should have no trouble getting your group members to identify with Jonah. Check which discussion questions from Day One you will use.

____ Have someone restate the assignment God gave to Jonah in verses 1 and 2.

____ Can you think of a purpose God has given to you at some time that you have struggled with?

____ How did God deal with Jonah's rebellion?

____ What do you think was going through Jonah's mind as he was running?

Main Objective in Day Two: In Day Two we learn the key principle, "If you don't get right when God sends the storm, you will get right when troubles grow far worse!" You'll want to make sure that your group understands that God is willing and able to turn up the heat if we are unwilling to submit to Him. Check the discussion questions below that might apply to your group.

____ What was Jonah's response to the storm God sent his way?

____ What are some of the storms God brings into our lives to get our attention?

____ Why do you think it took Jonah so long to surrender to the Lord's call?

____ We see that it wasn't until Jonah prayed that God commanded the fish to vomit him onto the land. What is the message for us in that?

____ The last statement of Day Two says, "When God brings calamity upon us for our rebellion, He will not relent until we repent." Do you agree or disagree with that statement?

Main Objective in Day Three: Day Three introduces us to the results of Jonah's repentance. The fruit his preaching at Nineveh bore is the greatest evangelistic response recorded in Scripture—greater even than Peter's preaching at Pentecost. Jonah's repentance allowed him to be a part of a mighty moving of God. Check which discussion questions from Day Three you will use.

____ What stands out to you from Jonah's message to Nineveh?

____ Why do you think the people of Nineveh responded as they did?

____ How does our preaching today differ from what you see here?

____ Verse 10 tells us that when the people repented, God relented concerning the calamity. How does that apply to us?

____ What do you think true repentance is?

Main Objective in Day Four: In Day Four we see more of Jonah's humanness. Sadly, though he was finally obedient to God's charge, he was disappointed that God did not judge the Ninevites anyway. Below, check any discussion questions from Day Four that may be appropriate for your group.

____ What are some reasons we don't rejoice when God shows mercy to the guilty?

____ What prejudices do you struggle with?

____ We see that Jonah's reluctance was rooted in the fact that he did not agree with God's plan. Are there any areas in your life where you struggle with disagreeing with God's plan?

____ Did you have any unanswered questions from this week's lesson?

Day Five—Key Points in Application: The most important application point from the life of Jonah is that God did not allow him to succeed in running away from His will. Check which discussion questions you will use from Day Five.

____ Can you think of a time where you ran from God's will?

____ Hebrews 12 indicates two wrong responses to God's disciplines: **a)** to regard it lightly, and **b)** to faint when we are reproved. What would these wrong responses look like in practical terms?

____ What are some areas where you struggle with recognizing people "*...according to the flesh*"?

CLOSING: 5–10 MINUTES

- ❑ **Summarize**—Restate the key points that were highlighted in the class. You may also want to briefly review the main objectives for each of the days found in these leader notes.
- ❑ **Remind** your group that the victorious Christian life is not attained when we try hard to be like Jesus, but when we surrender our lives to God and let Him work through us.
- ❑ **Ask** your group what they think the key applications from Day Five are.
- ❑ **Preview**—Take a few moments to preview next week's lesson on **"Hosea: Returning to the Lord."** Encourage your group to do their homework.
- ❑ **Pray**—Close in prayer.

Tools for Good Discussion

As mentioned earlier, there are certain people who show up in every discussion group. Last week we looked at "Talkative Timothy." Another person who is likely to show up is **"Silent Sally."** She does not readily speak up. Sometimes, her silence is because she doesn't yet feel comfortable enough with the group to share her thoughts. Other times, it is simply because she fears being rejected. Often, her silence is because she is too polite to interrupt and thus is headed off at the pass each time she wants to speak by more aggressive (and less sensitive) members of the group. In the "Helpful Hints" section of **How to Lead a Small Group Bible Study** (p. 213), you'll find some practical ideas on managing the "Silent Sally's" in your group.

Hosea

MEMORY **2 Corinthians 11:2–3** VERSES

"I am jealous for you with a godly jealousy; for I betrothed you to one husband, that to Christ I might present you as a pure virgin. But I am afraid, lest as the serpent deceived Eve by his craftiness, your minds should be led astray from the simplicity and purity of devotion to Christ."

Before the Session

- ❑ Resist the temptation to do all your homework in one sitting or to put it off until the last minute. You will not be fully prepared if you study in this fashion.
- ❑ Make sure to mark down any discussion questions that come to mind as you study.
- ❑ If you want to do further study, look at 1 and 2 Kings and 1 and 2 Chronicles and read about the kings who ruled while Hosea ministered.
- ❑ Remember your need to trust God with your study. The Holy Spirit is always the best teacher, so stay sensitive to Him!

What to Expect

In this lesson, assume that all your group members need to better understand how to return to the Lord when they stray. They will all eventually need this for their own walk, and they will all, sooner or later, be in a position to help someone else who will need it. Don't worry so much about covering all the details of the study. Make sure that you devote adequate time to clearly explaining and answering any questions they have about returning to the Lord.

THE MAIN POINT

The main call of Hosea is to "return to the Lord," and the main point to be seen in this lesson is how we do that.

In order to understand Hosea's instruction, it is necessary to look at the day in which he lived and the sins of Israel that he confronted. His powerful showdown with the spiritual adultery of Israel was made more personal by the physical adultery of his own wife.

During the Session

OPENING: 5–10 MINUTES

Opening Prayer—Remember to have one of your group members open your time together in prayer.

Opening Illustration—Winston Churchill, Prime Minister of Great Britain during World War II, not only was a great leader, but also earned a reputation as the "king of the verbal comeback." He seemed to be at his best while sparring with his main political adversary, Lady Astor. On one occasion, being quite put out with him, she uttered, "Sir Churchill, if I were your wife, I would put arsenic in your tea!" to which Churchill retorted, "Lady Astor, if I were your husband, I would drink it!" On another occasion at a party the two met in the elevator as they were leaving. Lady Astor remarked with contempt, "Sir Churchill, I perceive that you are drunk." The quick-witted Churchill returned, "Yes Lady Astor, and you are ugly," and then added, "and tomorrow I shall be sober!" No one, however, was armed with a greater comeback than the prophet Hosea. Every time someone would comment about his unfaithful, harlot wife, he could return, "And that is exactly what you are to God."

DISCUSSION: 30–40 MINUTES

By now, you should realize that your job is not to teach this lesson, but to facilitate discussion. Do your best to guide the group to the right answers, but don't be guilty of making a point **someone else** in the group could easily make.

Main Objective in Day One: In Day One, the main objective is to see how God worked His message into Hosea's life. Through his marriage to an unfaithful bride, he was able to feel the heart of God toward prodigal Israel. Check which questions you might use for your discussion on Day One.

____ Why do you think God wanted Hosea to have a harlot for a wife?

____ What struggles do you think Hosea had in ministry because of his wife?

____ How is Gomer's harlotry a good parallel to Israel's wanderings from God?

____ What do you think about Hosea's children?

____ Were there any questions raised by your study?

Main Objective in Day Two: In Day Two, we learn some of the specifics of the sins in Israel God confronted through the prophet Hosea. Make sure that your group grasps the concept that Israel had committing "spiritual" adultery by their dalliance with other religions. Not mentioned in the workbook study, but something worth discussing, is that the words used in Hosea 2:2 are similar to those used in the Jewish formula for divorce. Check which discussion questions you will use from Day Two.

____ What kinds of actions in Israel does God associate with "spiritual adultery"?

____ What are some equivalents to "spiritual adultery" in our day?

____ What correlation do you see between Israel's straying and their lack of gratitude for God's blessings?

____ Israel's unfaithfulness to the Lord included the hypocrisy of rituals with no meaning in their hearts. What are some things that can become meaningless rituals to us today?

Main Objective in Day Three: Day Three introduces us to the heart of God through His message to "return to the Lord." It is a powerful reminder that at the heart of the Scriptures is God's willingness to accept us back when we stray. Every member of your group will be able to relate in some way with wandering from the Lord, and will benefit from Hosea's invitation. It is worth reminding the group that the word "return" appears 22 times in Hosea. Check the discussion questions for Day Three that appeal to you.

____ What stands out to you most about the way God draws His unfaithful spouse back in Chapter 2?

____ What similarities do you see between Hosea and what God did with us through Christ?

____ Hosea 2:6 indicates that God would *"hedge up her way with thorns."* Have you ever experienced God doing that as you wandered?

____ Have you ever experienced God "winning" your love back? How?

____ Do you agree with the statement, "We don't 'find' God—He finds us"?

Main Objective in Day Four: In Day Four, we see how God woos His prodigal people back to Himself. Some key points you want your group members to catch are: **1)** confession is for our benefit, not just God's, **2)** repentance **always** accompanies true confession, and, most importantly, **3)** repentance will involve "plowing the fallow (unplowed) ground." Make sure they see that any area of our lives from which we exclude God will become hard, fallow ground. It takes a choice to allow the plow of His Word into those areas to break up the hardness. Check the questions for Day Four that you will use in your discussion on Hosea.

____ Why do we need to confess sin if God already knows everything?

____ Do you think it is possible to truly confess without repenting?

____ Hosea 14:5–8 pictures the freshness of life after repentance. Have you ever experienced this repentance?

____ How do you think "fallow" ground (hard, unplowed ground) develops in our lives?

____ Name some examples of "fallow ground" that you have seen or experienced.

Day Five—Key Points in Application: The most important application out of Day Five is that we are all prodigals, and therefore we all need to know how to return to the Lord. Express to your group that the keys to repentance and returning to God are: **a)** remembering what it was like to walk with God, and **b)** making a choice to return. Check which discussion questions from Day Five you will use.

____ What stands out to you about the parable of the prodigal son?

____ What gets in our way of returning to the Lord?

____ Have you ever tried to "return" to God, expecting God to place you on "probation"?

____ Is there anything you still don't understand about returning to the Lord when you stray?

CLOSING: 5–10 MINUTES

- ❑ **Summarize**—Restate the key points.
- ❑ **Ask** your group what they consider to be the key applications for Day Five.
- ❑ **Sing**—If your meeting space allows, you may want to sing together the last verse of "Come Thou Fount of Every Blessing." Explain the relevance of this song to the Hosea study. (See p. 77 in *Following God: Life Principles from the Prophets of the Old Testament*.)
- ❑ **Pray**—Ask someone in your group to close your session with prayer.

Tools for Good Discussion

Hopefully your group is functioning smoothly at this point, but perhaps you recognize the need for improvement. In either case, you will benefit from taking the time to evaluate yourself and your group. Without evaluation, you will judge your group on subjective emotions. You may think everything is fine and miss some opportunities to improve your effectiveness. You may be discouraged by problems you are confronting when you ought to be encouraged that you are doing the right things and making progress. A healthy Bible-study group is not one without problems, but is one that recognizes its problems and deals with them the right way. At this point in the course, as you and your group are nearly halfway completed with the study of the Old Testament prophets, it is important to examine yourself and see if there are any mid-course corrections that you feel are necessary to implement. Review the evaluation questions list found on page 218 of this Leader's Guide, and jot down two or three action points to begin implementing next week. Perhaps you have made steady improvements since the first time you answered the evaluation questions at the beginning of the course. If so, your improvements should challenge you to be an even better group leader for the final seven lessons in the study.

ACTION POINTS:

1. ______________________________

____

2. ______________________________

____

3. ______________________________

____

Isaiah

MEMORY **2 Timothy 2:21** VERSE

"Therefore, if a man cleanses himself from these things, he will be a vessel for honor, sanctified, useful to the Master, prepared for every good work."

Before the Session

- ❑ Remember the Boy Scout motto: **BE PREPARED!** The main reason a Bible study flounders is because the leader is unprepared and tries to "shoot from the hip," so to speak.
- ❑ Make sure to mark down any discussion questions that come to mind as you study.
- ❑ If you want to do further study, look at 1 and 2 Kings and 1 and 2 Chronicles, and read about the kings who ruled while Isaiah ministered. You may also benefit from doing the lesson on Hezekiah from *Following God: Life Principles from the Kings.* The revival during Hezekiah's reign was influenced by the ministry of Isaiah.
- ❑ Don't forget to pray for the members of your group and for your time of studying together. You don't want to be satisfied with what **you** can do. You want to see God do what only **He** can do!

What to Expect

In this lesson, realize that all of us, sooner or later, will fall prey to comparing ourselves to others around us instead of to the holy standards of God. Make sure you allow time for members of your group to share honestly about their struggles. Realize that there may be some sin God wants to deal with so that He can make each member more useable to Him in His work. Be sensitive to any questions this lesson may surface about ministry, and guard your group from applying it only to those with a "vocational" ministry.

THE MAIN POINT

The main point to be seen in this lesson is that, before God can use us, He must first make us useable.

In other words, before He can do a work **through** us, He must first do a work **in** us. Before Isaiah *"saw the Lord"* his message was *"woe"* to this person and *"woe"* to that person. But when he saw the Lord, his message changed to *"woe is me"* (Is. 6:5). His own sin had to be dealt with before he could get to the place of saying, *"Here am I, send me"* (Is. 6:8).

During the Session

OPENING: 5–10 MINUTES

Opening Prayer—Remember to have one of your group members open your time together in prayer.

Opening Illustration—A good way to begin your discussion time is by asking the question, "Why does a surgeon sterilize his scalpel before he operates?" This should get your group thinking. The main idea they should come to is that a surgeon sterilizes his scalpel to protect his patient from infection. Think about it. A surgeon operating with a dirty scalpel is going to do more harm than good. In fact, he may put the patient's life at risk unnecessarily. The parallel is obvious—God will not use us in someone else's life until He has first cleansed us and made us useable.

DISCUSSION: 30–40 MINUTES

Remember to pace your discussion so that you will be able to bring closure to the lesson in the time allotted. You are the one who must balance lively discussion with timely redirection to ensure that you don't end up finishing only part of the lesson.

Main Objective in Day One: In Day One, the main objective is to see what Isaiah's message was like before his encounter with the Lord. You don't necessarily need to spend a lot of time on Day One, but you want to make sure your group members make the connection that without a clear view of God, it is easy to let the sins of others cloud our view of our own sins. Check which discussion questions from Day One you find to be useful.

____ What common denominators did you see in Isaiah's early message?

____ Do you ever struggle with seeing the sins of others more clearly than your own? Why?

____ Ask your group if they have any questions from their study of Day One.

Main Objective in Day Two: In Day Two, we learn some of the specifics of Isaiah's relationship with King Uzziah and the impact his death may have had on Isaiah's view of himself and of God. The main principle here is that when those around us commit great sins, it is easy to judge our own righteousness by how we "stack up" against them. We will always win such a comparison. Instead, we must realize that sin is not relative—it is not how we are compared to other sinners. Sin is how far we fall short of God. Check which discussion questions from Day Two you will use.

____ What lessons can we learn from King Uzziah?

____ How do you think Isaiah felt about the failings of Uzziah?

____ What effect do you think Uzziah's sin had on Isaiah's view of himself?

____ How do you think Uzziah's death changed how Isaiah saw himself?

Main Objective in Day Three: Day Three introduces us to the transforming experience Isaiah had when he *"saw the Lord"* (Is. 6:1). There are two key points you want to make sure your group members see from Day Three: **1)** it is God who reveals Isaiah's sin, and **2)** it is God who deals with Isaiah's sin. Isaiah did not see his own sin before, focused as he was on the sins of others. But when he saw the Lord, God revealed to him his own sinfulness. God did not leave him there, though. God only reveals sin so that He can deal with it. Check which discussion questions from Day Three you will use.

____ Looking at the passage, what things stand out to Isaiah in this vision?

____ How would you feel if you were in Isaiah's place?

____ Why do you think Isaiah's lips were touched with fire from the altar?

____ What else stands out to you from Isaiah's encounter with the Lord?

Main Objective in Day Four: In Day Four, we see the all-important principle that **after** God has dealt with our sin, then He is able to use us. It is on the heels of Isaiah's forgiveness that he receives the invitation from God, "Whom shall I send?" Check which discussion questions from Day Four you will use.

____ What do you think about the statement, "until we see ourselves as useless, we really aren't useable"?

____ We usually think of ministry as a "call" (as if God picked us and we had no choice), but here we see it as an "invitation," something to which we can choose to say yes. What do you think about that?

____ We see that God's task for Isaiah was a ministry with no fruit. Have you ever experienced that?

____ What kind of struggles did it bring?

<u>**Day Five—Key Points in Application**</u>: The most important application point out of Day Five is that we cannot use "immediate results" as a yardstick to measure whether or not we are doing what God wants us to do. It is obedience to God, and not results that measure our successes or failures in His work. Check the discussion questions from Day Five that pertain to your study group.

- ____ Has a lack of results ever caused you to doubt that you were serving in the right place?
- ____ What is the right way to know if you are serving rightly?
- ____ Who are the Uzziah's in your life that you measure yourself against?
- ____ What is the biggest application point that you recognized this week?

CLOSING: 5–10 MINUTES

- ❑ **Summarize**—Highlight the key points.
- ❑ **Remind** those in your group that the victorious Christian life is not attained when we try hard to be like Jesus, but when we surrender our lives to God and let Him work through us.
- ❑ **Preview**—Take a few moments to preview next week's lesson on **"Micah: What Does the Lord Require of You."**
- ❑ **Pray**—Close in prayer.

TOOLS FOR GOOD DISCUSSION

As discussed earlier, there are certain people who show up in every discussion group that you will ever lead. We have already looked at "Talkative Timothy" and "Silent Sally." This week, let's talk about another person who also tends to show up. Let's call this person **"Tangent Tom."** He is the kind of guy who loves to talk even when he has nothing to say. Tangent Tom loves to "chase rabbits" regardless of where they go. When he gets the floor, you never know where the discussion will lead. You need to understand that not all tangents are bad. Sometimes, much can be gained from discussion "a little off the beaten path." But these diversions must be balanced against the purpose of the group. In the "Helpful Hints" section of **How to Lead a Small Group** (p. 213), you will find some practical ideas on managing the "Tangent Tom's" in your group. You will also get some helpful information on evaluating tangents as they arise.

Micah

"He has told you, O man, what is good; and what does the Lord require of you but to do justice, to love kindness, and to walk humbly with your God."

Before the Session

- ❑ It might be a good idea for you to try to get your homework done early in the week. This will allow time for you to reflect on what you have learned. Don't succumb to the temptation to procrastinate.
- ❑ Keep a highlight pen handy to highlight any things you want to be sure to discuss or any questions that you think your group may have trouble understanding. Mark down any good discussion questions that come to mind as you study.
- ❑ If you want to do further study, look at 1 and 2 Kings and 1 and 2 Chronicles, and read about the kings who ruled while Micah ministered. You may also benefit from doing the lesson on **Hezekiah** from *Following God: Life Principles from the Kings of the Old Testament.* The revival of Hezekiah's day was influenced by the ministry of Micah.
- ❑ Don't think of your ministry to the members of your group as something that only takes place during your group session. Pray for each group member by name during the week. Pray that each member learns much from his or her studies. Encourage all members of your group as you have opportunity.

What to Expect

In this lesson, we are afforded a very practical opportunity to teach our group members the right and wrong ways of dealing with sin. This is one of the most important tools you can place in their spiritual toolboxes. You will make it easier for your members to be open and honest with their own struggles with sin if you come prepared to share from your own experiences and struggles. Knowing that you have not "arrived" spiritually will make it easier for them to face the fact that they have not yet "arrived" and will give them courage to address this important issue.

Our study in Micah will help us focus on what it takes to please God. Micah's message comes as the Northern Kingdom (Israel) faced total annihilation because of that nation's rebellion against Jehovah. God speaks to the Southern Kingdom (Judah) and says, "Even though you are religious, you are just as sinful as rebellious Israel."

THE MAIN POINT

What God desires from us is not religious ritual, but a heart relationship with Him that produces justice and mercy in our actions.

DURING THE SESSION

OPENING: 5–10 MINUTES

Opening Prayer—It would be a good idea to have a different group member open your time together in prayer each week.

Opening Illustration—A good way to begin your discussion time is by asking the question, "What if someone offended you greatly, and instead of apologizing and asking forgiveness, they baked you a plate of cookies—would that make things right in your relationship?" After allowing some discussion, the point you want your group to see is that this is what we do with God when we try to deal with our sins our own way instead of His way.

DISCUSSION: 30–40 MINUTES

A key objective in how you manage your discussion time is to keep the big picture in view. Your job is not as a school teacher, grading their papers, but as a tutor, making sure they understand the subject. Keep the main point of the lesson in view and make sure they take that point home with them.

Main Objective in Day One: In the discussion for Day One, your main objective as group leader should be to help your group understand the context in which Micah lived and ministered. Nothing is meaningful without a context, and it is impossible to fully appreciate the message and ministry of Micah without understanding the days in which he lived. Since his message is directed to Judah, we will not take the time to study the rulers of the Northern Kingdom during his ministry. Check which discussion questions for Day One that you plan to use.

____ How do you think the people of Judah viewed the people of the Northern Kingdom (Israel)?

____ How do you think the people of Judah saw themselves?

____ How do you think God's judgment of Israel through the Assyrian conquest changed Judah's views?

____ How do you think Micah's messages changed their views?

____ What else stood out to you about the days in which Micah ministered?

Main Objective in Day Two: In Day Two, we learn some of the specifics of Micah's message of judgment and his explanations of why it would come. By looking at what he confronts in the people, and by seeing the explanations he gives, we can begin to understand why judgment had come upon Israel, why it would eventually come to Judah, and, in principle, we can see why it comes upon us today. It is important to understand that God judges the sin of His people. As Christians, our eternal destiny with Christ is never to be doubted, but that does not mean that God will not chasten us on earth for our sins. Check which discussion questions you will use from Day Two.

____ What do you think the people of Judah thought about the idea of God judging them?

____ On page 100 (workbook), the statement is made that, "A fundamental law of the universe is that we reap what we sow." How do you think that statement applies to Christians?

____ Why do you think God is so hard on his own people?

____ Second Timothy 4:3 talks about an inevitable time when people will *"accumulate for themselves teachers in accordance with their own desires."* What do you think this verse means?

Main Objective in Day Three: Day Three introduces us to the message of hope that accompanied Micah's preaching of judgment. Yes, Judah's sin would have to be addressed. But even though Israel and Judah had changed in how they followed God, Jehovah had not changed in any aspect whatsoever. He would still be faithful to fulfill all that he had promised. God was not (and is still not) finished with Israel. Check the discussion questions that you will use from Day Three.

____ Do you ever struggle with feeling hopeless when you see your own sin?

____ What stands out to you as you look at the promises that Micah emphasizes?

____ Do you expect that God will fulfill all that He has promised to Israel?

____ Were there any questions raised by your study in Day Three?

Main Objective in Day Four: In Day Four, Micah closes his message to us by drawing our eyes to God's forgiveness and how we are to experience it. Sooner or later, all believers will find themselves in need of a fresh experience of God's forgiveness. Micah shows us how to receive this forgiveness. Check the questions from Day Four that you will use in your discussion

____ What comes to mind when you hear the word "forgiveness"?

____ Why do you think forgiveness is still an issue for people who were forgiven at the cross (Christians)?

____ In Micah 6:6–7, we see some of the ways Israel and Judah tried to make up for their sins. How do we try to do that today?

____ What should we be doing?

____ What stands out to you from these last three verses of Micah (7:18-20)?

<u>**Day Five—Key Points in Application:**</u> The most important application from Day Five is that we cannot approach God on our own terms. We must approach Him as He requires. Micah 6:8 reiterates this thought of coming to God on His terms, and, in reality, we must approach this verse from the end and work our way backward. For example, before we can love mercy with others, and expect justice of ourselves, we must walk humbly with Him. Make sure your group fully understands Micah 6:8. Check which discussion questions from Day Five you will use.

____ What are some ways we fail to expect justice of ourselves?

____ What stands out to you about loving mercy in your relationships with others?

____ What things get in the way of walking humbly with God?

____ What is the biggest application point you saw this week?

CLOSING: 5–10 MINUTES

❑ **Summarize**—You may want to read the paragraph at the beginning of the leader's notes for this lesson, called "The Main Point" of Micah.

❑ **Preview**—If time allows, preview next week's lesson, **"Jeremiah: Trusting in God When Life Looks Hopeless."**

❑ **Pray**—Close in prayer.

Tools for Good Discussion

One of the issues you will eventually have to combat in any group Bible study is the enemy of **boredom.** This antagonist raises its ugly head from time to time, but it shouldn't. It is wrong to bore people with the Word of God! Often boredom results when leaders allow their processes to become too predictable. As small group leaders, we tend to do the same thing in the same way every single time. Yet God the Creator, who spoke everything into existence is infinitely creative! Think about it. He is the one who not only created animals in different shapes and sizes, but different colors as well. When He created food, He didn't make it all taste or feel the same. This God of creativity lives in us. We can trust Him to give us creative ideas that will keep our group times from becoming tired and mundane. In the "Helpful Hints" section of **How to Lead a Small Group** (pp. 215-216), you'll find some practical ideas on adding spice and creativity to your study time.

Jeremiah

MEMORY **Psalms 27:13** VERSE

"I would have despaired unless I had believed that I would see the goodness of the Lord in the land of the living."

Before the Session

- ❑ Your own preparation is key not only to your effectiveness in leading the group-discussion time, but also to your confidence in leading. It is hard to be confident if you know you are unprepared. These discussion questions and leader's notes are meant to be a helpful addition to your own study but should never become a substitute.
- ❑ As you do your homework, study with an eye to your own relationship with God. Resist the temptation to bypass this self-evaluation on your way to preparing to lead the group. Nothing will minister to your group more than the testimony of your own walk with God.
- ❑ Look at 1 and 2 Kings and 1 and 2 Chronicles, and read about the kings who ruled while Jeremiah ministered. You may also benefit from doing the lesson on **Josiah** from *Following God: Life Principles from the Kings of the Old Testament.*
- ❑ Don't think of your ministry to the members of your group as something that only takes place during your group time. Pray for each group member by name during the week, and, as you pray, ask God to enlighten them while they do their homework. Encourage your group as you have opportunity.

What to Expect

In this lesson, we will touch on an area of life that is sometimes painful and vulnerable. It is only fitting that this idea of "trusting God when life looks hopeless" comes later in the study, when relationships have been built to the point of allowing for a certain amount of vulnerability. Be prepared for the possibility that some in your group may be living in a situation that they feel is hopeless, perhaps with an unbelieving spouse or a prodigal child. While these truths from Jeremiah should be a great comfort, they may also bring to the surface some hidden pain. Don't be afraid of some honest emotion spilling out into the group time.

THE MAIN POINT

The main point in Jeremiah is the testimony he offers of faith in God in the midst of hopeless-looking circumstances.

Jeremiah ministered not so much to his own generation, but to the future remnant who would one day return to the promised land. Though he lamented the fall of Jerusalem, he stood on the promises of Jehovah that one day the people of God would return to the land and worship in righteousness. While the story of Jeremiah may seem like ancient history, the principles from his life are just as applicable today when you and I find ourselves in hopeless situations.

During the Session

OPENING: 5–10 MINUTES

Opening Prayer—A good prayer with which to open your time is the prayer of David in Psalms 119:18, *"Open my eyes, that I may behold wonderful things from Thy law."* Remember, if it took the illumination of God for men to write Scripture, it will take the same for us to understand it.

Opening Illustration—A good way to begin your discussion time is by asking the question, "What is the most hopeless situation you can think of?" After allowing some discussion, ask, "Is that situation hopeless for the Christian?" You want your group to understand that usually what is defined as hopeless is based on an earthly, circumstantial set of values instead of being based on an eternal perspective.

DISCUSSION: 30–40 MINUTES

Remember to pace your discussion so that you don't run out of time to get to the application questions in Day Five. This time for application is perhaps the most important part of your Bible study. It will be helpful if you are familiar enough with the lesson to be able to prioritize the days for which you want to place more emphasis, so that you are prepared to reflect this added emphasis in the time you devote to each day's reading.

Main Objective in Day One: In Day One, the main objective is to understand the context in which Jeremiah lived and ministered. Nothing is meaningful without a context, and it is impossible to fully appreciate the message and ministry of Jeremiah without understanding the days in which he lived. Review the discussion questions for Day One below, and check the ones that you will use for your discussion time:

____ What stands out to you about the last four kings of Judah?

____ What were the three things God did to Jeremiah before He formed him in the womb?

____ How do those three things apply to us today?

____ Have you ever felt "too young" for a responsibility God has given you? What does Jeremiah have to say about that?

Main Objective in Day Two: In Day Two, we learn some of the specifics of Jeremiah's preaching. By looking at what he confronts in the people, and by seeing the response for which he calls from them, we can have a sense of what God desires from His people throughout the ages. It is important to understand that God judges the sin of His people. Though we may be Christians who are eternally saved by God's grace, He will still chasten us for our transgressions. Check which discussion questions you will use from Day Two.

____ The two sins of Judah were **a)** forsaking the fountain of living waters (God), and **b)** hewing their own cisterns that would hold no water. What are some ways people do that today?

____ In speaking of their judgment, Jeremiah 2:19 says, *"Your own wickedness will correct you."* Can you think of some examples from your life or those you know where sin was its own punishment?

____ How do we distinguish true repentance over sin from remorse over sin's consequences?

____ What else stood out to you from Day Two?

Main Objective in Day Three: Day Three introduces us to the pain of speaking truth to those who reject it. Jeremiah's was not a pleasant ministry. His example ought to remind us that we do not judge the success or failure of a ministry or task based on how people respond, but rather, based on being faithful to God's assignment. Check the questions below from Day Three that you find to be essential to your group's discussion.

____ Jeremiah was faithful to preach truth even though he had no expectation that the people would respond. How does Jeremiah's faithfulness apply to us today?

____ Have you ever experienced grief like that of Jeremiah's over someone else who vehemently refused to repent?

____ What are some modern examples of persecution to those who preach truth?

____ Why do you think the unrepentant persecute the messenger when they hear truth?

____ Were there any questions raised by your study in Day Three?

<u>Main Objective in Day Four:</u> In Day Four, our study of Jeremiah takes us to the reality that, sooner or later, God will place us in a situation where we have to act in faith instead of by sight. He will call us to step out on truth instead of allowing us to react to our circumstances. Jeremiah also shows us the necessity of keeping our future hope in view as we face the present. Check the discussion questions from Day Four that you will use in your group session.

____ What stands out to you from this story of Jeremiah buying the farm?

____ Have you ever experienced "buyer's remorse" after stepping out in faith?

____ What do you learn from the future promises made to Israel?

____ What are some ways our present life on earth requires walking by faith rather than walking by sight?

____ What else stood out to you from Day Four?

<u>Day Five—Key Points in Application:</u> Among the applications introduced in Day Five, the most noteworthy concept is that we should not be as concerned with the visible results of our actions as in whether or not we are doing what God has called us to do. Make sure that your group understands that success in life always comes in doing what God says and leaving the results to Him. Check any questions that you would like to use for discussion on Day Five.

____ Of the three things God did before He formed Jeremiah (*"knew," "consecrated," "appointed"* [Jeremiah 1:5]), which stands out the most to you personally?

____ Is there a hopeless situation in your life you need to surrender to God? Do you need to accept what He has appointed for you?

____ Out of fear, have you failed to do something that you know God has called you to?

____ Is there anything you need to "recall to mind" about God in your present circumstances?

____ What other applications did you come to understand from this week's lesson?

CLOSING: 5–10 MINUTES

- ❑ **Summarize**—Restate the key points. You may want to read the paragraph at the beginning of the leader's notes for Jeremiah called "The Main Point."
- ❑ **Preview**—If time allows, preview next week's lesson on **"Habakkuk: Following God in the Low Places of Life."**
- ❑ **Pray**—Close in prayer.

Tools for Good Discussion

From time to time each of us can say stupid things. Some of us, however, are better at it than others. I suspect the apostle Peter fell into this category. One minute he was on the pinnacle of success saying, *"Thou art the Christ, the Son of the Living God"* (Matthew 16:16), and the next minute he was putting his foot in his mouth, trying to talk Jesus out of going to the cross. Proverbs 10:19 states, *"When there are many words, transgression is unavoidable. . . ."* What do you do when someone in the group says something that is obviously wrong? First of all, remember that how you deal with a situation like this not only affects the present, but the future. In the "Helpful Hints" section of **How to Lead a Small Group Bible Study** (p. 216), you'll find some practical ideas on managing the obviously mistaken comments that may be presented in your group discussion.

Habakkuk

MEMORY 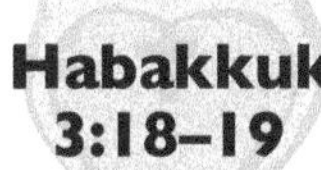 VERSES

Habakkuk 3:18–19

"Yet I will exult in the Lord, I will rejoice in the God of my salvation. The Lord God is my strength, And He . . . makes me walk on my high places."

Before the Session

- ❑ Pray each day for the members of your group—that they spend time in the Word, grasp the message God wants to bring to their lives, and that they surrender to what God is saying to them through their study of His Word.
- ❑ As you pray that your group members will grow in their study of the Scriptures, make sure you have searched the Scriptures carefully for each day's lesson as well.
- ❑ Walk through the discussion questions given throughout this Leader's Guide lesson, and select which questions you think might enhance your group discussion.
- ❑ **Suggestions for Additional Study**—To better understand the condition of Judah at this time you may want to review last week's lesson on **Jeremiah,** and look at *Following God: Life Principles from the Kings of the Old Testament,* (Lesson 9), entitled **"Josiah: The Impact of Following the Word of God."**
- ❑ Remain ever teachable. Look first for what God is saying to you. This will help you in understanding and relating to some of the struggles that your group members may be facing in the "low places" they are going through.

What to Expect

This lesson may reveal some evident struggles that one or a few members of your group may be facing. Do not feel like you have to be "The Answer Man" or "The Answer Woman." Sometimes the most faith-filled response to a question is "I don't know," followed by "but we know we can trust God. He is faithful and trustworthy." Some in your group will have some tremendous testimonies of victory or rejoicing in the midst of some very dark days. You may see and hear some wonderful testimonies of the grace of God at work. I knew a very dear man of God, Oscar Thompson, a professor of evangelism at Southwestern Seminary in Fort Worth, Texas in the 1970's. The ravaging effects of cancer plagued his body, and he faced some very rough days before his death. But he also experienced some wonderful days of grace. God allowed him to minister and counsel many people from all over the country who were facing the pains of chemotherapy or even the day of their death. He often spoke to them of the grace of God. He said, "God gives dying grace on dying days." He does not give dying grace on non-dying days. Oscar Thompson lived in that reality and died in that reality. God truly gives whatever grace and wisdom we need when we need it. Help your group members see this truth so that they may continue to follow God through the low places of their lives.

THE MAIN POINT

We will learn to live by faith in the "high places" of God's grace, as we walk through the "low places" of the dark circumstances in life.

DURING THE SESSION

OPENING: 5–10 MINUTES

Opening Prayer—Remember to ask the Lord for **His** wisdom. He promised to guide us into the truth.

Opening Illustration—The following hymn, "He Giveth More Grace" was written by Annie Johnson Flint:

"He giveth more grace when the burden grows greater;
He sendeth more strength when the labors increase.
To added affliction He addeth His mercy;
to multiplied trials, His multiplied peace.

"His love has no limit; His grace has no measure;
His pow'r has no boundary known unto men.
For out of His infinite riches in Jesus,
He giveth, and giveth, and giveth again!"

The second verse says,

"When we have exhausted our store of endurance,
When our strength has failed ere the day is half done,
When we reach the end of our hoarded resources,
Our Father's full giving is only begun."

How true these words are for the trials we face!

DISCUSSION: 30–40 MINUTES

Select one or two specific questions to get the group started. Keep the group focused along the main study of Habakkuk. By this point in the course (Week 9), you know both the talkative ones and the quiet ones. Continue to encourage members in the importance of their input. Some of the greatest life lessons we ever learn may come from someone who has said very little up to this point.

Main Objective in Day One: In Day One, the main-objective is to see the symptoms of being in a "low place," the darkness and distress sin has brought. Check the discussion questions for Day One that you will use.

____ What was the condition of Judah in the days of Habakkuk, especially around 609–605 B.C.? What parallels do you see today?

____ How does a leader affect those around him? What did you discover about King Jehoahaz?

____ How do the sins of others bring discouragement to you personally? What can we do to encourage one another to follow the Lord and obey His Word day-by-day?

____ How do you face the questions you have (especially the unanswered questions) about the way circumstances are turning out for you? How could you help others with their particular questions?

Main Objective in Day Two: Here we learn that the "low places" show us our hearts and our attitudes, especially the attitude of **pride**. Make sure everyone in your group sees the truth about pride in today's lesson. Check the discussion questions for Day Two that you will use.

____ What is the difference between living by sight (feelings, emotions, human logic) and living by faith (God's logic)? You may want to read 2 Corinthians 4:16–18, the testimony of Paul in the face of the pressure of circumstances.

____ Describe pride. What does a prideful person look like, sound like, act like?

____ How has God dealt with you about an area of pride? Can you recall a time when God was speaking specifically to you about your pride?

____ What are some ways we try to fix circumstances in others' lives or in our own instead of urging others to humble themselves before God or humbling ourselves before God?

____ What are some ways God may seek to bring us to humble ourselves?

Main Objective in Day Three: In Day Three, the study concentrates on Habakkuk's new attitude toward God. Select a question or two from the list below that you think might be useful for your discussion of Day Three.

____ Habakkuk truly heard the message that God spoke to him. What are some ways God speaks in the midst of our circumstances?

____ How can we make sure we are "all ears" when God is speaking?

____ How can we gain a clearer view of who God is and what He wants in our lives?

____ What are some ways God has worked in your life, both to your benefit and to the benefit of others around you?

____ Are there some things God has revealed about Himself that you would not have known had it not been for the rough days that God has allowed to enter your life?

Main Objective in Day Four: Here we see the triumph of Habakkuk in the midst of the coming calamities of his people. His focus was on the Lord and how the Lord would guide His people **through** the difficult days. Check a question or two from the list below that you find to be profitable to your discussion of Day Four.

____ Habakkuk trembled when he thought about what the future held. Yet, he also rejoiced. How do the ideas of trembling and rejoicing fit together?

____ How can a person have joy even in the midst of difficulties, including the loss of prosperity? What was Habakkuk's solution to all that he faced?

____ How can you personally focus more fully on the Lord, and how can you help others do the same?

Day Five—Key Points in Application: The most noteworthy application point from Day Five is that we make sure that our faith is directed upon God, not on people or earthly things. Encourage your group members to discern whether the motivations for their lifestyles come from God or from the world. Review the Day Five question list below, and select the ones that you feel will enhance your group discussion.

____ What shapes the way most people (even many Christians) look at life?

____ What do you know for sure about God's knowledge and wisdom? What are some world opinions that have gotten mixed in with what you see in Scripture?

____ How has God shown His love in your life?

____ What are some struggles you have faced, difficulties that are dark threads in the tapestry that God is weaving? What is God saying to you through Habakkuk?

CLOSING: 5–10 MINUTES

- ❑ **Summarize**—Restate the key points the group shared. Review the objectives for each of the days found at the beginning of these leader notes.
- ❑ **Focus**—Using the memory verses (Habakkuk 3:18–19), focus the group on the centrality of faith in the character and ways of God. As Psalm 119:68 says, *"Thou art good and doest good."* We can trust Him.
- ❑ **Ask** them to share their thoughts concerning Day Five, especially the truths about the "gates" that all God's decisions come through.
- ❑ **Encourage**—We have finished nine lessons. This is no time to slack off. Encourage your group to keep up the pace. We have three more lessons full of life-changing truths. Take a few moments to preview next week's lesson on **"Daniel: Confidence in the God of Heaven."** Encourage your group members to do their homework and to space it out over the week.
- ❑ Close in prayer.

Tools for Good Discussion

The Scriptures are full of examples of people who struggled with the problem of pride. Unfortunately, pride isn't a problem reserved for the history books. It shows up just as often today as it did in the days the Scriptures were written. In your group discussions, you may see traces of pride manifested in a "know-it-all" group member. **"Know-It-All Ned"** may have shown up in your group by this point. He may be an intellectual giant, or he may be a legend only in his own mind. He can be very prideful and argumentative. If you want some helpful hints on how to deal with "Know-It-All Ned," look in the "Helpful Hints" section of **How to Lead a Small Group Bible Study** (p. 214).

Daniel

MEMORY **Isaiah 66:2b** VERSE

"But to this one will I look, to him who is humble and contrite of spirit, and who trembles at My word."

Before the Session

- ❑ Never underestimate the importance of prayer for yourself and for the members of your group. Ask the Lord to give them understanding in their time in the Word and bring them to a new level of knowing Him.
- ❑ Remember to mark those ideas and questions you want to discuss or ask as you go through the study.
- ❑ Suggestions for Additional Study: To better understand the condition of Judah at this time you may want to look at two lessons in *Following God: Life Principles from the Kings of the Old Testament*. The first lesson is titled, **"Josiah: The Impact of Following the Word of God."** To see how God worked near the end of Daniel's life you may want to look at **"Zerubbabel and Ezra: Following God's Will."**
- ❑ Be sensitive to the needs of your group. Be prepared to stop and pray for a member who may be facing a difficult struggle or challenge.

What to Expect

Some in your group may recall some things they have heard about Daniel as a youth (i.e., the story of Daniel in the Lion's Den), while others may find the study completely new. There may be some tough questions that surface in dealing with the things God allows in our lives or in facing some matters dealing with authorities in our lives. Remember that your job is not to teach the lesson, but to guide discussion so that all can learn from each other. You will want to emphasize the faithfulness of God in Daniel's life and how God is ever faithful to each member in your group. Just because God is always faithful to us does not mean that He will reveal to us all of the why's and why not's of life. God's faithfulness to us means that He will take us all the way to the finish line in the race He has set out for us. He takes us there in His way, in His timing, along His paths. Those paths are always chosen out of His covenant love for us, and He has promised to **never** leave us nor forsake us—just as we see in Daniel's life. May this lesson be a real encouragement to your group to **see God** at work in their lives and to **seek God** in the circumstances they are facing.

THE MAIN POINT

We can place our total confidence and trust in the God of Heaven who rules over all. He is **always** at work fulfilling His purposes for His people.

During the Session

OPENING: 5–10 MINUTES

Opening Prayer—Have one of the group members open the time with prayer.

Opening Illustration—Confidence in the Word of God. King Josiah emphasized the importance of following **all** of the Word of God (2 Kings 23:25). Apparently he made an impact on young Daniel and Daniel's family. The Babylonian army was known for its fierce and proud soldiers. Their reputation had spread far and wide. Habakkuk had talked much about them. Now Daniel faced them and was a captive in their caravan back to Babylon. As a fourteen-year-old youth he discovered that the Word of God was sufficient wherever he was and in whatever circumstance he faced. His confidence in the God of Heaven meant a confidence in the Word of the God of Heaven. We can discover the same.

DISCUSSION: 30–40 MINUTES

Select one or two specific questions to get the group to start talking. This lesson on Daniel covers over 70 years of his life and has application points for every stage of life. Focus on the power and reign of the Lord in our lives. Keep the group directed on the **faithfulness of God** in Daniel's life as well as on the **faith of Daniel** in God's faithfulness. Continue to encourage each member in the importance of his or her input.

Main Objective in Day One: In Day One the main objective is to see the righteous God Daniel knew and Daniel's desire to follow His righteous Word. Check which discussion questions you will use from Day One .

____ What would it mean to have a king like Josiah leading the people (imagine you and your parents) in following all the Word of God? How would you respond if you were Daniel?

____ What would it be like to hear about coming judgment and then see the armies of Babylon? If you were Daniel's parents, what would you say to your children when you heard Habakkuk, Jeremiah, or Zephaniah proclaiming the message God had given him? How would you prepare yourself or your children in light of the messages of these prophets?

____ How do you face new circumstances? Think of all the "new" things Daniel and his friends faced. Have you experienced a major move with your family or some major change in your life? What can you learn from Daniel about what's important?

____ Sometimes we must take a stand or confront a person or group because of a personal conviction God has given us. What principles have you gleaned from the way Daniel responded to his situation?

Main Objective in Day Two: Sometimes we face situations that are beyond our own understanding or abilities, but they are not beyond God's. The Lord wants us to depend on Him and look to Him for His wisdom and grace for difficult situations. Check the discussion questions that you will use from Day Two.

____ What stood out to you about Daniel's attitude and confidence in God in the face of this trial?

____ What were priorities to Daniel and his three friends? What did they do first? second? third? What does that say to you about how you should face trials?

____ Can you think of a time when you faced a trial in which you needed wisdom, and how God gave you that wisdom?

____ Describe a time when you depended on man's wisdom, man's might or strength, or man's riches. What did God teach you (or what is He teaching you now about this) in light of Jeremiah 9:23–24?

____ What practical lessons can you glean from Daniel's confidence in God's ability to reveal the way to go, the choices to make, and the things to do? What about the things **not** to do?

Main Objective in Day Three: The main objective is to see that *"it is Heaven that rules"* and in seeing that to also see the attitude of humility and trust that God wants in us. Check the discussion questions from Day Three that are relevant to your group.

____ Nebuchadnezzar's dream was followed by twelve months of waiting. God was waiting to see his response, then He acted to carry out the dream He had given him. How have you seen the Lord's reign in your life through His timing of some event or answer to prayer?

____ Nebuchadnezzar's view of life was filled with pride. What are some ways that **pride** fills our view of life today? What do we need to do when we see this?

____ What are some ways God has humbled you in your pride?

____ Daniel served for many years under several rulers, some of whom were very proud. How did Daniel serve under such men? Where was his focus, and how did that focus get him through those years of service?

<u>**Main Objective in Day Four**</u>: Daniel's relationship with the Lord impacted all that he did—his job and his home life, not just his spiritual life. The same can be true of us. Place a check mark near the questions that are best suited for your discussion.

____ Daniel was marked by integrity on the job. How important is integrity? What difference did Daniel's integrity make to Darius or to Daniel's co-workers?

____ How can our relationship to God affect our relationships to those in authority over us? How can our relationships with those in authority over us affect our fellowship with God?

____ How important is the Word of God in our lives? In Daniel 9, we find that Daniel was reading the prophecy of Jeremiah. How do you think that affected how he prayed and what he prayed?

____ Where was Daniel focused as he thought of and prayed for Jerusalem and the people of Israel? How does that speak to you about your focus in life or your focus in prayer?

<u>**Day Five—Key Points in Application**</u>: The most important application point seen in the life of Daniel is this: we should make sure that we see life and its many circumstances from **God's point of view** rather than seeing life only from the level of our circumstances. Check which discussion questions you will use from Day Five.

____ In God's scheme of things, how we finish the race is far more important than how we start the race. How did Daniel finish his race? What can you do to insure a good finish in your life?

____ Daniel served under a variety of authorities—some idolatrous, some proud, some unpredictable. Paul the Apostle wrote Romans 13 (about authorities) during the reign of Nero, a very wicked ruler.

____ Where was the focus of Daniel or Paul? How did they deal with authorities in their lives? What can we learn from them?

____ What has God shown you about the "kingdom" where you are "ruling" or, in most cases, serving?

____ Daniel has some things to say about facing surprises in life. What do we know for sure about the surprises of life, things like sudden changes in our jobs, schools, locations, finances, relationships, friends or family?

CLOSING: 5–10 MINUTES

- ❑ **Summarize.**
- ❑ **Ask** your group to express their thoughts about the key applications from Day Five.
- ❑ **Preview**—Take time to preview next week's lesson, **"Haggai: A Call to Consider Your Ways."**
- ❑ **Pray**—Close in prayer.

Tools for Good Discussion

So, group leaders, how have the first nine weeks of this study been for you? Have you dealt with anyone in your group called **"Agenda Alice"**? She is the type that is focused on a Christian "hot-button" issue instead of the Bible study. If not managed properly, she (or he) will either sidetrack the group from its main study objective, or create a hostile environment in the group if she fails to bring people to her way of thinking. For help with "Agenda Alice," see the "Helpful Hints" section of **How to Lead a Small Group Bible Study** (pp. 214-215).

Haggai

MEMORY **2 Corinthians 6:16** VERSE

"For we are the temple of the living God; just as God said, 'I will dwell in them and walk among them; and I will be their God, and they shall by My people.'"

Before the Session

- ❑ Pray for your group as they walk through this week's lesson.
- ❑ Spread your study time over the week. Think of the lesson as a large meal. You need time to chew each truth and digest it fully.
- ❑ Remember to mark those ideas and questions you want to discuss or ask as you go.
- ❑ For additional study, you can better understand the condition of Jerusalem at the time of Zerubbabel by looking at the lesson, **"Zerubbabel and Ezra: Following God's Will"** (Lesson 10) in *Following God: Life Principles from the Kings of the Old Testament*.

What to Expect

Haggai will be a new name for some (perhaps for all) in your group. He appears only for a brief moment on the stage of the Old Testament, but what He said lingers throughout time into eternity. Along with the newness of Haggai, some will find the discussion about the Tabernacle or Temple to be new or at least unfamiliar. There may be a few questions about Zerubbabel or the "signet ring" or God's promises for the future that are not easily answered. Be patient. Study diligently in your preparation time. You may want to consult a Bible dictionary about some of these things. As you tread through the lesson, seek to keep the main point the main point. Emphasize what you clearly know and understand. Then you can move on to the things that are not as clear as the Lord gives time and insight.

THE MAIN POINT

God continually calls us to "consider" our "ways" in our walk with Him, and He calls us to adjust our ways to His ways through following His Word.

During the Session

OPENING: 5–10 MINUTES

Opening Prayer—Have one of the group members open the time with prayer.

Opening Illustration—It's the Little Things That Count. Often we are tempted to think that only the big things in life, or the big events, or the "big name" people are what is really important. But a small rudder turns the greatest of ships, and the tongue, though it is one of the smallest members of our bodies, is often the most powerful. How many times we have found that it is not a whole book or a whole chapter of the Bible that impacts—but a small verse or part of a verse or phrase empowered by the Spirit of God that pierces us in soul and spirit. This little book of Haggai (only two chapters, 38 verses) has this powerful potential. In this small book, the call to consider our ways rings clear with the promise that obedience will bring the blessing of God.

DISCUSSION: 30–40 MINUTES

This lesson on Haggai covers only a year of his life but looks at God's plans for the ages. Focus on the Lord's call to consider our ways in the light of His plans in our lives. Keep the group directed at the mercy and faithfulness of God. Help them see His "never give up" attitude with His people and with His plans. Every **call** for us to consider our ways is a **promise** that His mercy and grace are available to the obedient heart.

<u>Main Objective in Day One</u>: The main point here is to discover the preeminence of God's priorities and the importance of making those priorities ours. Check which discussion questions you will use from Day One.

____ Do you find it easy to focus on "taking care of business" (i.e., your own "business") and forgetting the things of God?

____ What things got in the way of building the Temple in Haggai's day? What things can get in the way of what God wants to do in and through our lives?

____ How can we follow the command to "set your heart on your ways"? How do we "set" our hearts or "consider" our ways?

____ God got their attention through their economy (the dew, the crops, and their expenses). How does the Lord get our attention today? How has he gotten your attention about your walk?

<u>Main Objective in Day Two</u>: In Day Two, we learn the importance of God's presence and what it means to walk practicing His presence. Check the discussion questions for Day Two that you will use.

____ How have you seen the difference between "existing" and "living" in your life or perhaps in your family's life?

____ What does it mean to you that God wants to "dwell with" **you**?

____ What does "fearing the Lord" mean to you? What are some ways you can (or do) show reverence for the Lord?

____ We see that the people of Jerusalem were energized by their obedience to the Word of the Lord. What does it mean to be "energized" by your obedience? What does that look like?

<u>Main Objective in Day Three</u>: Day Three focuses on the promise of the presence and provision of the Lord as the people obeyed. Decide which discussion questions for Day Three you will use from the list below:

____ What would the promise of the Lord's presence and provision mean to people walking out of Egypt into the Wilderness of Sinai? What would it mean to people rebuilding a temple from the rubble in a city with no walls and a depressed economy?

____ What is the one thing someone wants when they are really thirsty? What kind of thirst did Jesus talk about in John 7? Name some ways you have experienced thirst—physically or spiritually.

____ Name some ways Jesus has quenched your soul's thirst. What is the difference between the **"living water"** Jesus gives and the "waters" of the world?

____ Haggai's messages were meant to bring the people into a much greater understanding and experience of the presence and provision of God in daily life. What do the promises of God mean in your life today? How do the promises of God give you comfort or encouragement?

<u>Main Objective in Day Four</u>: Day Four looks at how the Lord treated Israel to bring them back to a full experience of His presence and power. Check which discussion questions you will use from Day Four.

____ **Whatever It Takes**—That is what we see again and again as Haggai speaks (Haggai 2:16–17) about how God uses different means to get our attention, to cause us to look up to Him in a fresh way, to come to a new day of full obedience. What does this tell you about the Lord?

____ The Lord not only used circumstances to speak to His people, He also sent His prophets with a clear message from His heart. God speaks through His Word to us today. What hinders us from obeying what is clear in His Word?

____ All that God did and said was meant to encourage and energize His people in their walk and for the tasks they would face in the days ahead. How can you be an encouragement and an energizer to others as opposed to a "discourager" and an "energy-drainer"?

____ The Lord did not stop His words of encouragement to Haggai. He had more to say through Zechariah. What does this tell you about the Lord's love and care for His people? What does this say about His care for you today? How can this encourage you and others in following God?

Day Five—Key Points in Application: The most important application point seen in the ministry of Haggai is found in the statement: *"consider your ways"* (Haggai 1:5). Is He real in the everyday affairs of your life, or do you just give Him a little attention on Sunday? Check which discussion questions from Day Five you will use.

____ We don't go to a Temple to acknowledge the presence of the Lord, we are the Temple of His Spirit. Everywhere we go, God and His Temple goes. How can the recognition of the truth that we are the Temple of God's Spirit affect your daily life?

____ What has this lesson said to you about your priorities? Are they the priorities that a disciple of Jesus Christ should have?

____ On page 179 in the workbook, the statement is made: "He wants us to walk—not **ahead** of Him, trying to control our own lives; not **behind** Him, rebelling against Him and His ways; but **with** Him, cooperating and enjoying the fellowship of the journey." What are some application points in that statement that touch your life?

____ God speaks in a language we understand. He uses the image of a tent to speak of dwelling with His people, of living with them like a family. Think of some pictures that describe the kind of relationship God wants with you (for example, a Father to a child).

CLOSING: 5–10 MINUTES

- ❑ **Summarize**—Restate the key points.
- ❑ **Ask** the group members to share their thoughts about the key applications from Day Five.
- ❑ **Preview**—Take time to preview next week's lesson on **"Christ the Prophet: Worshiping in Spirit and Truth."** Encourage them to do their homework for this final lesson in the study of the Old Testament prophets.
- ❑ **Pray**—Close in prayer.

Tools for Good Discussion

Well, it is evaluation time again! You may be saying to yourself, "Why bother evaluating at the end? If I did a bad job, it is too late to do anything about it now!" Well, it may be too late to change how you did on this course, but it is never too late to learn from this course what will help you on the next. Howard Hendricks, that peerless communicator from Dallas Theological Seminary, puts it this way: "The good teacher's greatest threat is satisfaction—the failure to keep asking, 'How can I improve?' The greatest threat to your ministry is **your ministry."** Any self-examination should be an accounting of your own strengths and weaknesses. As you consider your strengths and weaknesses, take some time to read through the evaluation questions list found in the **How to Lead a Small Group Bible Study** section (p.218-219) of this leader's guide. Make it your aim to continue growing as a discussion leader. Below, jot down two or three action points for you to implement in future classes.

ACTION POINTS:

1. ______________________________

____

2. ______________________________

____

3. ______________________________

____

Christ the Prophet

MEMORY John 5:24 VERSE

"Truly, truly, I say to you, he who hears My word, and believes Him who sent Me, has eternal life, and does not come into judgment, but has passed out of death into life."

Before the Session

- ❑ Never underestimate the importance of prayer for yourself and for the members of your group. Pray for each group member by name.
- ❑ Spread your study time over the week.
- ❑ Remember to mark those ideas and questions you want to discuss or ask as you go through the study. Add to those some of the questions listed below.
- ❑ Be sensitive to the working of the Spirit in your group meeting, ever watchful for ways to help one another truly follow God.

What to Expect

Like seeing the facets of a diamond or emerald from several angles, seeing Christ as The Prophet will hopefully give fresh perspective to the members in your group. Hopefully, all will experience a deeper level of obedience to the Lord and His Word, and with that, discover the reward of receiving a prophet (The Prophet) of the Lord. When we focus on Jesus Christ we often discover answers to the deepest cries of our heart. We also face new questions and desire greater understanding. Some questions may arise that you may not be able to answer or to answer as fully as you would like. Remember that you do not need to be "The Answer Man" or "The Answer Woman" for all the things that come up. Rejoice in the new insights and challenge the group to deeper study with the unknowns. As you move through the lesson, seek to keep the main focus the main focus. Emphasize what you clearly know and understand. Then you can move on to the things that are not as clear as the Lord gives time and insight.

THE MAIN POINT

As we study the life and ministry of Christ Jesus the Prophet, we will learn the necessity of honoring Him and His Word with a life of worship in spirit (heart) and truth.

During the Session

OPENING: 5–10 MINUTES

Opening Prayer—Psalm 119:18 says, *"Open my eyes, that I may behold wonderful things from Thy law."* Ask the Lord to open your eyes as you meet together. Have one of the group members open the time with prayer.

Opening Illustration—It has been said of George Whitefield, the great evangelist of the First Great

Awakening (1740s), that he could be clearly heard in a crowd of 20,000 with no means of amplification. More than that, his message thundered with the conviction of the Holy Spirit through the hearts of thousands. Imagine what it was like to hear the Lord Jesus when He spoke His Sermon on the Mount or when He spoke at the feeding of the 5,000. Matthew 7:28–29 says *"the multitudes were amazed at His teaching; for He was teaching them as one having authority, and not as their scribes."* As you look at Christ the Prophet, may He speak with authority and conviction to each one in your group.

DISCUSSION: 30–40 MINUTES

This lesson on Christ the Prophet focuses on Christ's clear grasp of the Word of His Father, how He faithfully proclaimed that Word, and the reward for an obedient response on the part of His hearers. For today, through this lesson, **we** are each His hearers. The admonition of Hebrews 12:1–2 cries out to all of us, *". . . let us run with endurance the race that is set before us,* **fixing our eyes on Jesus,** *the author and perfecter of faith. . . ."* As you and your group set your eyes on Christ the Prophet, hearing and heeding His Word will result in a greater walk of faith and a deeper experience of His joy.

Main Objective in Day One: The main point here is to see how the Lord raises up those who speak the truth because He longs for His people to walk in that truth. Ultimately, He sent His Son, the Lord Jesus. Choose one or more discussion questions from Day One that is relevant to your group.

____ God warned about deception and lies in the Canaanite culture. What are some of the sources of falsehood, lies, and deception we face in our lives today?

____ How does the fact that God wants you to know the truth bring encouragement to you? What are some of His sources of truth for us today?

____ How important is it to come to the Lord and His Word with an open, listening heart? How can we do that more consistently?

____ Have you ever heard someone speak "straw" as opposed to "grain," like Jeremiah talked about? How have you seen the difference in your life or in what you have heard?

Main Objective in Day Two: In Day Two, the main objective is to see how Christ fulfilled the promise given to Moses—God would raise up a prophet like Moses who would speak **all** the Word He gave Him to speak. Check the questions that you might consider using for your group discussion for Day Two.

____ What would it be like to know that the one teaching you was absolutely true in everything he said? What do you think the people thought as they heard Jesus?

____ What is it like when you learn that someone has told you something that was deceptive in any way?

____ Jesus spoke with authority. How does your confidence in the Lord Jesus and His Word bring comfort or encouragement to you?

____ Jesus had an open, honest relationship with His Father. He walked in the freedom of the truth. How has His truth given you freedom in some area?

Main Objective in Day Three: Day Three focuses on **the focus** of the Lord Jesus—a right relationship with God the Father and right worship. Check the discussion questions that you will use for Day Three.

____ What are some things that get in the way of people seeing God as He really is? Or to put it another way: What are some of the substitutes for true worship? With what do people try to replace true worship?

____ How do Christians sometimes fail to worship in spirit and truth? What gets in the way in their relationship with God the Father?

____ Why does the Lord want us to deal honestly with our sin? What good is that? How important is that?

____ What is the result of dealing with sin and focusing on pure worship in spirit and truth?

Main Objective in Day Four: Day Four looks at the importance of receiving The Prophet and the message He brings. Check which discussion questions from Day Four you will use.

____ Many believed Jesus to be a prophet, but refused to heed what He said. What does it mean to receive Him and His Word?

____ A personal relationship with Jesus Christ involves walking with Him in the truth. What should we do when we do not fully understand Him or His Word?

____ Practically speaking, how do we continue receiving His Word?

____ What has it meant to you to receive Jesus Christ as your Lord and Savior, as the Prophet, the Way, the Truth, and the Life?

Day Five—Key Points in Application: The most important application point in the study of Christ the Prophet is the practical application of His Word to our lives. Place a checkmark next to the questions for Day Two that you will use in your discussion time.

____ What can you do to insure that you are continuing to hear Christ the Prophet?

____ Is there an area where you are struggling, where there is little or no freedom, where you don't know the truth that deals with that struggle?

____ What are you doing to prepare for His prophesied return?

____ What has the Lord showed you about your worship and obedience of Him?

CLOSING: 5–10 MINUTES

❑ **Summarize**—Restate the key points.

❑ **Focus**—Using the memory verse (John 5:24), focus the group on what it means to truly hear and believe His Word.

❑ **Ask** some of your group members to share their thoughts about the key applications from Day Five.

❑ **Pray**—Close your time in prayer by thanking the Lord for the journey of learning on which He has led you over the past 12 weeks.

TOOLS FOR GOOD DISCUSSION

Congratulations! You have successfully navigated the waters of small group discussion. You have finished all 12 lessons in *Following God: Life Principles from the Prophets of the Old Testament*, but there is so much more to learn, so many more paths to take on our journey with the Lord, so much more to discover about what it means to follow Him. Now What? It may be wise for you and your group to continue with another study. In the front portion of this leader's guide (in the "Helpful Hints" section of **How to Lead a Small Group Bible Study** (pp. 216-217), there is information on how you can transition to the next study and share those insights with your group. Encourage your group to continue in some sort of consistent Bible study. Time in the Word is much like time at the dinner table. If we are to stay healthy, we will never get far from physical food, and if we are to stay nourished on "sound" or "healthy" doctrine, then we must stay close to the Lord's "dinner table" found in His Word. Job said it well, *"I have not departed from the command of His lips; I have treasured the words of His mouth more than my necessary food"* (Job 23:12).